AF252135

SUPER HOROSCOPE

ARIES 1996

March 21 - April 20

BERKLEY BOOKS, NEW YORK

CONTENTS

ISBN: 0-425-14902-1

NOTE TO THE CUSP-BORN

First find the year of your birth, and then find the sign under which you were born according to your day of birth. Thus, you can determine if you are a true Aries (or Pisces or Taurus), according to the variations of the dates of the Zodiac. (See also page 7.)

Are you *really* an Aries? If your birthday falls during the fourth week of March, at the beginning of Aries, will you still retain the traits of Pisces, the sign of the Zodiac before Aries? And what if you were born late in April—are you more Taurus than Aries? Many people born at the edge, or cusp, of a sign have difficulty determining exactly what sign they are. If you are one of these people, here's how you can figure it out, once and for all.

Consult the following table. It will tell you the precise days on which the Sun entered and left your sign for the year of your birth. If you were born at the beginning or end of Aries, yours is a lifetime reflecting a process of subtle transformation. Your life on Earth will symbolize a significant change in consciousness, for you are either about to enter a whole new way of living or are leaving one behind.

If your birthday falls at the end of March, you may want to read the horoscope book for Pisces as well as Aries, for Pisces holds the keys to many of your hidden uncertainties, past guilts, weaknesses, sorrows, unspoken wishes, and your cosmic unfoldment.

You are eager to start living, and possess, in a way, the secret of eternal youth. Obstacles enrage you but never beat you, for you usually feel you have sacrificed more than your share. In some way (after waiting) you will assert yourself and your right to make your own decisions.

However, you are often drawn back through Pisces into a sense of responsibility, a duty to others, a selflessness that at times eats away at your confidence and undermines your character. Honor and the vitality of life are your gifts.

If you were born late in April, you may want to read the horoscope book for Taurus as well as Aries. The investment could be revealing and profitable, for Taurus is often your means of putting your talents to practical use and turning your ideas into actual, tangible rewards.

You are headstrong and determined; you have a sense of independence and fight that nothing can destroy. Sometimes you can vacillate and be worried and negative, but you never give up. You have the earthy sense of all your needs to meet responsibilities, do your duties, build, acquire, and collect. You are attracted to all you possess, and the more you possess, the more permanent your life. You are thus less able to simply pick up and go back to zero; what you start you must try to finish.

DATES SUN ENTERS ARIES
(LEAVES PISCES)

March 20 every year from 1900 to 2000, except for the following:

March 21:

1901	1911	1923	1938	1955
02	13	26	39	59
03	14	27	42	63
05	15	30	43	67
06	18	31	46	71
07	19	34	47	75
09	22	35	51	79
10				

DATES SUN LEAVES ARIES
(ENTERS TAURUS)

April 20 every year from 1900 to 2000, except for the following:

April 19:			April 21:
1948	1972	1988	1903
52	76	89	07
56	80	92	11
60	81	93	19
64	84	96	
68	85	97	

HISTORY AND USES
OF ASTROLOGY

Does astrology have a place in the fast-moving, ultra-scientific world we live in today? Can it be justified in a sophisticated society whose outriders are already preparing to step off the moon into the deep space of the planets themselves? Or is it just a hangover of ancient superstition, a psychological dummy for neurotics and dreamers of every historical age?

These are the kind of questions that any inquiring person can be expected to ask when they approach a subject like astrology which goes beyond, but never excludes, the materialistic side of life.

The simple, single answer is that astrology works. It works for tens of millions of people in the western world alone. In the United States there are 10 million followers and in Europe, an estimated 25 million. America has more than 4000 practicing astrologers, Europe nearly three times as many. Even down-under Australia has its hundreds of thousands of adherents. The importance of such vast numbers of people from diverse backgrounds and cultures is recognized by the world's biggest newspapers and magazines who probably devote more of their space to this subject in a year than to any other. In the eastern countries, astrology has enormous followings, again, because it has been proved to work. In countries like India, brides and grooms for centuries have been chosen on the basis of astrological compatibility. The low divorce rate there, despite today's heavy westernizing influence, is attributed largely to this practice.

In the western world, astrology today is more vital than ever before; more practicable because it needs a sophisticated society like ours to understand and develop its contribution to the full; more valid because science itself is confirming the precepts of astrological knowledge with every new exciting step. The ordinary person who daily applies astrology intelligently does not have to wonder whether it is true nor believe in it blindly. He can see it working for himself. And, if he can use it—and this book is designed to help the reader to do just that—he can make living a far richer experience, and become a more developed personality and a better person.

Astrology is the science of relationships. It is not just a study of planetary influences on man and his environment. It is the study of man himself.

We are at the center of our personal universe, of all our relationships. And our happiness or sadness depends on how we act, how we relate to the people and things that surround us. The emotions that we generate have a distinct affect—for better or worse—on the world around us. Our friends and our enemies will confirm this. Just look in the mirror the next time you are angry. In other words, each of us is a kind of sun or planet or star and our influence on our personal universe, whether loving, helpful or destructive, varies with our changing moods, expressed through our individual character.

And to an extent that includes the entire galaxy, this is true of the planetary bodies. Their radiations affect each other, including the earth and all the things on it. And in comparatively recent years, giant constellations called "quasars" have been discovered. These exist far beyond the night stars that we can observe, and science says these quasars are emitting radiating influences more powerful and different than ever recorded on earth. Their effect on man from an astrological point of view is under deep study. Compared with these inter-stellar forces, our personal "radiations" are negligible on the planetary scale. But ours are just as potent in the way they affect our moods, and our ability to control them. To this extent they determine much of the happiness and satisfaction in our lives. For instance, if we were bound and gagged and had to hold some strong emotion within us without being able to move, we would soon start to feel very uncomfortable. We are obviously pretty powerful radiators inside, in our own way. But usually, we are able to throw off our emotion in some sort of action—we have a good cry, walk it off, or tell someone our troubles—before it can build up too far and make us physically ill. Astrology helps us to understand the universal forces working on us, and through this understanding, we can become more properly adjusted to our surroundings and find ourselves coping where others may flounder.

Closely related to our emotions is the "other side" of our personal universe, our physical welfare. Our body, of course, is largely influenced by things around us over which we have very little control. The phone rings, we hear it. The train runs late. We snag our stocking or cut our face shaving. Our body is under a constant bombardment of events that influence our lives to varying degrees.

The question that arises from all this is, what makes each of us act so that we have to involve other people and keep the ball of activity and evolution rolling? This is the question that both science and astrology are involved with. The scientists have attacked it from different angles: anthropology, the study of human evolution as body, mind and response to environment; anatomy, the study of bodily structure; psychology, the science of the human mind; and so on. These studies have produced very impressive classifications and valuable information, but because the approach to the problem is fragmented, so is the result. They remain "branches" of science. Science generally studies effects. It keeps turning up wonderful answers but no lasting solutions. Astrology, on the other hand approaches the question from the broader viewpoint. Astrology began its inquiry with the totality of human experience and saw it as an effect. It then looked to find the cause, or at least the prime movers, and during thousands of years of observation of man and his *universal* environment, came up with the extraordinary principle of planetary influence—or astrology, which, from the Greek, means the science of the stars.

Modern science, as we shall see, has confirmed much of astrology's foundations—most of it unintentionally, some of it reluctantly, but still, indisputably.

It is not difficult to imagine that there must be a connection between outer space and the earth. Even today, scientists are not too sure how our earth was created, but it is generally agreed that it is only a tiny part of the universe. And as a part of the universe, people on earth see and feel the influence of heavenly bodies in almost every aspect of our existence. There is no doubt that the sun has the greatest influence on life on this planet. Without it there would be no life, for without it there would be no warmth, no division into day and night, no cycles of time or season at all. This is clear and easy to see. The influence of the moon, on the other hand, is more subtle, though no less definite.

There are many ways in which the influence of the moon manifests itself here on earth, both on human and animal life. It is a well-known fact, for instance, that the large movements of water on our planet—that is the ebb and flow of the tides—are caused by the moon's gravitational pull. Since this is so, it follows that these water movements do not occur only in the oceans, but that all bodies of water are affected, even down to the tiniest puddle.

The human body, too, which consists of about 70 percent water, falls within the scope of this lunar influence. For example the menstrual cycle of most women corresponds to the lunar month; the period of pregnancy in humans is 273 days, or equal to nine lunar months. Similarly, many illnesses reach a crisis at the change of the moon, and statistics in many countries have shown that the crime rate is highest at the time of the full moon. Even human sexual desire has been associated with the phases of the moon. But, it is in the movement of the tides that we get the clearest demonstration of planetary influence, and the irresistible correspondence between the so-called metaphysical and the physical.

Tide tables are prepared years in advance by calculating the future positions of the moon. Science has known for a long time that the moon is the main cause of tidal action. But only in the last few years has it begun to realize the possible extent of this influence on mankind. To begin with, the ocean tides do not rise and fall as we might imagine from our personal observations of them. The moon as it orbits around the earth, sets up a circular wave of attraction which pulls the oceans of the world after it, broadly in an east to west direction. This influence is like a phantom wave crest, a loop of power stretching from pole to pole which passes over and around the earth like an invisible shadow. It travels with equal effect across the land masses and, as scientists were recently amazed to observe, caused oysters placed in the dark in the middle of the United States where there is no sea, to open their shells to receive the non-existent tide. If the land-locked oysters react to this invisible signal, what effect does it have on us who not so long ago in evolutionary time, came out of the sea and still have its salt in our blood and sweat?

Less well known is the fact that the moon is also the primary force behind the circulation of blood in human beings and animals, and the movement of sap in trees and plants. Agriculturists have established that the moon has a distinct influence on crops, which explains why for centuries people have planted according to moon cycles. The habits of many animals, too, are directed by the movement of the moon. Migratory birds, for instance, depart only at or near the time of the full moon. Just as certain fish, eels in particular, move only in accordance with certain phases of the moon.

Know Thyself—Why?

In today's fast-changing world, everyone still longs to know what the future holds. It is the one thing that everyone has in common: rich and poor, famous and infamous, all are deeply concerned about tomorrow.

But the key to the future, as every historian knows, lies in the past. This is as true of individual people as it is of nations. You cannot understand your future without first understanding your past, which is simply another way of saying that you must first of all know yourself.

The motto "know thyself" seems obvious enough nowadays, but it was originally put forward as the foundation of wisdom by the ancient Greek philosophers. It was then adopted by the "mystery religions" of the ancient Middle East, Greece and Rome, and is still used in all genuine schools of mind training or mystical discipline, both in those of the East, based on yoga, and those of the West. So it is universally accepted now, and has been through the ages.

But how do you go about discovering what sort of person you are? The first step is usually classification into some sort of system of types. Astrology did this long before the birth of Christ. Psychology has also done it. So has modern medicine, in its way.

One system classifies men according to the source of the impulses they respond to most readily: the muscles, leading to direct bodily action; the digestive organs, resulting in emotion, or the brain and nerves. Another such system says that character is determined by the endocrine glands, and gives us labels like "pituitary," "thyroid" and "hyperthyroid" types. These different systems are neither contradictory nor mutually exclusive. In fact, they are very often different ways of saying the same thing.

Very popular and useful classifications were devised by Dr. C. G. Jung, the eminent disciple of Freud. Jung observed among the different faculties of the mind, four which have a predominant influence on character. These four faculties exist in all of us without exception, but not in perfect balance. So when we say, for instance, that a man is a "thinking type," it means that in any situation he tries to be rational. It follows that emotion, which some say is the opposite of thinking, will be his weakest function. This type can be sensible and reasonable, or calculating and unsympathetic. The emotional type, on the other hand, can often be recognized by exaggerated language—everything is either marvelous or terrible—and in extreme cases they even invent dramas and quarrels out of nothing just to make life more interesting.

The other two faculties are intuition and physical sensation. The sensation type does not only care for food and drink, nice clothes and furniture; he is also interested in all forms of physical experience. Many scientists are sensation types as are athletes and nature-lovers. Like sensation, intuition is a form of perception and we all possess it. But it works through that part of the mind which is not under conscious control—consequently it sees meanings and connections which are not obvious to thought or emotion. Inventors and original thinkers are always intuitive, but so, too, are superstitious people who see meanings where none exist.

Thus, sensation tells us what is going on in the world, feeling (that is, emotion) tells us how important it is to ourselves, thinking enables us to interpret it and work out what we should do about it, and intuition tells us what it means to ourselves and others. All four faculties are essential, and all are present in every one of us. But some people are guided chiefly by one, others by another.

Besides these four types, Jung observed a division into extrovert and introvert, which cuts across them. By and large, the introvert is one who finds truth inside himself rather than outside. He is not, therefore, ideally suited to a religion or a political party which tells him what to believe. Original thinkers are almost necessarily introverts. The extrovert, on the other hand, finds truth coming to him from outside. He believes in experts and authorities, and wants to think that nature and the laws of nature really exists, that they are what they appear to be and not just generalities made by men.

A disadvantage of all these systems of classification, is that one cannot tell very easily where to place oneself. Some people are reluctant to admit that they act to please their emotions. So they deceive themselves for years by trying to belong to whichever type they think is the "best." Of course, there is no best; each has its faults and each has its good points.

The advantage of the signs of the Zodiac is that they simplify classification. Not only that, but your date of birth is personal—it is unarguably yours. What better way to know yourself than by going back as far as possible to the very moment of your birth? And this is precisely what your horoscope is all about.

What Is a Horoscope?

If you had been able to take a picture of the heavens at the moment of your birth, that photograph would be your horoscope. Lacking such a snapshot, it is still possible to recreate the picture—and this is at the basis of the astrologer's art. In other words, your horoscope is a representation of the skies with the planets in the exact positions they occupied at the time you were born.

This information, of course, is not enough for the astrologer. He has to have a background of significance to put the photograph on. You will get the idea if you imagine two balls—one inside the other. The inner one is transparent. In the center of both is the astrologer, able to look up, down and around in all directions. The outer sphere is the Zodiac which is divided into twelve approximately equal segments, like the segments of an orange. The inner ball is our photograph. It is transparent except for the images of the planets. Looking out from the center, the astrologer sees the planets in various segments of the Zodiac. These twelve segments are known as the signs or houses.

The position of the planets when each of us is born is always different. So the photograph is always different. But the Zodiac and its signs are fixed.

Now, where in all this are you, the subject of the horoscope?

Your character is largely determined by the sign the sun is in. So that is where the astrologer looks first in your horoscope.

There are twelve signs in the Zodiac and the sun spends approximately one month in each. As the sun's motion is almost perfectly regular, the astrologers have been able to fix the dates governing each sign. There are not many people who do not know which sign of the Zodiac they were born under or who have not been amazed at some time or other at the accuracy of the description of their own character. Here are the twelve signs, the ancient zodiacal symbol, and their dates for the year 1996.*

ARIES	Ram	March 20–April 19
TAURUS	Bull	April 19–May 20
GEMINI	Twins	May 20–June 20
CANCER	Crab	June 20–July 22
LEO	Lion	July 22–August 22
VIRGO	Virgin	August 22–September 22
LIBRA	Scales	September 22–October 22
SCORPIO	Scorpion	October 22–November 21
SAGITTARIUS	Archer	November 21–December 21
CAPRICORN	Sea-Goat	December 21–January 20
AQUARIUS	Water-Bearer	January 20–February 19
PISCES	Fish	February 19–March 20

The time of birth—part from the date—is important in advanced astrology because the planets travel at such great speed that the patterns they form change from minute to minute. For this reason, each person's horoscope is his and his alone. Further on we will see that the practicing astrologer has ways of determining and reading these minute time changes which dictate the finer character differences in us all.

However, it is still possible to draw significant conclusions and make meaningful predictions based simply on the sign of the Zodiac a person is born under. In a horoscope, the signs do not necessarily correspond with the divisions of the houses. It could be that a house begins halfway across a sign. It is the interpretation of such combinations of different influences that distinguishes the professional astrologer from the student and the follower.

However, to gain a workable understanding of astrology, it is not necessary to go into great detail. In fact, the beginner is likely to find himself confused if he attempts to absorb too much too quickly. It should be remembered that this is a science and to become proficient at it, and especially to grasp the tremendous scope of possibilities in man and his affairs and direct them into a worthwhile reading, takes a great deal of study and experience.

*These dates are fluid and change with the motion of the Earth from year to year.

If you do intend to pursue it seriously you will have to learn to figure the exact moment of birth against the degrees of longitude and latitude of the planets at that precise time. This involves adapting local time to Greenwich Mean Time (G.M.T.), reference to tables of houses to establish the Ascendant, as well as making calculations from Ephemeris—the tables of the planets' positions.

After reading this introduction, try drawing up a rough horoscope to get the "feel" of reading some elementary characteristics and natal influences.

Draw a circle with twelve equal segments. Write in counterclockwise the names of the signs—Aries, Taurus, Gemini etc.—one for each segment. Look up an ephemeris for the year of the person's birth and note down the sign each planet was in on the birthday. Do not worry about the number of degrees (although if a planet is on the edge of a sign its position obviously should be considered). Write the name of the planet in the segment/sign on your chart. Write the number 1 in the sign where the sun is. This is the first house. Number the rest of the houses, counterclockwise till you finish at 12. Now you can investigate the probable basic expectation of experience of the person concerned. This is done first of all by seeing what planet or planets is/are in what sign and house. (See also page 72.)

The 12 houses control these functions:

1st.	Individuality, body appearance, general outlook on life	(Personality house)
2nd.	Finance, business	(Money house)
3rd.	Relatives, education, correspondence	(Relatives house)
4th.	Family, neighbors	(Home house)
5th.	Pleasure, children, attempts, entertainment	(Pleasure house)
6th.	Health, employees	(Health house)
7th.	Marriage, partnerships	(Marriage house)
8th.	Death, secret deals, difficulties	(Death house)
9th.	Travel, intellectual affairs	(Travel house)
10th.	Ambition, social standing	(Business and Honor house)
11th.	Friendship, social life, luck	(Friends house)
12th.	Troubles, illness, loss	(Trouble house)

The characteristics of the planets modify the influence of the Sun according to their natures and strengths.

Sun: Source of life. Basic temperament according to sun sign. The will.

Moon: Superficial nature. Moods. Changeable. Adaptive. Mother.

Mercury: Communication. Intellect. Reasoning power. Curiosity. Short travels.

Venus: Love. Delight. Art. Beautiful possessions.

Mars: Energy. Initiative. War. Anger. Destruction. Impulse.

Jupiter: Good. Generous. Expansive. Opportunities. Protection.

Saturn: Jupiter's opposite. Contraction. Servant. Delay. Hardwork. Cold. Privation. Research. Lasting rewards after long struggle.

Uranus: Fashion. Electricity. Revolution. Sudden changes. Modern science.

Neptune: Sensationalism. Mass emotion. Devastation. Delusion.

Pluto: Creates and destroys. Lust for power. Strong obsessions.

Superimpose the characteristics of the planets on the functions of the house in which they appear. Express the result through the character of the birth (sun) sign, and you will get the basic idea of how astrology works.

Of course, many other considerations have been taken into account in producing the carefully worked out predictions in this book: The aspects of the planets to each other; their strength according to position and sign; whether they are in a house of exaltation or decline; whether they are natural enemies or not; whether a planet occupies his own sign; the position of a planet in relation to its own house or sign; whether the planet is male, female or neuter; whether the sign is a fire, earth, water or air sign. These are only a few of the colors on the astrologer's pallet which he must mix with the inspiration of the artist and the accuracy of the mathematician.

The Problem of Love

Love, of course, is never a problem. The problem lies in recognizing the difference between infatuation, emotion, sex and, sometimes, the downright deceit of the other person. Mankind, with its record of broken marriages, despair and disillusionment, is obviously not very good at making these distinctions.

Can astrology help?

Yes. In the same way that advance knowledge can usually help in any human situation. And there is probably no situation as human, as poignant, as pathetic and universal, as the failure of man's love.

Love, of course, is not just between man and woman. It involves love of children, parents, home and so on. But the big problems usually involve the choice of partner.

Astrology has established degrees of compatibility that exist between people born under the various signs of the Zodiac. Because people are individuals, there are numerous variations and modifications and the astrologer, when approached on mate and marriage matters makes allowances for them. But the fact remains that some groups of people are suited for each other and some are not and astrology has expressed this in terms of characteristics which all can study and use as a personal guide.

No matter how much enjoyment and pleasure we find in the different aspects of each other's character, if it is not an overall compatibility, the chances of our finding fulfillment or enduring happiness in each other are pretty hopeless. And astrology can help us to find someone compatible.

History of Astrology

The origins of astrology have been lost far back in history, but we do know that reference is made to it as far back as the first written records of the human race. It is not hard to see why. Even in primitive times, people must have looked for an explanation for the various happenings in their lives. They must have wanted to know why people were different from one to another. And in their search they turned to the regular movements of the sun, moon and stars to see if they could provide an answer.

It is interesting to note that as soon as man learned to use his tools in any type of design, or his mind in any kind of calculation, he turned his attention to the heavens. Ancient cave dwellings reveal dim crescents and circles representative of the sun and moon, rulers of day and night. Mesopotamia and the civilization of Chaldea, in itself the foundation of those of Babylonia and Assyria, show a complete picture of astronomical observation and well-developed astrological interpretation.

Humanity has a natural instinct for order. The study of anthropology reveals that primitive people—even as far back as prehistoric times—were striving to achieve a certain order in their lives. They tried to organize the apparent chaos of the universe. They had the desire to attach meaning to things. This demand for order has persisted throughout the history of man. So that observing the regularity of the heavenly bodies made it logical that primitive peoples should turn heavenwards in their search for an understanding of the world in which they found themselves so random and alone.

And they did find a significance in the movements of the stars. Shepherds tending their flocks, for instance, observed that when the cluster of stars now known as the constellation Aries was in sight, it was the time of fertility and they associated it with the Ram. And they noticed that the growth of plants and plant life corresponded with different phases of the moon, so that certain times were favorable for the planting of crops, and other times were not. In this way, there grew up a tradition of seasons and causes connected with the passage of the sun through the twelve signs of the Zodiac.

Astrology was valued so highly that the king was kept informed of the daily and monthly changes in the heavenly bodies, and the results of astrological studies regarding events of the future. Head astrologers were clearly men of great rank and position, and the office was said to be a hereditary one.

Omens were taken, not only from eclipses and conjunctions of the moon or sun with one of the planets, but also from storms and earthquakes. In the eastern civilizations, particularly, the reverence inspired by astrology appears to have remained unbroken since the very earliest days. In ancient China, astrology, astronomy and religion went hand in hand. The astrologer, who was also an astronomer, was part of the official government service and had his own corner in the Imperial Palace. The duties of the Imperial astrologer, whose office was one of the most important in the land, were clearly defined, as this extract from early records shows:

"This exalted gentleman must concern himself with the stars in the heavens, keeping a record of the changes and movements of the Planets, the Sun and the Moon, in order to examine the movements of the terrestial world with the object of prognosticating good and bad fortune. He divides the territories of the nine regions of the empire in accordance with their dependence on particular celestial bodies. All the fiefs and principalities are connected with the stars and from this their prosperity or misfortune should be ascertained. He makes prognostications according to the twelve years of the Jupiter cycle of good and evil of the terrestial world. From the colors of the five kinds of clouds, he determines the coming of floods or droughts, abundance or famine. From the twelve winds, he draws conclusions about the state of harmony of heaven and earth, and takes note of good and bad signs that result from their accord or disaccord. In general, he concerns himself with five kinds of phenomena so as to warn the Emperor to come to the aid of the government and to allow for variations in the ceremonies according to their circumstances."

The Chinese were also keen observers of the fixed stars, giving them such unusual names as Ghost Vehicle, Sun of Imperial Concubine, Imperial Prince, Pivot of Heaven, Twinkling Brilliance or Weaving Girl. But, great astrologers though they may have been, the Chinese lacked one aspect of mathematics that the Greeks applied to astrology—deductive geometry. Deductive geometry was the basis of much classical astrology in and after the time of the Greeks, and this explains the different methods of prognostication used in the East and West.

Down through the ages the astrologer's art has depended, not so much on the uncovering of new facts, though this is important, as on the interpretation of the facts already known. This is the essence of his skill. Obviously one cannot always tell how people will react (and this underlines the very important difference between astrology and predestination which will be discussed later on) but one can be prepared, be forewarned, to know what to expect.

But why should the signs of the zodiac have any effect at all on the formation of human character? It is easy to see why people thought they did, and even now we constantly use astrological expressions in our everyday speech. The thoughts of "lucky star," "ill-fated," "star-crossed," "mooning around," are interwoven into the very structure of our language.

In the same way that the earth has been created by influences from outside, there remains an indisputable togetherness in the working of the universe. The world, after all, is a coherent structure, for if it were not, it would be quite without order and we would never know what to expect. A dog could turn into an apple, or an elephant sprout wings and fly at any moment without so much as a by your leave. But nature, as we know, functions according to laws, not whims, and the laws of nature are certainly not subject to capricious exceptions.

This means that no part of the universe is ever arbitrarily cut off from any other part. Everything is therefore to some extent linked with everything else. The moon draws an imperceptible tide on every puddle; tiny and trivial events can be effected by outside forces (such as the fall of a feather by the faintest puff of wind). And so it is fair to think that the local events at any moment reflect to a very small extent the evolution of the world as a whole.

From this principle follows the possibility of divination, and also knowledge of events at a distance, provided one's mind were always as perfectly undisturbed, as ideally smooth, as a mirror or unruffled lake. Provided, in other words, that one did not confuse the picture with hopes, guesses, and expectations. When people try to foretell the future by cards or crystal ball gazing they find it much easier to confuse the picture with expectations than to reflect it clearly.

But the present does contain a good deal of the future to which it leads—not all, but a good deal. The diver halfway between bridge and water is going to make a splash; the train whizzing towards the station will pass through it unless interfered with; the burglar breaking a pane of glass has exposed himself to the possibility of a prison sentence. Yet this is not a doctrine of determinism, as was emphasized earlier. Clearly, there are forces already at work in the present, and any one of them could alter the situation in some way. Equally, a change of decision could alter the whole situation as well. So the future depends, not on an irresistible force, but on a small act of free will.

An individual's age, physique, and position on the earth's surface are remote consequences of his birth. Birth counts as the original cause for all that happens subsequently. The horoscope, in this case, means "this person represents the further evolution of the state of the universe pictured in this chart." Such a chart can apply equally to man or woman, dog, ship or even limited company.

If the evolution of an idea, or of a person, is to be understood as a totality, it must continue to evolve from its own beginnings, which is to say, in the terms in which it began. The brown-eyed person will be faithful to brown eyes all his life; the traitor is being faithful to some complex of ideas which has long been evolving in him; and the person born at sunset will always express, as he evolves, the psychological implications or analogies of the moment when the sun sinks out of sight.

This is the doctrine that an idea must continue to evolve in terms of its origin. It is a completely non-materialist doctrine, though it never fails to apply to material objects. And it implies, too, that the individual will continue to evolve in terms of his moment of origin, and therefore possibly of the sign of the Zodiac rising on the eastern horizon at his birth. It also implies that the signs of the Zodiac themselves will evolve in the collective mind of the human race in the same terms that they were first devised and not in the terms in which modern astrologers consciously think they ought to work.

For the human race, like every other k. l of animal, has a collective mind, as Professor Jung discovered in his investigation of dreams. If no such collective mind existed, no infant could ever learn anything, for communication would be impossible. Furthermore, it is absurd to suggest that the conscious mind could be older than the "unconscious," for an infant's nervous system functions correctly before it has discovered the difference between "myself" and "something else" or discovered what eyes and hands are for. Indeed, the involuntary muscles function correctly even before birth, and will never be under conscious control. They are part of what we call the "unconscious" which is not really "unconscious" at all. To the contrary, it is totally aware of itself and everything else; it is merely that part of the mind that cannot be controlled by conscious effort.

And human experience, though it varies in detail with every individual, is basically the same for each one of us, consisting of sky and earth, day and night, waking and sleeping, man and woman, birth and death. So there is bound to be in the mind of the human race a very large number of inescapable ideas, which are called our natural archetypes.

There are also, however, artificial or cultural archetypes which are not universal or applicable to everyone, but are nevertheless inescapable within the limits of a given culture. Examples of these are the cross in Christianity, and the notion of "escape from the wheel of rebirth" in India. There was a time when these ideas did not exist. And there was a time, too, when the scheme of the Zodiac did not exist. One would not expect the Zodiac to have any influence on remote and primitive peoples, for example, who have never heard of it. If the Zodiac is only an archetype, their horoscopes probably would not work and it would not matter which sign they were born under.

But where the Zodiac is known, and the idea of it has become worked into the collective mind, then there it could well appear to have an influence, even if it has no physical existence. For ideas do not have a physical existence, anyway. No physical basis has yet been discovered for the telepathy that controls an anthill; young swallows migrate before, not after, their parents; and the weaver-bird builds its intricate nest without being taught. Materialists suppose, but cannot prove, that "instinct" (as it is called, for no one knows how it works) is controlled by nucleic acid in the chromosomes. This is not a genuine explanation, though, for it only pushes the mystery one stage further back.

Does this mean, then, that the human race, in whose civilization the idea of the twelve signs of the Zodiac has long been embedded, is divided into only twelve types? Can we honestly believe that it is really as simple as that? If so, there must be pretty wide ranges of variation within each type. And if, to explain the variation, we call in heredity and environment, experiences in early childhood, the thyroid and other glands, and also the four functions of the mind mentioned at the beginning of this introduction, and extroversion and introversion, then one begins to wonder if the original classification was worth making at all. No sensible person believes that his favorite system explains everything. But even so, he will not find it much use at all if it does not even save him the trouble of bothering with the others.

Under the Jungian system, everyone has not only a dominant or principal function, but also a secondary or subsidiary one, so that the four can be arranged in order of potency. In the intuitive type, sensation is always the most inefficient function, but the second most inefficient function can be either thinking (which tends to make original thinkers such as Jung himself) or else feeling (which tends to make artistic people). Therefore, allowing for introversion and extroversion, there are at least four kinds of intuitive types, and sixteen types in all. Furthermore, one can see how the sixteen types merge into each other, so that there are no unrealistic or unconvincingly rigid divisions.

In the same way, if we were to put every person under only one sign of the Zodiac, the system becomes too rigid and unlike life. Besides, it was never intended to be used like that. It may be convenient to have only twelve types, but we know that in practice there is every possible gradation between aggressiveness and timidity, or between conscientiousness and laziness. How, then, do we account for this?

The Tyrant and the Saint

Just as the thinking type of man is also influenced to some extent by sensation and intuition, but not very much by emotion, so a person born under Leo can be influenced to some extent by one or two (but not more) of the other signs. For instance, famous persons born under the sign of Gemini include Henry VIII, whom nothing and no-one could have induced to abdicate, and Edward VIII, who did just that. Obviously, then, the sign Gemini does not fully explain the complete character of either of them.

Again, under the opposite sign, Sagittarius, were both Stalin, who was totally consumed with the notion of power, and Charles V, who freely gave up an empire because he preferred to go into a monastery. And we find under Scorpio, many uncompromising characters such as Luther, de Gaulle, Indira Gandhi and Montgomery, but also Petain, a successful commander whose name later became synonymous with collaboration.

A single sign is therefore obviously inadequate to explain the differences between people; it can only explain resemblances, such as the combativeness of the Scorpio group, or the far-reaching devotion of Charles V and Stalin to their respective ideals—the Christian heaven and the Communist utopia.

But very few people are born under one sign only. As well as the month of birth, as was mentioned earlier, the day matters, and, even more, the hour, which ought, if possible, to be noted to the nearest minute. Without this, it is impossible to have an actual horoscope, for the word horoscope means literally, "a consideration of the hour."

The month of birth tells you only which sign of the Zodiac was occupied by the sun. The day and hour tell you what sign was occupied by the moon. And the minute tells you which sign was rising on the eastern horizon. This is called the Ascendant, and it is supposed to be the most important thing in the whole horoscope.

If you were born at midnight, the sun is then in an important position, although invisible. But at one o'clock in the morning the sun is not important, so the moment of birth will not matter much. The important thing then will be the Ascendant, and possibly one or two of the planets. At a given day and hour, say, dawn on January 1st, or 9:00 p.m. on the longest day, the Ascendant will always be the same at any given place. But the moon and planets alter from day to day, at different speeds and have to be looked up in an astronomical table.

The sun is said to signify one's heart, that is to say, one's deepest desires and inmost nature. This is quite different from the moon, which, as we have seen, signifies one's superficial way of behaving. When the ancient Romans referred to the Emperor Augustus as a Capricornian, they meant that he had the moon in Capricorn; they did not pay much attention to the sun, although he was born at sunrise. Or, to take another example, a modern astrologer would call Disraeli a Scorpion because he had Scorpio rising, but most people would call him Sagittarian because he had the sun there. The Romans would have called him Leo because his moon was in Leo.

The sun, as has already been pointed out, is important if one is born near sunrise, sunset, noon or midnight, but is otherwise not reckoned as the principal influence. So if one does not seem to fit one's birth month, it is always worthwhile reading the other signs, for one may have been born at a time when any of them were rising or occupied by the moon. It also seems to be the case that the influence of the sun develops as life goes on, so that the month of birth is easier to guess in people over the age of forty. The young are supposed to be influenced mainly by their Ascendant which characterizes the body and physical personality as a whole.

It should be clearly understood that it is nonsense to assume that all people born at a certain time will exhibit the same characteristics, or that they will even behave in the same manner. It is quite obvious that, from the very moment of its birth, a child is subject to the effects of its environment, and that this in turn will influence its character and heritage to a decisive extent. Also to be taken into account are education and economic conditions, which play a very important part in the formation of one's character as well.

However, it is clearly established that people born under one sign of the Zodiac do have certain basic traits in their character which are different from those born under other signs. It is obvious to every thinking person that certain events produce different reactions in various people. For instance, if a man slips on a banana skin and falls heavily on the pavement, one passer-by may laugh and find this extremely amusing, while another may just walk on, thinking: "What a fool falling down like that. He should look where he is going." A third might also walk away saying to himself: "It's none of my business—I'm glad it wasn't me." A fourth might walk past and think: "I'm sorry for that man, but I haven't the time to be bothered with helping him." And a fifth might stop to help the fallen man to his feet, comfort him and take him home. Here is just one event which could produce entirely different reactions in different people. And, obviously, there are many more. One that comes to mind immediately is the violently opposed views to events such as wars, industrial strikes, and so on. The fact that people have different attitudes to the same event is simply another way of saying that they have different characters. And this is not something that can be put down to background, for people of the same race, religion, or class, very often express quite different reactions to happenings or events. Similarly, it is often the case that members of the same family, where there is clearly uniform background of economic and social standing, education, race and religion, often argue bitterly among themselves over political and social issues.

People have, in general, certain character traits and qualities which, according to their environment, develop in either a positive or a negative manner. Therefore, selfishness (inherent selfishness, that is) might emerge as unselfishness; kindness and consideration as cruelty and lack of consideration towards others. In the same way, a naturally constructive person, may, through frustration, become destructive, and so on. The latent characteristics with which people are born can, therefore, through environment and good or bad training, become something that would appear to be its opposite, and so give the lie to the astrologer's description of their character. But this is not the case. The true character is still there, but it is buried deep beneath these external superficialities.

Careful study of the character traits of different signs can be immeasurable help, and can render beneficial service to the intelligent person. Undoubtedly, the reader will already have discovered that, while he is able to get on very well with some people, he just "cannot stand" others. The causes sometimes seem inexplicable. At times there is intense dislike, at other times immediate sympathy. And there is, too, the phenomenon of love at first sight, which is also apparently inexplicable. People appear to be either sympathetic or unsympathetic towards each other for no apparent reason.

Now if we look at this in the light of the Zodiac, we find that people born under different signs are either compatible or incompatible with each other. In other words, there are good and bad interrelating factors among the various signs. This does not, of course, mean that humanity can be divided into groups of hostile camps. It would be quite wrong to be hostile or indifferent toward people who happen to be born under an incompatible sign. There is no reason why everybody should not, or cannot, learn to control and adjust their feelings and actions, especially after they are aware of the positive qualities of other people by studying their character analyses, among other things.

Every person born under a certain sign has both positive and negative qualities, which are developed more or less according to his free will. Nobody is entirely good or entirely bad, and it is up to each one of us to learn to control himself on the one hand, and at the same time to endeavor to learn about himself and others.

It cannot be repeated often enough that, though the intrinsic nature of man and his basic character traits are born in him, nevertheless it is his own free will that determines whether he will make really good use of his talents and abilities—whether, in other words, he will overcome his vices or allow them to rule him. Most of us are born with at least a streak of laziness, irritability, or some other fault in our nature, and it is up to each one of us to see that we exert sufficient willpower to control our failings so that they do not harm ourselves or others.

Astrology can reveal our inclinations and tendencies. Our weaknesses should not be viewed as shortcomings that are impossible to change. The horoscope of a man may show him to have criminal leanings, for instance, but this does not mean he will definitely become a criminal.

The ordinary man usually finds it difficult to know himself. He is often bewildered. Astrology can frequently tell him more about himself than the different schools of psychology are able to do. Knowing his failings and shortcomings, he will do his best to overcome them, and make himself a better and more useful member of society and a helpmate to his family and friends. It can also save him a great deal of unhappiness and remorse.

And yet it may seem absurd that an ancient philosophy, something that is known as a "pseudo-science," could be a prop to the men and women of the twentieth century. But below the materialistic surface of modern life, there are hidden streams of feeling and thought. Symbology is reappearing as a study worthy of the scholar; the psychosomatic factor in illness has passed from the writings of the crank to those of the specialist; spiritual healing in all its forms is no longer a pious hope but an accepted phenomenon. And it is into this context that we consider astrology, in the sense that it is an analysis of human types.

Astrology and medicine had a long journey together, and only parted company a couple of centuries ago. There still remain in medical language such astrological terms as "saturnine," "choleric," and "mercurial," used in the diagnosis of physical tendencies. The herbalist, for long the handyman of the medical profession, has been dominated by astrology since the days of the Greeks. Certain herbs traditionally respond to certain planetary influences, and diseases must therefore be treated to ensure harmony between the medicine and the disease.

No one expects the most eccentric of modern doctors to go back to the practices of his predecessors. We have come a long way since the time when phases of the moon were studied in illness. Those days were a medical nightmare, with epidemics that were beyond control, and an explanation of the Black Death sought in conjunction with the planets. Nowadays, astrological diagnosis of disease has literally no parallel in modern life. And yet, age-old symbols of types and of the vulnerability of, say, the Saturnian to chronic diseases or the choleric to apoplexy and blood pressure and so on, are still applicable.

But the stars are expected to foretell and not only to diagnose. The astrological forecaster has a counterpart on a highly conventional level in the shape of the weather prophet, racing tipster and stock market forecaster, to name just three examples. All in their own way are aiming at the same result. They attempt to look a little further into the pattern of life and also try to determine future patterns accurately.

Astrological forecasting has been remarkably accurate, but often it is wide of the mark. The brave man who cares to predict world events takes dangerous chances. Individual forecasting is less clear cut; it can be a help or a disillusionment. Then welcome to the nagging question: if it is possible to foreknow, is it right to foretell? A complex point of ethics on which it is hard to pronounce judgment. The doctor faces the same dilemma if he finds that symptoms of a mortal disease are present in his patient and that he can only prognosticate a steady decline. How much to tell an individual in a crisis is a problem that has perplexed many distinguished scholars. Honest and conscientious astrologers in this modern world, where so many people are seeking guidance, face the same problem.

The ancient cults, the symbols of old religions, are eclipsed for the moment. They may return with their old force within a decade or two. But at present the outlook is dark. Human beings badly need assurance, as they did in the past, that all is not chaos. Somewhere, somehow, there is a pattern that must be worked out. As to the why and wherefore, the astrologer is not expected to give judgment. He is just someone who, by dint of talent and training, can gaze into the future.

Five hundred years ago it was customary to call in a learned man who was an astrologer who was probably also a doctor and a philosopher. By his knowledge of astrology, his study of planetary influences, he felt himself qualified to guide those in distress. The world has moved forward at a fantastic rate since then, and in this twentieth century speed has been the keyword everywhere. Tensions have increased, the spur of ambition has been applied indiscriminately. People are uncertain of themselves. At first sight it seems fantastic in the light of modern thinking that they turn to the most ancient of all studies, and get someone to calculate a horoscope for them. But is it *really* so fantastic if you take a second look? For astrology is concerned with tomorrow, with survival. And in a world such as ours, those two things are the keywords of the time in which we live.

HOW TO USE THESE PREDICTIONS

A person reading the predictions in this book should understand that they are produced from the daily position of the planets for a group of people and are not, of course, individually specialized. To get the full benefit of them he should relate the predictions to his own character and circumstances, co-ordinate them, and draw his own conclusions from them.

If he is a serious observer of his own life he should find a definite pattern emerge that will be a helpful and reliable guide.

The point is that we always retain our free will. The stars indicate certain directional tendencies but we are not compelled to follow. We can do or not do, and wisdom must make the choice.

We all have our good and bad days. Sometimes they extend into cycles of weeks. It is therefore advisable to study daily predictions in a span ranging from the day before to several days ahead; also to re-read the monthly predictions for similar cycles.

Daily predictions should be taken very generally. The word "difficult" does not necessarily indicate a whole day of obstruction or inconvenience. It is a warning to you to be cautious. Your caution will often see you around the difficulty before you are involved. This is the correct use of astrology.

In another section, detailed information is given about the influence of the moon as it passes through the various signs of the Zodiac. It includes instructions on how to use the Moon Tables. This information should be used in conjunction with the daily forecasts to give a fuller picture of the astrological trends.

THE MOON

Moon is the nearest planet to the earth. It exerts more observable influence on us from day to day than any other planet. The effect is very personal, very intimate, and if we are not aware of how it works it can make us quite unstable in our ideas. And the annoying thing is that at these times we often see our own instability but can do nothing about it. A knowledge of what can be expected may help considerably. We can then be prepared to stand strong against the moon's negative influences and use its positive ones to help us to get ahead. Who has not heard of going with the tide?

Moon reflects, has no light of its own. It reflects the sun—the life giver—in the form of vital movement. Moon controls the tides, the blood rhythm, the movement of sap in trees and plants. Its nature is inconstancy and change so it signifies our moods, our superficial behavior—walking, talking and especially thinking. Being a true reflector of other forces, moon is cold, watery like the surface of a still lake, brilliant and scintillating at times, but easily ruffled and disturbed by the winds of change.

The moon takes 28½ days to circle the earth and the Zodiac. It spends just over 2¼ days in each sign. During that time it reflects the qualities, energies and characteristics of the sign and, to a degree, the planet which rules the sign. While the moon in its transit occupies a sign incompatible with our own birth sign, we can expect to feel a vague uneasiness, perhaps a touch of irritableness. We should not be discouraged nor let the feeling get us down, or, worse still, allow ourselves to take the discomfort out on others. Try to remember that the moon has to change signs within 55 hours and, provided you are not physically ill, your mood will probably change with it. It is amazing how frequently depression lifts with the shift in the moon's position. And, of course, when the moon is transiting a sign compatible or sympathetic to yours you will probably feel some sort of stimulation or just plain happy to be alive.

In the horoscope, the moon is such a powerful indicator that competent astrologers often use the sign it occupied at birth as the birth sign of the person. This is done particularly when the sun is on the cusp, or edge, of two signs. Most experienced astrologers, however, coordinate both sun and moon signs by reading and confirming from one to the other and secure a far more accurate and personalized analysis.

For these reasons, the moon tables which follow this section (see pages 28–35) are of great importance to the individual. They show the days and the exact times the moon will enter each sign of the Zodiac for the year. Remember, you have to adjust the indicated times to local time. The corrections, already calculated for most of the main cities, are at the beginning of the tables. What follows now is a guide to the influences that will be reflected to the earth by the moon while it transits each of the twelve signs. The influence is at its peak about 26 hours after the moon enters a sign.

MOON IN ARIES

This is a time for action, for reaching out beyond the usual self-imposed limitations and faint-hearted cautions. If you have plans in your head or on your desk, put them into practice. New ventures, applications, new jobs, new starts of any kind—all have a good chance of success. This is the period when original and dynamic impulses are being reflected onto the earth. The energies are extremely vital and favor the pursuit of pleasure and adventure in practically every form. Sick people should feel an improvement. Those who are well will probably find themselves exuding confidence and optimism. People fond of physical exercise should find their bodies growing with tone and well-being. Boldness, strength, determination should characterize most of your activities with a readiness to face up to old challenges. Yesterday's problems may seem petty and exaggerated—so deal with them. Strike out alone. Self-reliance will attract others to you. This is a good time for making friends. Business and marriage partners are more likely to be impressed with the man and woman of action. Opposition will be overcome or thrown aside with much less effort than usual. CAUTION: Be dominant but not domineering.

MOON IN TAURUS

The spontaneous, action-packed person of yesterday gives way to the cautious, diligent, hardworking "thinker." In this period ideas will probably be concentrated on ways of improving finances. A great deal of time may be spent figuring out and going over schemes and plans. It is the right time to be careful with detail. People will find themselves working longer than usual at their desks. Or devoting more time to serious thought about the future. A strong desire to put order into business and financial arrangements may cause extra work. Loved ones may complain of being neglected and may fail to appreciate that your efforts are for their ultimate benefit. Your desire for system may extend to criticism of arrangements in the home and lead to minor upsets. Health may be affected through overwork. Try to secure a reasonable amount of rest and relaxation, although the tendency will be to "keep going" despite good advice. Work done conscientiously in this period should result in a solid contribution to your future security. CAUTION: Try not to be as serious with people as the work you are engaged in.

MOON IN GEMINI

The humdrum of routine and too much work should suddenly end. You are likely to find yourself in an expansive, quicksilver world of change and self-expression. Urges to write, to paint, to experience the freedom of some sort of artistic outpouring, may be very strong. Take full advantage of them. You may find yourself finishing something you began and put aside long ago. Or embarking on something new which could easily be prompted by a chance meeting, a new acquaintance, or even an advertisement. There may be a yearning for a change of scenery, the feeling to visit another country (not too far away), or at least to get away for a few days. This may result in short, quick journeys. Or, if you are planning a single visit, there may be some unexpected changes or detours on the way. Familiar activities will seem to give little satisfaction unless they contain a fresh element of excitement or expectation. The inclination will be towards untried pursuits, particularly those that allow you to express your inner nature. The accent is on new faces, new places. CAUTION: Do not be too quick to commit yourself emotionally.

MOON IN CANCER

Feelings of uncertainty and vague insecurity are likely to cause problems while the moon is in Cancer. Thoughts may turn frequently to the warmth of the home and the comfort of loved ones. Nostalgic impulses could cause you to bring out old photographs and letters and reflect on the days when your life seemed to be much more rewarding and less demanding. The love and understanding of parents and family may be important, and, if it is not forthcoming you may have to fight against a bit of self-pity. The cordiality of friends and the thought of good times with them that are sure to be repeated will help to restore you to a happier frame of mind. The feeling to be alone may follow minor setbacks or rebuffs at this time, but solitude is unlikely to help. Better to get on the telephone or visit someone. This period often causes peculiar dreams and up-surges of imaginative thinking which can be very helpful to authors of occult and mystical works. Preoccupation with the more person-al world of simple human needs should overshadow any material strivings. CAUTION: Do not spend too much time thinking—seek the company of loved ones or close friends.

MOON IN LEO

New horizons of exciting and rather extravagant activity open up. This is the time for exhilarating entertainment, glamorous and lavish parties, and expensive shopping sprees. Any merrymaking that relies upon your generosity as a host has every chance of being a spectacular success. You should find yourself right in the center of the fun, either as the life of the party or simply as a person whom happy people like to be with. Romance thrives in this heady at-mosphere and friendships are likely to explode unexpectedly into serious attachments. Children and younger people should be at-tracted to you and you may find yourself organizing a picnic or a visit to a fun-fair, the cinema or the seaside. The sunny company and vitality of youthful companions should help you to find some unsuspected energy. In career, you could find an opening for pro-motion or advancement. This should be the time to make a direct approach. The period favors those engaged in original research. CAUTION: Bask in popularity but not in flattery.

MOON IN VIRGO

Off comes the party cap and out steps the busy, practical worker. He wants to get his personal affairs straight, to rearrange them, if necessary, for more efficiency, so he will have more time for more work. He clears up his correspondence, pays outstanding bills, makes numerous phone calls. He is likely to make inquiries, or sign up for some new insurance and put money into gilt-edged invest-ment. Thoughts probably revolve around the need for future secur-ity—to tie up loose ends and clear the decks. There may be a ten-dency to be "finicky," to interfere in the routine of others, particu-larly friends and family members. The motive may be a genuine desire to help with suggestions for updating or streamlining their affairs, but these will probably not be welcomed. Sympathy may be felt for less fortunate sections of the community and a flurry of some sort of voluntary service is likely. This may be accompanied by strong feelings of responsibility on several fronts and health may suffer from extra efforts made. CAUTION: Everyone may not want your help or advice.

MOON IN LIBRA

These are days of harmony and agreement and you should find yourself at peace with most others. Relationships tend to be smooth and sweet-flowing. Friends may become closer and bonds deepen in mutual understanding. Hopes will be shared. Progress by cooperation could be the secret of success in every sphere. In business, established partnerships may flourish and new ones get off to a good start. Acquaintances could discover similar interests that lead to congenial discussions and rewarding exchanges of some sort. Love, as a unifying force, reaches its optimum. Marriage partners should find accord. Those who wed at this time face the prospect of a happy union. Cooperation and tolerance are felt to be stronger than dissension and impatience. The argumentative are not quite so loud in their bellowings, nor as inflexible in their attitudes. In the home, there should be a greater recognition of the other point of view and a readiness to put the wishes of the group before selfish insistence. This is a favorable time to join an art group. CAUTION: Do not be too independent—let others help you if they want to.

MOON IN SCORPIO

Driving impulses to make money and to economize are likely to cause upsets all round. No area of expenditure is likely to be spared the axe, including the household budget. This is a time when the desire to cut down on extravagance can become near fanatical. Care must be exercised to try to keep the aim in reasonable perspective. Others may not feel the same urgent need to save and may retaliate. There is a danger that possessions of sentimental value will be sold to realize cash for investment. Buying and selling of stock for quick profit is also likely. The attention may turn to having a good clean up round the home and at the office. Neglected jobs could suddenly be done with great bursts of energy. The desire for solitude may intervene. Self-searching thoughts could disturb. The sense of invisible and mysterious energies at work could cause some excitability. The reassurance of loves ones may help. CAUTION: Be kind to the people you love.

MOON IN SAGITTARIUS

These are days when you are likely to be stirred and elevated by discussions and reflections of a religious and philosophical nature. Ideas of far-away places may cause unusual response and excitement. A decision may be made to visit someone overseas, perhaps a person whose influence was important to your earlier character development. There could be a strong resolution to get away from present intellectual patterns, to learn new subjects and to meet more interesting people. The superficial may be rejected in all its forms. An impatience with old ideas and unimaginative contacts could lead to a change of companions and interests. There may be an upsurge of religious feeling and metaphysical inquiry. Even a new insight into the significance of astrology and other occult studies is likely under the curious stimulus of the moon in Sagittarius. Physically, you may express this need for fundamental change by spending more time outdoors: sports, gardening or going for long walks. CAUTION: Try to channel any restlessness into worthwhile study.

MOON IN CAPRICORN

Life in these hours may seem to pivot around the importance of gaining prestige and honor in the career, as well as maintaining a spotless reputation. Ambitious urges may be excessive and could be accompanied by quite acquisitive drives for money. Effort should be directed along strictly ethical lines where there is no possibility of reproach or scandal. All endeavors are likely to be characterized by great earnestness, and an air of authority and purpose which should impress those who are looking for leadership or reliability. The desire to conform to accepted standards may extend to sharp criticism of family members. Frivolity and unconventional actions are unlikely to amuse while the moon is in Capricorn. Moderation and seriousness are the orders of the day. Achievement and recognition in this period could come through community work or organizing for the benefit of some amateur group. CAUTION: Dignity and esteem are not always self-awarded.

MOON IN AQUARIUS

Moon in Aquarius is in the second last sign of the Zodiac where ideas can become disturbingly fine and subtle. The result is often a mental "no-man's land" where imagination cannot be trusted with the same certitude as other times. The dangers for the individual are the extremes of optimism and pessimism. Unless the imgination is held in check, situations are likely to be misread, and rosy conclusions drawn where they do not exist. Consequences for the unwary can be costly in career and business. Best to think twice and not speak or act until you think again. Pessimism can be a cruel self-inflicted penalty for delusion at this time. Between the two extremes are strange areas of self-deception which, for example, can make the selfish person think he is actually being generous. Eerie dreams which resemble the reality and even seem to continue into the waking state are also possible. CAUTION: Look for the fact and not just for the image in your mind.

MOON IN PISCES

Everything seems to come to the surface now. Memory may be crystal clear, throwing up long-forgotten information which could be valuable in the career or business. Flashes of clairvoyance and intuition are possible along with sudden realizations of one's own nature, which may be used for self-improvement. A talent, never before suspected, may be discovered. Qualities not evident before in friends and marriage partners are likely to be noticed. As this is a period in which the truth seems to emerge, the discovery of false characteristics is likely to lead to disenchantment or a shift in attachments. However, where qualities are realized it should lead to happiness and deeper feeling. Surprise solutions could bob up for old problems. There may be a public announcement of the solving of a crime or mystery. People with secrets may find someone has "guessed" correctly. The secrets of the soul or the inner self also tend to reveal themselves. Religious and philosophical groups may make some interesting discoveries. CAUTION: Not a time for activities that depend on secrecy.

MOON TABLES

CORRECTION FOR NEW YORK TIME,
FIVE HOURS WEST OF GREENWICH

Atlanta, Boston, Detroit, Miami, Washington, Montreal,
Ottawa, Quebec, Bogota, Havana, Lima, Santiago . . . . Same time

Chicago, New Orleans, Houston, Winnipeg, Churchill,
Mexico City . . . . Deduct 1 hour

Albuquerque, Denver, Phoenix, El Paso, Edmonton,
Helena . . . . Deduct 2 hours

Los Angeles, San Francisco, Reno, Portland,
Seattle, Vancouver . . . . Deduct 3 hours

Honolulu, Anchorage, Fairbanks, Kodiak . . . . Deduct 5 hours

Nome, Samoa, Tonga, Midway . . . . Deduct 6 hours

Halifax, Bermuda, San Juan, Caracas, La Paz,
Barbados . . . . Add 1 hour

St. John's, Brasilia, Rio de Janeiro, Sao Paulo,
Buenos Aires, Montevideo . . . . Add 2 hours

Azores, Cape Verde Islands . . . . Add 3 hours

Canary Islands, Madeira, Reykjavik . . . . Add 4 hours

London, Paris, Amsterdam, Madrid, Lisbon, Gibraltar,
Belfast, Rabat . . . . Add 5 hours

Frankfurt, Rome, Oslo, Stockholm, Prague,
Belgrade . . . . Add 6 hours

Bucharest, Beirut, Tel Aviv, Athens, Istanbul, Cairo,
Alexandria, Cape Town, Johannesburg . . . . Add 7 hours

Moscow, Leningrad, Baghdad, Dhahran, Addis Ababa,
Nairobi, Teheran, Zanzibar . . . . Add 8 hours

Bombay, Calcutta, Sri Lanka . . . . Add 10½ hours

Hong Kong, Shanghai, Manila, Peking, Perth . . . . Add 13 hours

Tokyo, Okinawa, Darwin, Pusan . . . . Add 14 hours

Sydney, Melbourne, Port Moresby, Guam . . . . Add 15 hours

Auckland, Wellington, Suva, Wake . . . . Add 17 hours

1996 MOON TABLES—NEW YORK TIME

JANUARY		FEBRUARY		MARCH	
Day Moon Enters		**Day Moon Enters**		**Day Moon Enters**	
1. Gemini	9:30 pm	1. Cancer		1. Leo	11:48 am
2. Gemini		2. Cancer		2. Leo	
3. Gemini		3. Leo	4:47 am	3. Virgo	11:14 pm
4. Cancer	9:57 am	4. Leo		4. Virgo	
5. Cancer		5. Virgo	4:23 pm	5. Virgo	
6. Leo	10:31 pm	6. Virgo		6. Libra	8:41 am
7. Leo		7. Virgo		7. Libra	
8. Leo		8. Libra	2:31 am	8. Scorp.	4:06 pm
9. Virgo	10:30 am	9. Libra		9. Scorp.	
10. Virgo		10. Scorp.	10:36 am	10. Sagitt.	9:33 pm
11. Libra	8:56 pm	11. Scorp.		11. Sagitt.	
12. Libra		12. Sagitt.	3:59 pm	12. Sagitt.	
13. Libra		13. Sagitt.		13. Capric.	1:09 am
14. Scorp.	4:31 am	14. Capric.	6:30 pm	14. Capric.	
15. Scorp.		15. Capric.		15. Aquar.	3:16 am
16. Sagitt.	8:26 am	16. Aquar.	7:01 pm	16. Aquar.	
17. Sagitt.		17. Aquar.		17. Pisces	4:51 am
18. Capric.	9:08 am	18. Pisces	7:10 pm	18. Pisces	
19. Capric.		19. Pisces		19. Aries	7:16 am
20. Aquar.	8:16 am	20. Aries	8:59 pm	20. Aries	
21. Aquar.		21. Aries		21. Taurus	0:00 pm
22. Pisces	8:03 am	22. Aries		22. Taurus	
23. Pisces		23. Taurus	2:09 am	23. Gemini	8:00 pm
24. Aries	10:38 am	24. Taurus		24. Gemini	
25. Aries		25. Gemini	11:15 am	25. Gemini	
26. Taurus	5:17 pm	26. Gemini		26. Cancer	7:07 am
27. Taurus		27. Cancer	11:11 pm	27. Cancer	
28. Taurus		28. Cancer		28. Leo	7:38 pm
29. Gemini	3:43 am	29. Cancer		29. Leo	
30. Gemini				30. Leo	
31. Cancer	4:12 pm			31. Virgo	7:16 am

Summer time to be considered where applicable.

1996 MOON TABLES—NEW YORK TIME

APRIL		MAY		JUNE	
Day Moon Enters		**Day Moon Enters**		**Day Moon Enters**	
1. Virgo		1. Libra		1. Sagitt	
2. Libra	4:27 pm	2. Scorp.	7:43 am	2. Capric.	9:30 pm
3. Libra		3. Scorp.		3. Capric.	
4. Scorp.	10:58 pm	4. Sagitt.	11:06 am	4. Aquar.	9:46 pm
5. Scorp.		5. Sagitt.		5. Aquar.	
6. Scorp.		6. Capric.	12:55 pm	6. Pisces	11:20 pm
7. Sagitt.	3:22 am	7. Capric.		7. Pisces	
8. Sagitt.		8. Aquar.	2:40 pm	8. Pisces	
9. Capric.	6:31 am	9. Aquar.		9. Aries	3:24 am
10. Capric.		10. Pisces	5:30 pm	10. Aries	
11. Aquar.	9:10 am	11. Pisces		11. Taurus	10:12 am
12. Aquar		12. Aries	10:01 pm	12. Taurus	
13. Pisces	12:01 pm	13. Aries		13. Gemini	7:17 pm
14. Pisces		14. Aries		14. Gemini	
15. Aries	3:44 pm	15. Taurus	4:26 am	15. Gemini	
16. Aries		16. Taurus		16. Cancer	6:09 am
17. Taurus	9:06 pm	17. Gemini	12:49 pm	17. Cancer	
18. Taurus		18. Gemini		18. Leo	6:23 pm
19. Taurus		19. Cancer	11:17 pm	19. Leo	
20. Gemini	4:55 am	20. Cancer		20. Leo	
21. Gemini		21. Cancer		21. Virgo	7:08 am
22. Cancer	3:26 pm	22. Leo	11:29 am	22. Virgo	
23. Cancer		23. Leo		23. Libra	6:38 pm
24. Cancer		24. Virgo	11:59 pm	24. Libra	
25. Leo	3:45 am	25. Virgo		25. Libra	
26. Leo		26. Virgo		26. Scorp.	2:54 am
27. Virgo	3:50 pm	27. Libra	10:34 am	27. Scorp.	
28. Virgo		28. Libra		28. Sagitt.	7:02 pm
29. Virgo		29. Scorp.	5:31 pm	29. Sagitt.	
30. Libra	1:28 am	30. Scorp.		30. Capric.	7:48 pm
		31. Sagitt.	8:44 pm		

Summer time to be considered where applicable.

1996 MOON TABLES—NEW YORK TIME

JULY		AUGUST		SEPTEMBER	
Day Moon Enters		**Day Moon Enters**		**Day Moon Enters**	
1. Capric.		1. Pisces		1. Taurus	7:21 am
2. Aquar.	7:06 am	2. Aries	6:06 pm	2. Taurus	
3. Aquar.		3. Aries		3. Gemini	2:09 pm
4. Pisces	7:08 am	4. Taurus	10:34 pm	4. Gemini	
5. Pisces		5. Taurus		5. Gemini	
6. Aries	9:43 am	6. Taurus		6. Cancer	0:30 am
7. Aries		7. Gemini	6:50 am	7. Cancer	
8. Taurus	3:44 pm	8. Gemini		8. Leo	
9. Taurus		9. Cancer	5:58 pm	9. Leo	12:55 pm
10. Taurus		10. Cancer		10. Leo	
11. Gemini	0:53 am	11. Cancer		11. Virgo	1:29 am
12. Gemini		12. Leo	6:30 am	12. Virgo	
13. Cancer	12:09 pm	13. Leo		13. Libra	12:52 pm
14. Cancer		14. Virgo	7:08 pm	14. Libra	
15. Cancer		15. Virgo		15. Scorp.	10:21 pm
16. Leo	0:32 am	16. Virgo		16. Scorp.	
17. Leo		17. Libra	6:56 am	17. Scorp.	
18. Virgo	1:17 pm	18. Libra		18. Sagitt.	5:32 am
19. Virgo		19. Scorp.	4:51 pm	19. Sagitt.	
20. Virgo		20. Scorp.		20. Capric.	10:13 am
21. Libra	1:15 am	21. Sagitt.	11:49 pm	21. Capric.	
22. Libra		22. Sagitt.		22. Aquar.	12:40 pm
23. Scorp.	10:44 am	23. Sagitt.		23. Aquar.	
24. Scorp.		24. Capric.	3:23 am	24. Pisces	1:44 pm
25. Sagitt.	4:25 pm	25. Capric.		25. Pisces	
26. Sagitt.		26. Aquar.	4:11 am	26. Aries	2:47 pm
27. Capric.	6:18 pm	27. Aquar.		27. Aries	
28. Capric.		28. Pisces	3:50 am	28. Taurus	5:25 pm
29. Aquar.	5:48 pm	29. Pisces		29. Taurus	
30. Aquar.		30. Aries	4:16 am	30. Gemini	11:02 pm
31. Pisces	5:02 pm	31. Aries			

Summer time to be considered where applicable.

1996 MOON TABLES—NEW YORK TIME

OCTOBER		NOVEMBER		DECEMBER	
Day Moon Enters		**Day Moon Enters**		**Day Moon Enters**	
1. Gemini		1. Cancer		1. Leo	
2. Gemini		2. Leo	4:17 am	2. Virgo	1:12 am
3. Cancer	8:15 am	3. Leo		3. Virgo	
4. Cancer		4. Virgo	4:58 pm	4. Libra	1:24 pm
5. Leo	8:13 pm	5. Virgo		5. Libra	
6. Leo		6. Virgo		6. Scorp.	10:40 pm
7. Leo		7. Libra	4:30 am	7. Scorp.	
8. Virgo	8:50 am	8. Libra		8. Scorp.	
9. Virgo		9. Scorp.	1:03 pm	9. Sagitt.	3:59 am
10. Libra	8:01 pm	10. Scorp.		10. Sagitt.	
11. Libra		11. Sagitt.	6:27 pm	11. Capric.	6:15 am
12. Libra		12. Sagitt.		12. Capric.	
13. Scorp.	4:47am	13. Capric.	9:45 pm	13. Aquar.	7:15 am
14. Scorp.		14. Capric.		14. Aquar.	
15. Sagitt.	11:08 am	15. Capric.		15. Pisces	8:45 am
16. Sagitt.		16. Aquar.	0:15 am	16. Pisces	
17. Capric.	3:38 pm	17. Aquar.		17. Aries	11:56 am
18. Capric.		18. Pisces	3:01 am	18. Aries	
19. Aquar.	6:52 pm	19. Pisces		19. Taurus	5:11 pm
20. Aquar.		20. Aries	6:35 am	20. Taurus	
21. Pisces	9:23 pm	21. Aries		21. Taurus	
22. Pisces		22. Taurus	11:13 am	22. Gemini	0:18 am
23. Aries	11:51 pm	23. Taurus		23. Gemini	
24. Aries		24. Gemini	5:21 pm	24. Cancer	9:15 am
25. Aries		25. Gemini		25. Cancer	
26. Taurus	3:12 am	26. Gemini		26. Cancer	
27. Taurus		27. Cancer	1:38 am	27. Leo	3:03 pm
28. Gemini	8:36 am	28. Cancer		28. Leo	
29. Gemini		29. Leo	12:31 pm	29. Virgo	8:46 am
30. Cancer	4:57 pm	30. Leo		30. Virgo	
31. Cancer				31. Libra	9:33 pm

Summer time to be considered where applicable.

1996 PHASES OF THE MOON—NEW YORK TIME

New Moon	First Quarter	Full Moon	Last Quarter
Dec. 5 ('95)	Dec. 28 ('95)	Jan. 5	Jan. 13
Jan. 20	Jan. 27	Feb. 4	Feb. 12
Feb. 18	Feb. 25	Mar. 4	Mar. 12
Mar. 19	Mar. 26	Apr. 3	Apr. 10
Apr. 17	Apr. 25	May 3	May 10
May 17	May 25	June 1	June 8
June 15	June 24	June 30	July 7
July 15	July 23	July 30	Aug. 6
Aug. 14	Aug. 21	Aug. 28	Sep. 4
Sep. 12	Sept. 20	Sept. 26	Oct. 4
Oct. 12	Oct. 19	Oct. 26	Nov. 3
Nov. 10	Nov. 17	Nov. 24	Dec. 3
Dec. 10	Dec. 17	Dec. 24	Jan. 2 ('97)

Each phase of the Moon lasts approximately seven to eight days, during which the Moon's shape gradually changes as it comes out of one phase and goes into the next.

There will be a partial solar eclipse during the New Moon phase on April 17 and October 12. There will be a lunar eclipse during the Full Moon phase on April 3 and September 26.

1996 PLANTING GUIDE

	Aboveground Crops	Root Crops	Pruning	Weeds Pests
January	1-23-27-28	6-12-13-14-15-19	6-14-15	7-8-9-10-11-17
February	1-2-19-20-23-24-28-29	8-9-10-11-15-16	11	5-6-7-13-14-17-18
March	22-23-27-28	7-8-9-10-13-14-17-18	9-10-17-18	5-11-12-15-16
April	3-18-19-23-24-30	4-5-6-10-14	5-6-14	7-8-12-16-17
May	1-2-20-21-28-29-30-31	7-11-12-15-16	11-12	4-5-9-10-13-14
June	17-18-24-25-26-27	3-4-7-8-12-13	7-8	2-5-6-9-10-14-15
July	21-22-23-24-28-29	1-5-9-10-14	5-14	3-7-11-12
August	18-19-20-21-24-25	1-2-5-6-10-11-29	1-2-10-11-29	3-4-8-9-13-30-31
September	14-15-16-17-21-25	2-6-7-12-29-30	6-7	1-4-5-9-10-11-12-27-28
October	13-14-18-19-22-23	4-5-11-27-31	4-5-31	1-2-6-7-8-9-10-29
November	14-15-18-19-23-24	1-7-8-9-10-27-28	1-9-10-27-28	2-3-4-5-6-25-26-30
December	12-16-20-21	5-6-7-8-25-26	7-8-25-26	1-2-3-9-28-29-30-31

1996 FISHING GUIDE

	Good	Best
January	2-3-4-7-8-20	5-6-13-27
February	3-4-5-6-7-12-18-25	1-2
March	2-3-4-5-6-12-19	7-8-27
April	1-2-7-17-25	3-4-5-6-10-30
May	4-5-6-10-17-25	1-2-3-29-30-31
June	1-2-16-28-29-30	3-4-8-24
July	2-3-4-7-27-30-31	1-15-23-28-29
August	14-22-26-27-30-31	1-2-6-25-28-29
September	4-12-20-24-26-27-28	25-29-30
October	24-25-28-29	4-12-19-23-26-27
November	3-22-25-26	11-18-23-24-27-28
December	3-10-17-22-23-24-27	21-25-26

MOON'S INFLUENCE OVER DAILY AFFAIRS

The Moon makes a complete transit of the Zodiac every 27 days 7 hours and 43 minutes. In making this transit the Moon forms different aspects with the planets and consequently has favorable or unfavorable bearings on affairs and events for persons according to the sign of the Zodiac under which they were born. Whereas the Sun exclusively represents fire, the Moon rules water. The action of the Moon may be described as fluctuating, variable, absorbent and receptive.

When the Moon is in conjunction with the Sun it is called a New Moon; when the Moon and Sun are in opposition it is called a Full Moon. From New Moon to Full Moon, first and second quarter—which takes about two weeks—the Moon is increasing or waxing. From Full Moon to New Moon, third and fourth quarter, the Moon is decreasing or waning. The Moon Table indicates the New Moon and Full Moon and the quarters.

ACTIVITY	MOON IN
Business:	
buying and selling	Sagittarius, Aries, Gemini, Virgo
new, requiring public support	1st and 2nd quarter
meant to be kept quiet	3rd and 4th quarter
Investigation	3rd and 4th quarter
Signing documents	1st & 2nd quarter, Cancer, Scorpio, Pisces
Advertising	2nd quarter, Sagittarius
Journeys and trips	1st & 2nd quarter, Gemini, Virgo
Renting offices, etc.	Taurus, Leo, Scorpio, Aquarius
Painting of house/apartment	3rd & 4th quarter, Taurus, Scorpio, Aquarius
Decorating	Gemini, Libra, Aquarius
Buying clothes and accessories	Taurus, Virgo
Beauty salon or barber shop visit	1st & 2nd quarter, Taurus, Leo, Libra, Scorpio, Aquarius
Weddings	1st & 2nd quarter

MOON'S INFLUENCE OVER YOUR HEALTH

ARIES	Head, brain, face, upper jaw
TAURUS	Throat, neck, lower jaw
GEMINI	Hands, arms, lungs, shoulders, nervous system
CANCER	Esophagus, stomach, breasts, womb, liver
LEO	Heart, spine
VIRGO	Intestines, liver
LIBRA	Kidneys, lower back
SCORPIO	Sex and eliminative organs
SAGITTARIUS	Hips, thighs, liver
CAPRICORN	Skin, bones, teeth, knees
AQUARIUS	Circulatory system, lower legs
PISCES	Feet, tone of being

Try to avoid work being done on that part of the body when the Moon is in the sign governing that part.

MOON'S INFLUENCE OVER PLANTS

Centuries ago it was established that seeds planted when the Moon is in certain signs and phases called Fruitful will produce more growth than seeds planted when the Moon is in a Barren sign.

FRUITFUL SIGNS	BARREN SIGNS	DRY SIGNS
Taurus	Aries	Aries
Cancer	Gemini	Gemini
Libra	Leo	Sagittarius
Scorpio	Virgo	Aquarius
Capricorn	Sagittarius	
Pisces	Aquarius	

ACTIVITY	MOON IN
Mow lawn, trim plants	**Fruitful sign:** 1st & 2nd quarter
Plant flowers	**Fruitful sign:** 2nd quarter; best in Cancer and Libra
Prune	**Fruitful sign:** 3rd & 4th quarter
Destroy pests; spray	**Barren sign:** 4th quarter
Harvest potatoes, root crops	**Dry sign:** 3rd & 4th quarter; Taurus, Leo, and Aquarius

THE SIGNS: DOMINANT CHARACTERISTICS

March 21–April 20

The Positive Side of Aries

The Arien has many positive points to his character. People born under this first sign of the Zodiac are often quite strong and enthusiastic. On the whole, they are forward-looking people who are not easily discouraged by temporary setbacks. They know what they want out of life and they go out after it. Their personalities are strong. Others are usually quite impressed by the Arien's way of doing things. Quite often they are sources of inspiration for others traveling the same route. Aries men and women have a special zest for life that is often contagious; for others, they are often the example of how life should be lived.

The Aries person usually has a quick and active mind. He is imaginative and inventive. He enjoys keeping busy and active. He generally gets along well with all kinds of people. He is interested in mankind, as a whole. He likes to be challenged. Some would say he thrives on opposition, for it is when he is set against that he often does his best. Getting over or around obstacles is a challenge he generally enjoys. All in all, the Arien is quite positive and young-thinking. He likes to keep abreast of new things that are happening in the world. Ariens are often fond of speed. They like things to be done quickly and this sometimes aggravates their slower colleagues and associates.

The Aries man or woman always seems to remain young. Their whole approach to life is youthful and optimistic. They never say die, no matter what the odds. They may have an occasional setback, but it is not long before they are back on their feet again.

The Negative Side of Aries

Everybody has his less positive qualities—and Aries is no exception. Sometimes the Aries man or woman is not very tactful in communicating with others; in his hurry to get things done he is apt to

be a little callous or inconsiderate. Sensitive people are likely to find him somewhat sharp-tongued in some situations. Often in his eagerness to achieve his aims, he misses the mark altogether. At times the Arien is too impulsive. He can occasionally be stubborn and refuse to listen to reason. If things do not move quickly enough to suit the Aries man or woman, he or she is apt to become rather nervous or irritable. The uncultivated Arien is not unfamiliar with moments of doubt and fear. He is capable of being destructive if he does not get his way. He can overcome some of his emotional problems by steadily trying to express himself as he really is, but this requires effort.

April 21–May 20

The Positive Side of Taurus

The Taurus person is known for his ability to concentrate and for his tenacity. These are perhaps his strongest qualities. The Taurus man or woman generally has very little trouble in getting along with others; it's his nature to be helpful toward people in need. He can always be depended on by his friends, especially those in trouble.

The Taurean generally achieves what he wants through his ability to persevere. He never leaves anything unfinished but works on something until it has been completed. People can usually take him at his word; he is honest and forthright in most of his dealings. The Taurus person has a good chance to make a success of his life because of his many positive qualities. The Taurean who aims high seldom falls short of his mark. He learns well by experience. He is thorough and does not believe in short-cuts of any kind. The Taurean's thoroughness pays off in the end, for through his deliberateness he learns how to rely on himself and what he has learned. The Taurus person tries to get along with others, as a rule. He is not overly critical and likes people to be themselves. He is a tolerant person and enjoys peace and harmony—especially in his home life.

The Taurean is usually cautious in all that he does. He is not a person who believes in taking unnecessary risks. Before adopting any one line of action, he will weigh all of the pros and cons. The

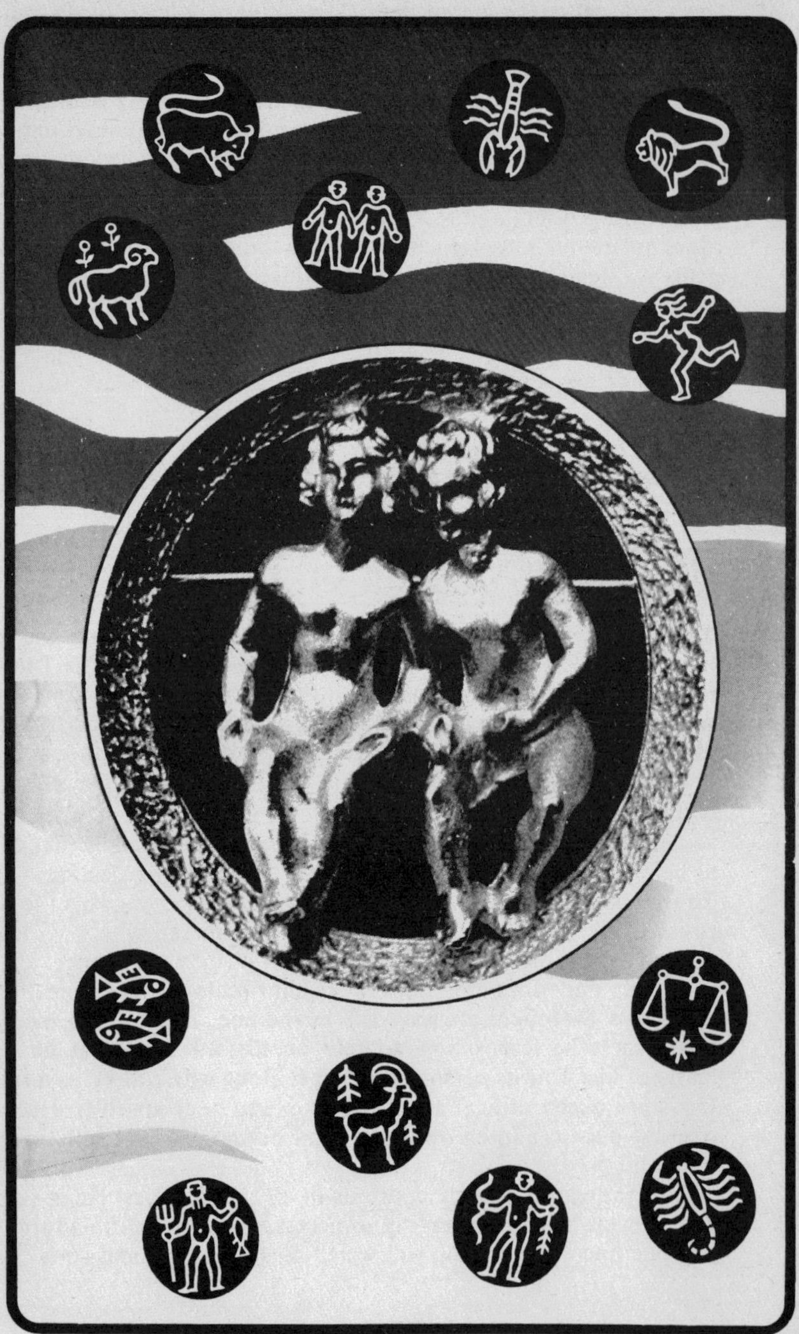

Taurus person is steadfast. Once his mind is made up it seldom changes. The person born under this sign usually is a good family person—reliable and loving.

The Negative Side of Taurus

Sometimes the Taurus man or woman is a bit too stubborn. He won't listen to other points of view if his mind is set on something. To others, this can be quite annoying. The Taurean also does not like to be told what to do. He becomes rather angry if others think him not too bright. He does not like to be told he is wrong, even when he is. He dislikes being contradicted.

Some people who are born under this sign are very suspicious of others—even of those persons close to them. They find it difficult to trust people fully. They are often afraid of being deceived or taken advantage of. The Taurean often finds it difficult to forget or forgive. His love of material things sometimes makes him rather avaricious and petty.

May 21–June 20

The Positive Side of Gemini

The person born under this sign of the Heavenly Twins is usually quite bright and quick-witted. Some of them are capable of doing many different things. The Gemini person very often has many different interests. He keeps an open mind and is always anxious to learn new things.

The Geminian is often an analytical person. He is a person who enjoys making use of his intellect. He is governed more by his mind than by his emotions. He is a person who is not confined to one view; he can often understand both sides to a problem or question. He knows how to reason; how to make rapid decisions if need be.

He is an adaptable person and can make himself at home almost anywhere. There are all kinds of situations he can adapt to. He is a person who seldom doubts himself; he is sure of his talents and his

ability to think and reason. The Geminian is generally most satisfied when he is in a situation where he can make use of his intellect. Never short of imagination, he often has strong talents for invention. He is rather a modern person when it comes to life; the Geminian almost always moves along with the times—perhaps that is why he remains so youthful throughout most of his life.

Literature and art appeal to the person born under this sign. Creativity in almost any form will interest and intrigue the Gemini man or woman.

The Geminian is often quite charming. A good talker, he often is the center of attraction at any gathering. People find it easy to like a person born under this sign because he can appear easygoing and usually has a good sense of humor.

The Negative Side of Gemini

Sometimes the Gemini person tries to do too many things at one time—and as a result, winds up finishing nothing. Some Geminians are easily distracted and find it rather difficult to concentrate on one thing for too long a time. Sometimes they give in to trifling fancies and find it rather boring to become too serious about any one thing. Some of them are never dependable, no matter what they promise.

Although the Gemini man or woman often appears to be well-versed on many subjects, this is sometimes just a veneer. His knowledge may be only superficial, but because he speaks so well he gives people the impression of erudition. Some Geminians are sharp-tongued and inconsiderate; they think only of themselves and their own pleasure.

June 21–July 20

The Positive Side of Cancer

The Cancerians's most positive point is his understanding nature. On the whole, he is a loving and sympathetic person. He would never go out of his way to hurt anyone. The Cancer man or woman

is often very kind and tender; they give what they can to others. They hate to see others suffering and will do what they can to help someone in less fortunate circumstances than themselves. They are often very concerned about the world. Their interest in people generally goes beyond that of just their own families and close friends; they have a deep sense of brotherhood and respect humanitarian values. The Cancerian means what he says, as a rule; he is honest about his feelings.

The Cancer man or woman is a person who knows the art of patience. When something seems difficult, he is willing to wait until the situation becomes manageable again. He is a person who knows how to bide his time. The Cancerian knows how to concentrate on one thing at a time. When he has made his mind up he generally sticks with what he does, seeing it through to the end.

The Cancerian is a person who loves his home. He enjoys being surrounded by familiar things and the people he loves. Of all the signs, Cancer is the most maternal. Even the men born under this sign often have a motherly or protective quality about them. They like to take care of people in their family—to see that they are well loved and well provided for. They are usually loyal and faithful. Family ties mean a lot to the Cancer man or woman. Parents and in-laws are respected and loved. The Cancerian has a strong sense of tradition. He is very sensitive to the moods of others.

The Negative Side of Cancer

Sometimes the Cancerian finds it rather hard to face life. It becomes too much for him. He can be a little timid and retiring, when things don't go too well. When unfortunate things happen, he is apt to just shrug and say, "Whatever will be will be." He can be fatalistic to a fault. The uncultivated Cancerian is a bit lazy. He doesn't have very much ambition. Anything that seems a bit difficult he'll gladly leave to others. He may be lacking in initiative. Too sensitive, when he feels he's been injured, he'll crawl back into his shell and nurse his imaginary wounds. The Cancer woman often is given to crying when the smallest thing goes wrong.

Some Cancerians find it difficult to enjoy themselves in environments outside their homes. They make heavy demands on others, and need to be constantly reassured that they are loved.

July 21–August 21

The Positive Side of Leo

Often Leos make good leaders. They seem to be good organizers and administrators. Usually they are quite popular with others. Whatever group it is that he belongs to, the Leo man is almost sure to be or become the leader.

The Leo person is generous most of the time. It is his best characteristic. He or she likes to give gifts and presents. In making others happy, the Leo person becomes happy himself. He likes to splurge when spending money on others. In some instances it may seem that the Leo's generosity knows no boundaries. A hospitable person, the Leo man or woman is very fond of welcoming people to his house and entertaining them. He is never short of company.

The Leo person has plenty of energy and drive. He enjoys working toward some specific goal. When he applies himself correctly, he gets what he wants most often. The Leo person is almost never unsure of himself. He has plenty of confidence and aplomb. He is a person who is direct in almost everything he does. He has a quick mind and can make a decision in a very short time.

He usually sets a good example for others because of his ambitious manner and positive ways. He knows how to stick to something once he's started. Although the Leo person may be good at making a joke, he is not superficial or glib. He is a loving person, kind and thoughtful.

There is generally nothing small or petty about the Leo man or woman. He does what he can for those who are deserving. He is a person others can rely upon at all times. He means what he says. An honest person, generally speaking, he is a friend that others value.

The Negative Side of Leo

Leo, however, does have his faults. At times, he can be just a bit too arrogant. He thinks that no one deserves a leadership position except him. Only he is capable of doing things well. His opinion of himself is often much too high. Because of his conceit, he is sometimes rather unpopular with a good many people. Some Leos are too materialistic; they can only think in terms of money and profit.

Some Leos enjoy lording it over others—at home or at their place of business. What is more, they feel they have the right to. Egocentric to an impossible degree, this sort of Leo cares little about how others think or feel. He can be rude and cutting.

August 22–September 22

The Positive Side of Virgo

The person born under the sign of Virgo is generally a busy person. He knows how to arrange and organize things. He is a good planner. Above all, he is practical and is not afraid of hard work.

The person born under this sign, Virgo, knows how to attain what he desires. He sticks with something until it is finished. He never shirks his duties, and can always be depended upon. The Virgo person can be thoroughly trusted at all times.

The man or woman born under this sign tries to do everything to perfection. He doesn't believe in doing anything half-way. He always aims for the top. He is the sort of a person who is constantly striving to better himself—not because he wants more money or glory, but because it gives him a feeling of accomplishment.

The Virgo man or woman is a very observant person. He is sensitive to how others feel, and can see things below the surface of a situation. He usually puts this talent to constructive use.

It is not difficult for the Virgoan to be open and earnest. He believes in putting his cards on the table. He is never secretive or under-handed. He's as good as his word. The Virgo person is generally plain-spoken and down-to-earth. He has no trouble in expressing himself.

The Virgo person likes to keep up to date on new developments in his particular field. Well-informed, generally, he sometimes has a keen interest in the arts or literature. What he knows, he knows well. His ability to use his critical faculties is well-developed and sometimes startles others because of its accuracy.

The Virgoan adheres to a moderate way of life; he avoids excesses. He is a responsible person and enjoys being of service.

The Negative Side of Virgo

Sometimes a Virgo person is too critical. He thinks that only he can do something the way it should be done. Whatever anyone else does is inferior. He can be rather annoying in the way he quibbles over insignificant details. In telling others how things should be done, he can be rather tactless and mean.

Some Virgos seem rather emotionless and cool. They feel emo-

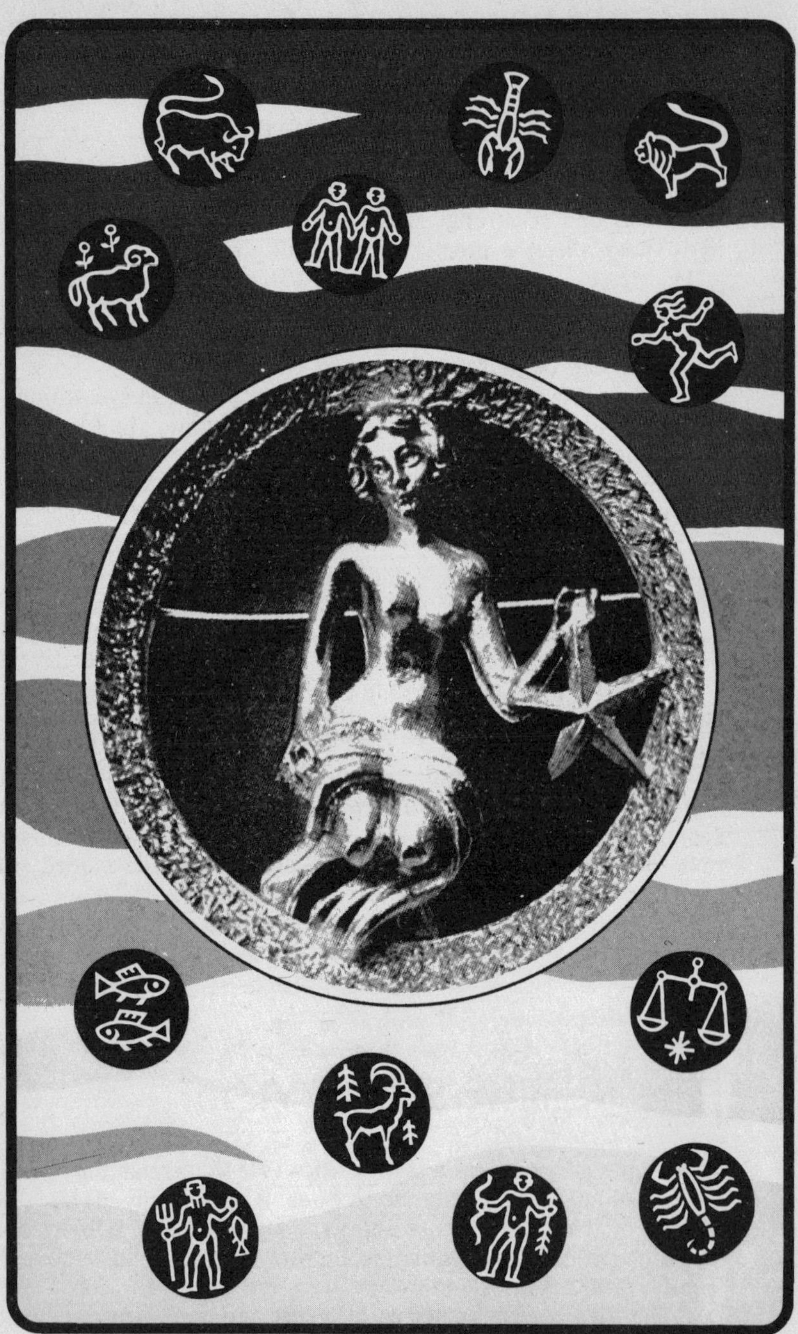

tional involvement is beneath them. They are sometimes too tidy, too neat. With money they can be rather miserly. Some try to force their opinions and ideas on others.

September 23–October 22

The Positive Side of Libra

Librans love harmony. It is one of their most outstanding character traits. They are interested in achieving balance; they admire beauty and grace in things as well as in people. Generally speaking, they are kind and considerate people. Librans are usually very sympathetic. They go out of their way not to hurt another person's feelings. They are outgoing and do what they can to help those in need.

People born under the sign of Libra almost always make good friends. They are loyal and amiable. They enjoy the company of others. Many of them are rather moderate in their views; they believe in keeping an open mind, however, and weighing both sides of an issue fairly before making a decision.

Alert and often intelligent, the Libran, always fair-minded, tries to put himself in the position of the other person. They are against injustice; quite often they take up for the underdog. In most of their social dealings, they try to be tactful and kind. They dislike discord and bickering, and most Libras strive for peace and harmony in all their relationships.

The Libra man or woman has a keen sense of beauty. They appreciate handsome furnishings and clothes. Many of them are artistically inclined. Their taste is usually impeccable. They know how to use color. Their homes are almost always attractively arranged and inviting. They enjoy entertaining people and see to it that their guests always feel at home and welcome.

The Libran gets along with almost everyone. He is well-liked and socially much in demand.

The Negative Side of Libra

Some people born under this sign tend to be rather insincere. So eager are they to achieve harmony in all relationships that they will even go so far as to lie. Many of them are escapists. They find facing

the truth an ordeal and prefer living in a world of make-believe.

In a serious argument, some Librans give in rather easily even when they know they are right. Arguing, even about something they believe in, is too unsettling for some of them.

Librans sometimes care too much for material things. They enjoy possessions and luxuries. Some are vain and tend to be jealous.

October 23–November 22

The Positive Side of Scorpio

The Scorpio man or woman generally knows what he or she wants out of life. He is a determined person. He sees something through to the end. The Scorpion is quite sincere, and seldom says anything he doesn't mean. When he sets a goal for himself he tries to go about achieving it in a very direct way.

The Scorpion is brave and courageous. They are not afraid of hard work. Obstacles do not frighten them. They forge ahead until they achieve what they set out for. The Scorpio man or woman has a strong will.

Although the Scorpion may seem rather fixed and determined, inside he is often quite tender and loving. He can care very much for others. He believes in sincerity in all relationships. His feelings about someone tend to last; they are profound and not superficial.

The Scorpio person is someone who adheres to his principles no matter what happens. He will not be deterred from a path he believes to be right.

Because of his many positive strengths, the Scorpion can often achieve happiness for himself and for those that he loves.

He is a constructive person by nature. He often has a deep understanding of people and of life, in general. He is perceptive and unafraid. Obstacles often seem to spur him on. He is a positive person who enjoys winning. He has many strengths and resources; challenge of any sort often brings out the best in him.

The Negative Side of Scorpio

The Scorpio person is sometimes hypersensitive. Often he imagines injury when there is none. He feels that others do not bother to

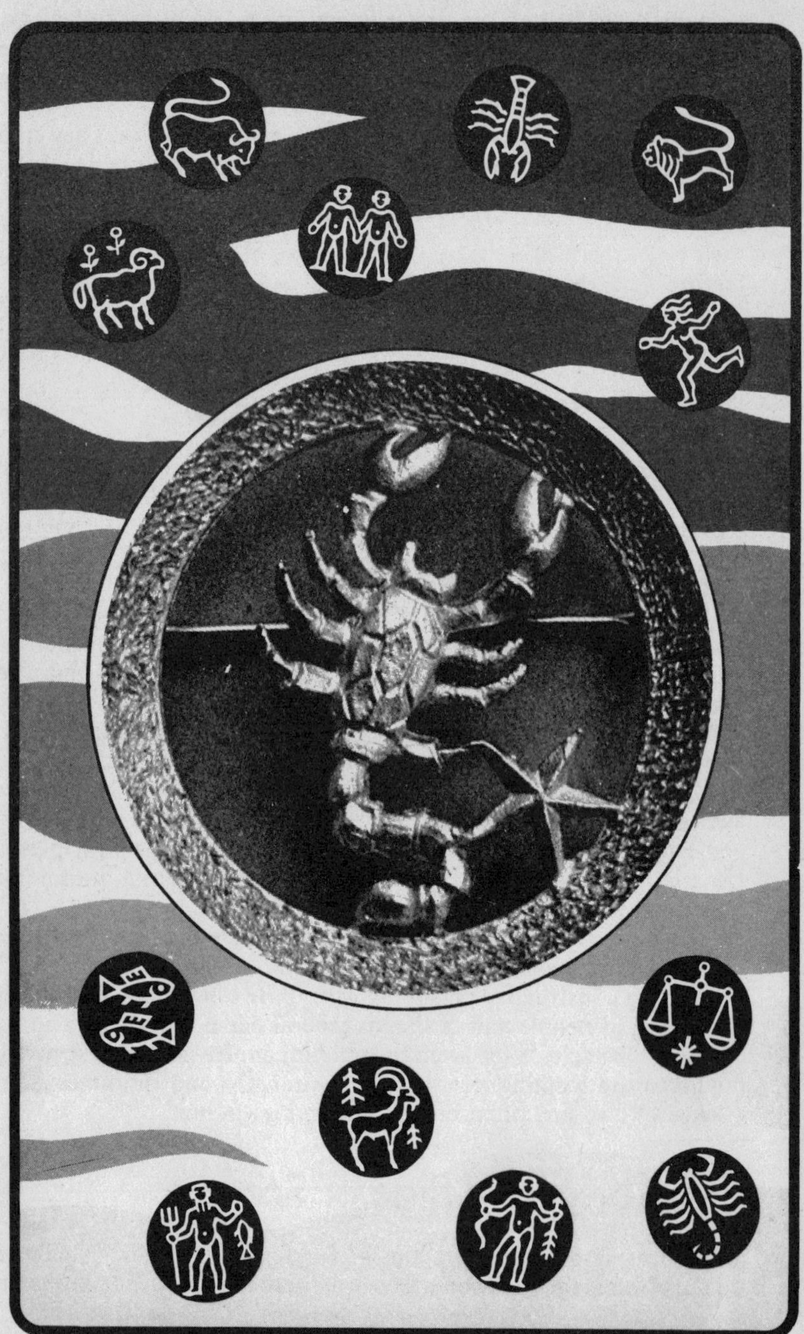

recognize him for his true worth. Sometimes he is given to excessive boasting in order to compensate for what he feels is neglect

The Scorpio person can be rather proud and arrogant. They can be rather sly when they put their minds to it and they enjoy outwitting persons or institutions noted for their cleverness.

Their tactics for getting what they want are sometimes devious and ruthless. They don't care too much about what others may think. If they feel others have done them an injustice, they will do their best to seek revenge. The Scorpion often has a sudden, violent temper; and this person's interest in sex is sometimes quite unbalanced or excessive.

November 23–December 20

The Positive Side of Sagittarius

People born under this sign are often honest and forthright. Their approach to life is earnest and open. The Sagittarian is often quite adult in his way of seeing things. They are broadminded and tolerant people. When dealing with others the person born under the sign of Sagittarius is almost always open and forthright. He doesn't believe in deceit or pretension. His standards are high. People who associate with the Sagittarian, generally admire and respect him.

The Sagittarian trusts others easily and expects them to trust him. He is never suspicious or envious and almost always thinks well of others. People always enjoy his company because he is so friendly and easy-going. The Sagittarius man or woman is often good-humored. He can always be depended upon by his friends, family, and co-workers.

The person born under this sign of the Zodiac likes a good joke every now and then; he is keen on fun and this makes him very popular with others.

A lively person, he enjoys sports and outdoor life. The Sagittarian is fond of animals. Intelligent and interesting, he can begin an animated conversation with ease. He likes exchanging ideas and discussing various views.

He is not selfish or proud. If someone proposes an idea or plan that is better than his, he will immediately adopt it. Imaginative yet practical, he knows how to put ideas into practice.

He enjoys sport and game, and it doesn't matter if he wins or loses. He is a forgiving person, and never sulks over something that has not worked out in his favor.

He is seldom critical, and is almost always generous.

The Negative Side of Sagittarius

Some Sagittarians are restless. They take foolish risks and seldom learn from the mistakes they make. They don't have heads for money and are often mismanaging their finances. Some of them devote much of their time to gambling.

Some are too outspoken and tactless, always putting their feet in their mouths. They hurt others carelessly by being honest at the wrong time. Sometimes they make promises which they don't keep. They don't stick close enough to their plans and go from one failure to another. They are undisciplined and waste a lot of energy.

December 21–January 19

The Positive Side of Capricorn

The person born under the sign of Capricorn is usually very stable and patient. He sticks to whatever tasks he has and sees them through. He can always be relied upon and he is not averse to work.

An honest person, the Capricornian is generally serious about whatever he does. He does not take his duties lightly. He is a practical person and believes in keeping his feet on the ground.

Quite often the person born under this sign is ambitious and knows how to get what he wants out of life. He forges ahead and never gives up his goal. When he is determined about something, he almost always wins. He is a good worker—a hard worker. Although things may not come easy to him, he will not complain, but continue working until his chores are finished.

He is usually good at business matters and knows the value of money. He is not a spendthrift and knows how to put something away for a rainy day; he dislikes waste and unnecessary loss.

The Capricornian knows how to make use of his self-control. He

can apply himself to almost anything once he puts his mind to it. His ability to concentrate sometimes astounds others. He is diligent and does well when involved in detail work.

The Capricorn man or woman is charitable, generally speaking, and will do what is possible to help others less fortunate. As a friend, he is loyal and trustworthy. He never shirks his duties or responsibilities. He is self-reliant and never expects too much of the other fellow. He does what he can on his own. If someone does him a good turn, then he will do his best to return the favor.

The Negative Side of Capricorn

Like everyone, the Capricornian, too, has his faults. At times, he can be over-critical of others. He expects others to live up to his own high standards. He thinks highly of himself and tends to look down on others.

His interest in material things may be exaggerated. The Capricorn man or woman thinks too much about getting on in the world and having something to show for it. He may even be a little greedy.

He sometimes thinks he knows what's best for everyone. He is too bossy. He is always trying to organize and correct others. He may be a little narrow in his thinking.

January 20–February 18

The Positive Side of Aquarius

The Aquarius man or woman is usually very honest and forthright. These are his two greatest qualities. His standards for himself are generally very high. He can always be relied upon by others. His word is his bond.

The Aquarian is perhaps the most tolerant of all the Zodiac personalities. He respects other people's beliefs and feels that everyone is entitled to his own approach to life.

He would never do anything to injure another's feelings. He is never unkind or cruel. Always considerate of others, the Aquarian is always willing to help a person in need. He feels a very strong tie between himself and all the other members of mankind.

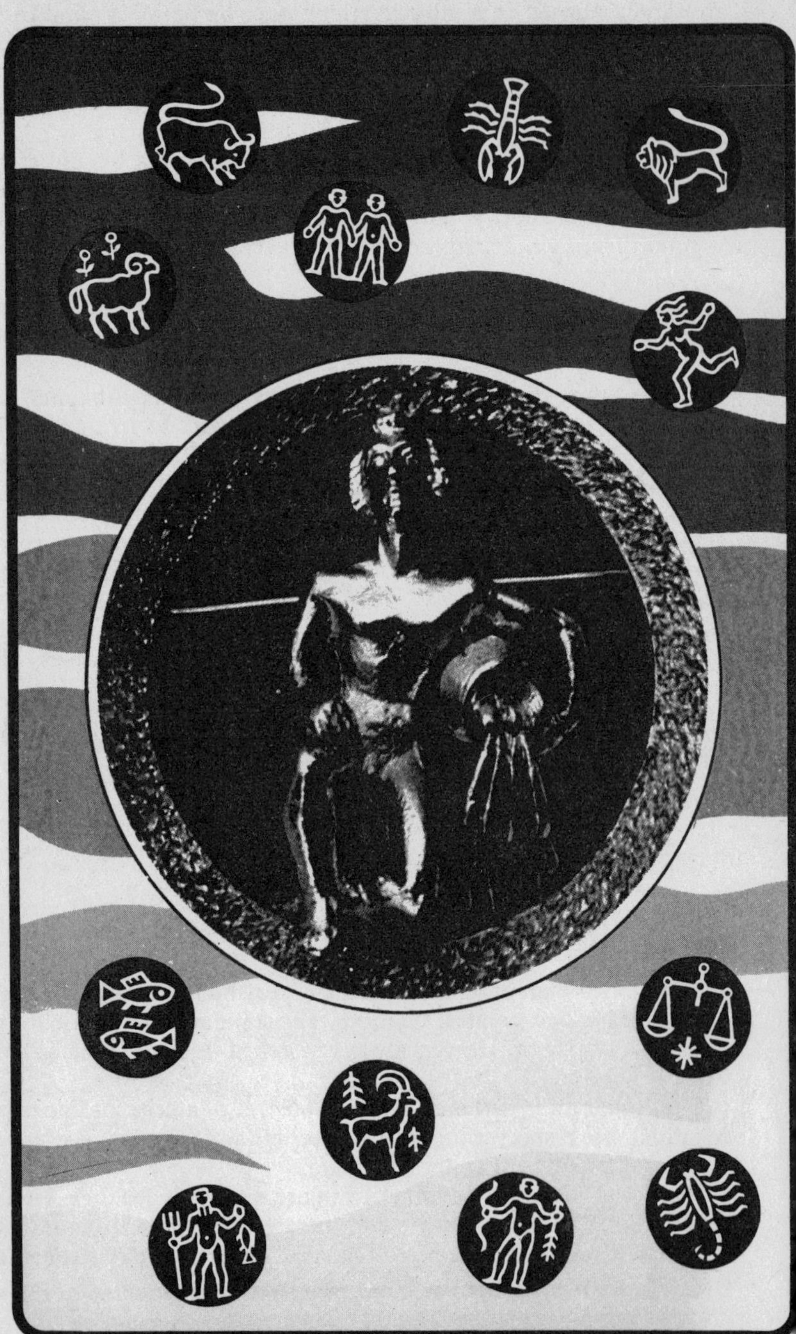

The person born under this sign is almost always an individualist. He does not believe in teaming up with the masses, but prefers going his own way. His ideas about life and mankind are often quite advanced. There is a saying to the effect that the average Aquarian is fifty years ahead of his time.

He is broadminded. The problems of the world concern him greatly. He is interested in helping others no matter what part of the globe they live in. He is truly a humanitarian sort. He likes to be of service to others.

Giving, considerate, and without prejudice, Aquarians have no trouble getting along with others.

The Negative Side of Aquarius

The Aquarian may be too much of a dreamer. He makes plans but seldom carries them out. He is rather unrealistic. His imagination has a tendency to run away with him. Because many of his plans are impractical, he is always in some sort of a dither.

Others may not approve of him at all times because of his unconventional behavior. He may be a bit eccentric. Sometimes he is so busy with his own thoughts, that he loses touch with the realities of existence.

Some Aquarians feel they are more clever and intelligent than others. They seldom admit to their own faults, even when they are quite apparent. Some become rather fanatic in their views. Their criticism of others is sometimes destructive and negative.

February 19–March 20

The Positive Side of Pisces

The Piscean can often understand the problems of others quite easily. He has a sympathetic nature. Kindly, he is often dedicated in the way he goes about helping others. The sick and the troubled often turn to him for advice and assistance.

He is very broadminded and does not criticize others for their faults. He knows how to accept people for what they are. On the whole, he is a trustworthy and earnest person. He is loyal to his

friends and will do what he can to help them in time of need. Generous and good-natured, he is a lover of peace; he is often willing to help others solve their differences. People who have taken a wrong turn in life often interest him and he will do what he can to persuade them to rehabilitate themselves.

He has a strong intuitive sense and most of the time he knows how to make it work for him; the Piscean is unusually perceptive and often knows what is bothering someone before that person, himself, is aware of it. The Pisces man or woman is an idealistic person, basically, and is interested in making the world a better place in which to live. The Piscean believes that everyone should help each other. He is willing to do more than his share in order to achieve cooperation with others.

The person born under this sign often is talented in music or art. He is a receptive person; he is able to take the ups and downs of life with philosophic calm.

The Negative Side of Pisces

Some Pisceans are often depressed; their outlook on life is rather glum. They may feel that they have been given a bad deal in life and that others are always taking unfair advantage of them. The Piscean sometimes feel that the world is a cold and cruel place. He is easily discouraged. He may even withdraw from the harshness of reality into a secret shell of his own where he dreams and idles away a good deal of his time.

The Piscean can be rather lazy. He lets things happen without giving the least bit of resistance. He drifts along, whether on the high road or on the low. He is rather short on willpower.

Some Pisces people seek escape through drugs or alcohol. When temptation comes along they find it hard to resist. In matters of sex, they can be rather permissive.

THE SIGNS AND THEIR KEY WORDS

		POSITIVE	NEGATIVE
ARIES	self	courage, initiative, pioneer instinct	brash rudeness, selfish impetuosity
TAURUS	money	endurance, loyalty, wealth	obstinacy, gluttony
GEMINI	mind	versatility	capriciousness, unreliability
CANCER	family	sympathy, homing instinct	clannishness, childishness
LEO	children	love, authority, integrity	egotism, force
VIRGO	work	purity, industry, analysis	fault-finding, cynicism
LIBRA	marriage	harmony, justice	vacillation, superficiality
SCORPIO	sex	survival, regeneration	vengeance, discord
SAGITTARIUS	travel	optimism, higher learning	lawlessness
CAPRICORN	career	depth	narrowness, gloom
AQUARIUS	friends	human fellowship, genius	perverse unpredictability
PISCES	confinement	spiritual love, universality	diffusion, escapism

THE ELEMENTS AND QUALITIES OF THE SIGNS

ELEMENT	SIGN	QUALITY	SIGN
FIRE..................	ARIES LEO SAGITTARIUS	CARDINAL.........	ARIES LIBRA CANCER CAPRICORN
EARTH...............	TAURUS VIRGO CAPRICORN	FIXED................	TAURUS LEO SCORPIO AQUARIUS
AIR.....................	GEMINI LIBRA AQUARIUS	MUTABLE.........	GEMINI VIRGO SAGITTARIUS PISCES
WATER..............	CANCER SCORPIO PISCES		

Every sign has both an element and a quality associated with it. The element indicates the basic makeup of the sign, and the quality describes the kind of activity associated with each.

Signs can be grouped together according to their *element* and *quality*. Signs of the same element share many basic traits in common. They tend to form stable configurations and ultimately harmonious relationships. Signs of the same quality are often less harmonious, but they share many dynamic potentials for growth as well as profound fulfillment.

THE FIRE SIGNS

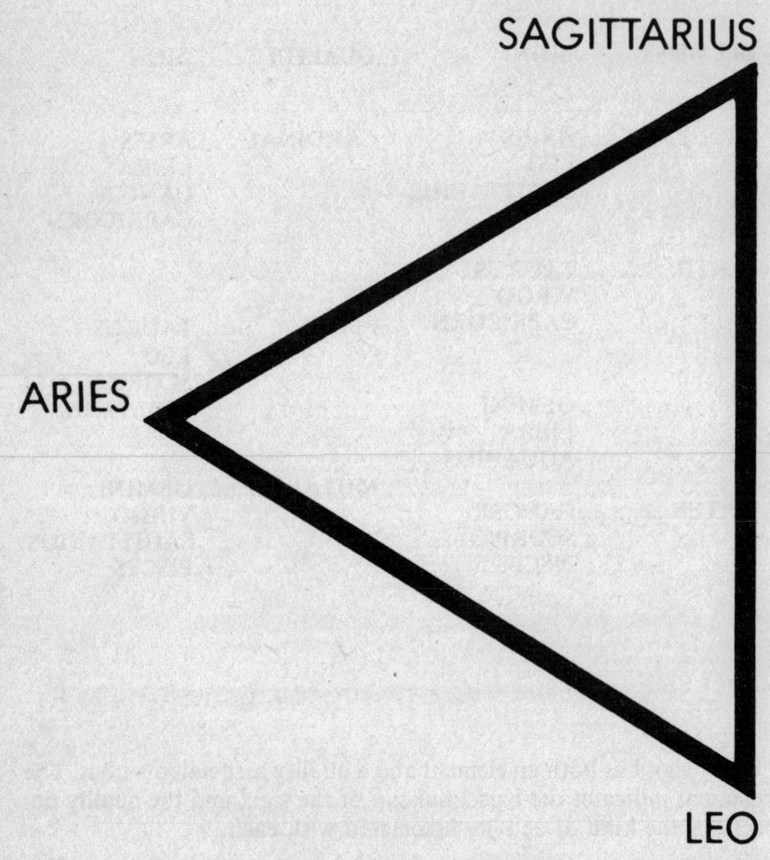

This is the fire group. On the whole these are emotional, volatile types, quick to anger, quick to forgive. They are adventurous, powerful people and .act as a source of inspiration for everyone. They spark into action with immediate exuberant impulses. They are intelligent, self-involved, creative and idealistic. They all share a certain vibrancy and glow that outwardly reflects an inner flame and passion for living.

THE EARTH SIGNS

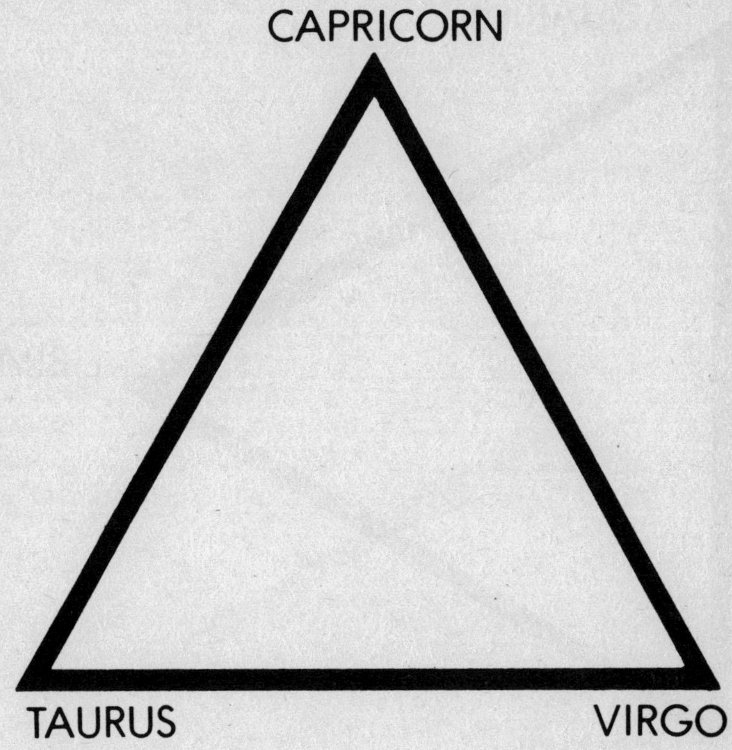

This is the earth group. They are in constant touch with the material world and tend to be conservative. Although they are all capable of spartan self-discipline, they are earthy, sensual people who are stimulated by the tangible, elegant and luxurious. The thread of their lives is always practical, but they do fantasize and are often attracted to dark, mysterious, emotional people. They are like great cliffs overhanging the sea, forever married to the ocean but always resisting erosion from the dark, emotional forces that thunder at their feet.

THE AIR SIGNS

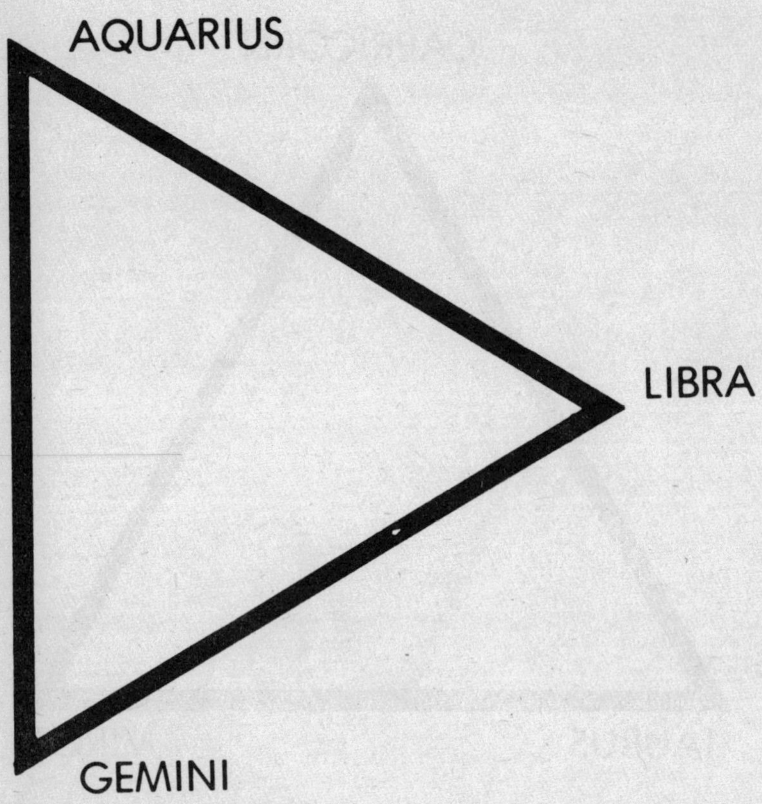

This is the air group. They are light, mental creatures desirous of contact, communication and relationship. They are involved with people and the forming of ties on many levels. Original thinkers, they are the bearers of human news. Their language is their sense of word, color, style and beauty. They provide an atmosphere suitable and pleasant for living. They add change and versatility to the scene, and it is through them that we can explore new territory of human intelligence and experience.

THE WATER SIGNS

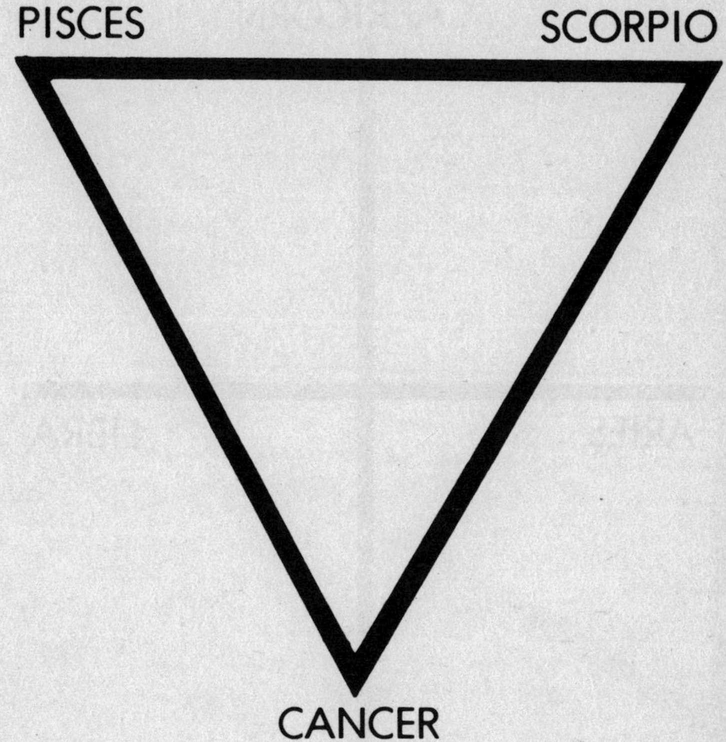

This is the water group. Through the water people, we are all joined together on emotional, non-verbal levels. They are silent, mysterious types whose magic hypnotizes even the most determined realist. They have uncanny perceptions about people and are as rich as the oceans when it comes to feeling, emotion or imagination. They are sensitive, mystical creatures with memories that go back beyond time. Through water, life is sustained. These people have the potential for the depths of darkness or the heights of mysticism and art.

THE CARDINAL SIGNS

Put together, this is a clear-cut picture of dynamism, activity, tremendous stress and remarkable achievement. These people know the meaning of great change since their lives are often characterized by significant crises and major successes. This combination is like a simultaneous storm of summer, fall, winter and spring. The danger is chaotic diffusion of energy; the potential is irrepressible growth and victory.

THE FIXED SIGNS

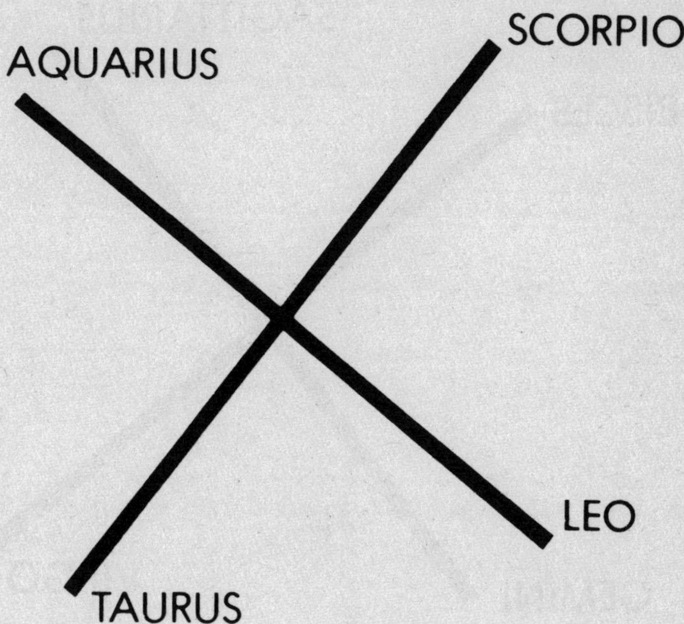

Fixed signs are always establishing themselves in a given place or area of experience. Like explorers who arrive and plant a flag, these people claim a position from which they do not enjoy being deposed. They are staunch, stalwart, upright, trusty, honorable people, although their obstinacy is well-known. Their contribution is fixity, and they are the angels who support our visible world.

THE MUTABLE SIGNS

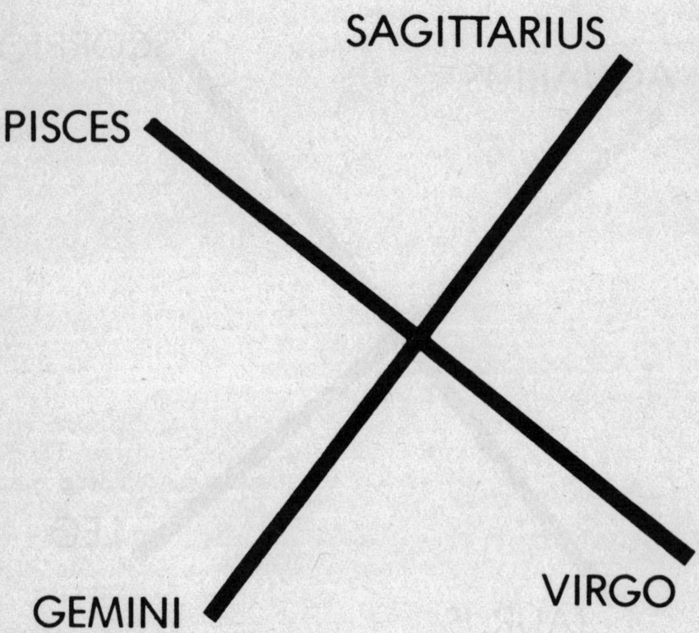

Mutable people are versatile, sensitive, intelligent, nervous and deeply curious about life. They are the translators of all energy. They often carry out or complete tasks initiated by others. Combinations of these signs have highly developed minds; they are imaginative and jumpy and think and talk a lot. At worst their lives are a Tower of Babel. At best they are adaptable and ready creatures who can assimilate one kind of experience and enjoy it while anticipating coming changes.

HOW TO APPROXIMATE YOUR RISING SIGN

Apart from the month and day of birth, the exact *time* of birth is another vital factor in the determination of an accurate horoscope. Not only do the planets move with great speed, but one must know how far the Earth has turned during the day. That way you can determine exactly where the planets are located with respect to the precise birthplace of an individual. This makes *your* horoscope *your* horoscope. In addition to these factors, another grid is laid upon that of the Zodiac and the planets: the houses. After all three have been considered, specific planetary relationships can be measured and analyzed in accordance with certain ordered procedures. It is the skillful translation of all this complex astrological language that a serious astrologer strives for in his attempt at coherent astrological synthesis. Keep this in mind.

The horoscope sets up a kind of framework around which the life of an individual grows like wild ivy, this way and that, weaving its way around the trellis of the natal positions of the planets. The year of birth tells us the positions of the distant, slow-moving planets like Jupiter, Saturn, Uranus and Pluto. The month of birth indicates the Sun sign, or birth sign as it is commonly called, as well as indicating the positions of the rapidly moving planets like Venus, Mercury and Mars. The day of birth locates the position of our Moon, and the moment of birth determines the houses through what is called the Ascendant, or Rising Sign.

As the Earth rotates on its axis once every 24 hours, each one of the twelve signs of the Zodiac appears to be "rising" on the horizon, with a new one appearing about every two hours. Actually it is the turning of the Earth that exposes each sign to view, but you will remember that in much of our astrological work we are discussing "apparent" motion. This *Rising Sign* marks the Ascendant and it colors the whole orientation of a horoscope. It indicates the sign governing the first house of the chart, and will thus determine which signs will govern all the other houses. The idea is a bit complicated at first, and we needn't dwell on complications in this introduction, but if you can imagine two color wheels with twelve divisions superimposed upon each other, one moving slowly and the other remaining still, you will have some idea of how the signs keep shifting the "color" of the houses as the Rising Sign continues to change every two hours.

The important point is that the birth chart, or horoscope, actually does define specific factors of a person's makeup. It contains a picture of being, much the way the nucleus of a tiny cell contains the potential for an entire elephant, or a packet of seeds contains a rosebush. If there were no order or continuity to the world, we could plant roses and get elephants. This same order that gives continuous flow to our lives often annoys people if it threatens to determine too much of their lives. We must grow from what we were planted, and there's no reason why we can't do that magnificently. It's all there in the horoscope. Where there is limitation, there is breakthrough; where there is crisis, there is transformation. Accurate analysis of a horoscope can help you find these points of breakthrough and transformation, and it requires knowledge of subtleties and distinctions that demand skillful judgment in order to solve even the simplest kind of personal question.

It is still quite possible, however, to draw some conclusions based upon the sign occupied by the Sun alone. In fact, if you're just being introduced to this vast subject, you're better off keeping it simple. Otherwise it seems like an impossible jumble, much like trying to read a novel in a foreign language without knowing the basic vocabulary. As with anything else, you can progress in your appreciation and understanding of astrology in direct proportion to your interest. To become really good at it requires study, experience, patience and above all—and maybe simplest of all—a fundamental understanding of what is actually going on right up there in the sky over your head. It is a vital living process you can observe, contemplate and ultimately understand. You can start by observing sunrise, or sunset, or even the full Moon.

In fact you can do a simple experiment after reading this introduction. You can erect a rough chart by following the simple procedure below:

1. Draw a circle with twelve equal segments.

2. Starting at what would be the nine o'clock position on a clock, number the segments, or houses, from 1 to 12 in a *counterclockwise direction*.

3. Label house number 1 in the following way: 4 A.M.-6 A.M.

4. In a counterclockwise direction, label the rest of the houses: 2 A.M.-4 A.M., MIDNIGHT-2 A.M., 10 P.M-MIDNIGHT, 8 P.M.-10 P.M., 6 P.M.-8 P.M., 4 P.M.-6 P.M., 2 P.M.-4 P.M., NOON-2 P.M., 10 A.M.-NOON, 8 A.M.-10 A.M., and 6 A.M.-8 A.M.

5. Now find out what time you were born and place the sun in the appropriate house.

6. Label the edge of that house with your Sun sign. You now have a description of your basic character and your fundamental drives. You can also see in what areas of life on Earth you will be most likely to focus your constant energy and center your activity.

7. If you are really feeling ambitious, label the rest of the houses with the signs, starting with your Sun sign, in order, still in a *counterclockwise direction*. When you get to Pisces, start over with Aries and keep going until you reach the house behind the Sun.

8. Look to house number 1. The sign that you have now labeled and attached to house number 1 is your Rising sign. It will color your self-image, outlook, physical constitution, early life and whole orientation to life. Of course this is a mere approximation, since there are many complicated calculations that must be made with respect to adjustments for birth time, but if you read descriptions of the sign preceding and the sign following the one you have calculated in the above manner, you may be able to identify yourself better. In any case, when you get through labeling all the houses, your drawing should look something like this:

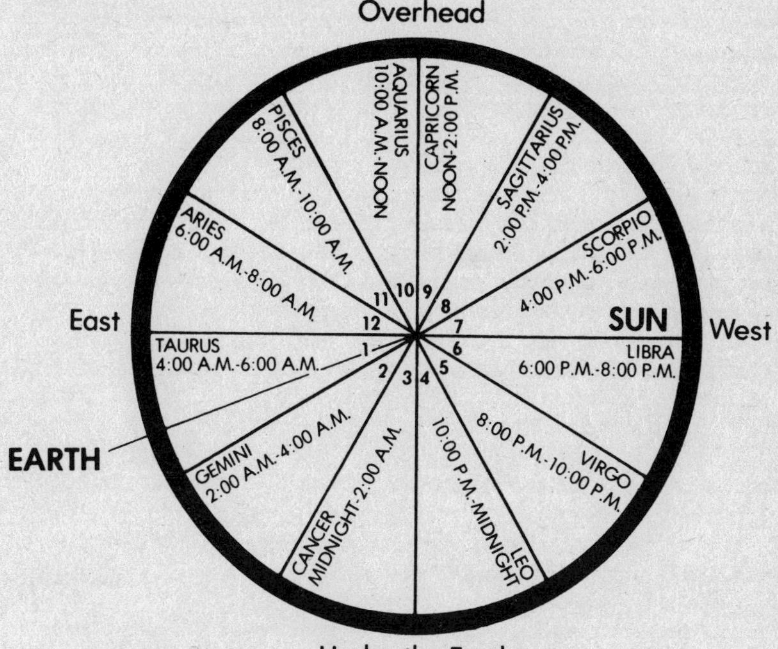

Basic chart illustrating the position of the Sun in Scorpio, with the Ascendant Taurus as the Rising Sign.

This individual was born at 5:15 P.M. on October 31 in New York City. The Sun is in Scorpio and is found in the 7th house. The Rising sign, or the sign governing house number 1, is Taurus, so this person is a blend of Scorpio and Taurus.

Any further calculation would necessitate that you look in an ephemeris, or table of planetary motion, for the positions of the rest of the planets for your particular birth year. But we will take the time to define briefly all the known planets of our Solar System and the Sun to acquaint you with some more of the astrological vocabulary that you will be meeting again and again. (See page 21 for a full explanation of the Moon in all the Signs.)

THE PLANETS AND SIGNS THEY RULE

The signs of the Zodiac are linked to the planets in the following way. Each sign is governed or ruled by one or more planets. No matter where the planets are located in the sky at any given moment, they still rule their respective signs, and when they travel through the signs they rule, they have special dignity and their effects are stronger.

Following is a list of the planets and the signs they rule. After looking at the list, go back over the definitions of the planets and see if you can determine how the planet ruling *your* Sun sign has affected your life.

SIGNS	RULING PLANETS
Aries	Mars, Pluto
Taurus	Venus
Gemini	Mercury
Cancer	Moon
Leo	Sun
Virgo	Mercury
Libra	Venus
Scorpio	Mars, Pluto
Sagittarius	Jupiter
Capricorn	Saturn
Aquarius	Saturn, Uranus
Pisces	Jupiter, Neptune

THE PLANETS OF THE SOLAR SYSTEM

Here are the planets of the Solar System. They all travel around the Sun at different speeds and different distances. Taken with the Sun, they all distribute individual intelligence and ability throughout the entire chart.

The planets modify the influence of the Sun in a chart according to their own particular natures, strengths and positions. Their positions must be calculated for each year and day, and their function and expression in a horoscope will change as they move from one area of the Zodiac to another.

Following, you will find brief statements of their pure meanings.

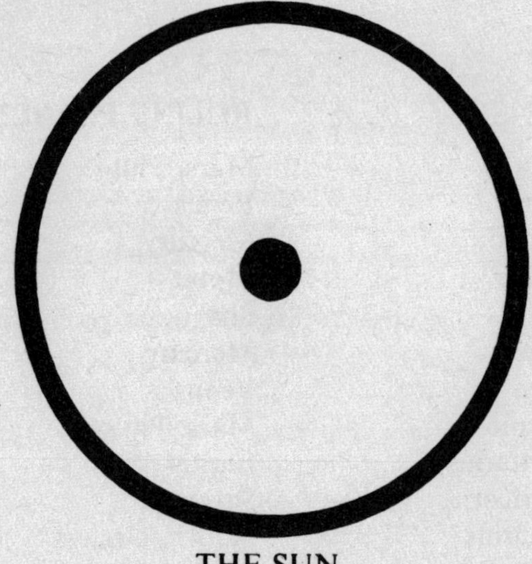

THE SUN

SUN

This is the center of existence. Around this flaming sphere all the planets revolve in endless orbits. Our star is constantly sending out its beams of light and energy without which no life on Earth would be possible. In astrology it symbolizes everything we are trying to become, the center around which all of our activity in life will always revolve. It is the symbol of our basic nature and describes the natural and constant thread that runs through everything that we do from birth to death on this planet.

To early astrologers, the sun seemed to be another planet because it crossed the heavens every day, just like the rest of the bodies in the sky.

It is the only star near enough to be seen well—it is, in fact, a dwarf star. Approximately 860,000 miles in diameter, it is about ten times as wide as the giant planet Jupiter. The next nearest star is nearly 300,000 times as far away, and if the Sun were located as far away as most of the bright stars, it would be too faint to be seen without a telescope.

Everything in the horoscope ultimately revolves around this singular body. Although other forces may be prominent in the charts of some individuals, still the Sun is the total nucleus of being and symbolizes the complete potential of every human being alive. It is vitality and the life force. Your whole essence comes from the position of the Sun.

You are always trying to express the Sun according to its position by house and sign. Possibility for all development is found in the Sun, and it marks the fundamental character of your personal radiations all around you.

It is the symbol of strength, vigor, wisdom, dignity, ardor and generosity, and the ability for a person to function as a mature individual. It is also a creative force in society. It is consciousness of the gift of life.

The underdeveloped solar nature is arrogant, pushy, undependable and proud, and is constantly using force.

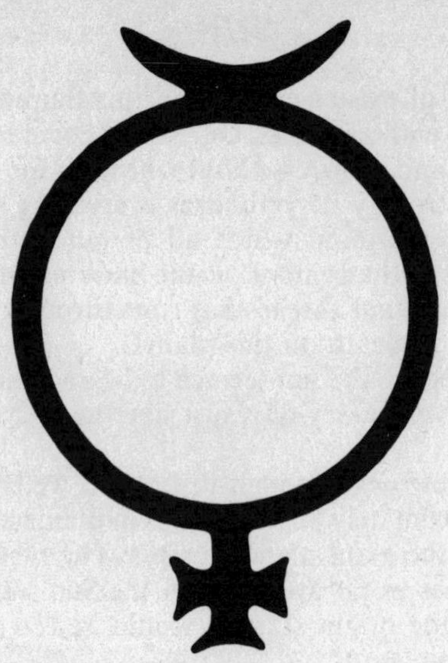

MERCURY

Mercury is the planet closest to the Sun. It races around our star, gathering information and translating it to the rest of the system. Mercury represents your capacity to understand the desires of your own will and to translate those desires into action.

In other words it is the planet of Mind and the power of communication. Through Mercury we develop an ability to think, write, speak and observe—to become aware of the world around us. It colors our attitudes and vision of the world, as well as our capacity to communicate our inner responses to the outside world. Some people who have serious disabilities in their power of verbal communication have often wrongly been described as people lacking intelligence.

Although this planet (and its position in the horoscope) indicates your power to communicate your thoughts and perceptions to the world, intelligence is something deeper. Intelligence is distributed throughout all the planets. It is the relationship of the planets to each other that truly describes what we call intelligence. Mercury rules speaking, language, mathematics, draft and design, students, messengers, young people, offices, teachers and any pursuits where the mind of man has wings.

VENUS

Venus is beauty. It symbolizes the harmony and radiance of a rare and elusive quality: beauty itself. It is refinement and delicacy, softness and charm. In astrology it indicates grace, balance and the aesthetic sense. Where Venus is we see beauty, a gentle drawing in of energy and the need for satisfaction and completion. It is a special touch that finishes off rough edges. It is sensitivity, and affection, and it is always the place for that other elusive phenomenon: love. Venus describes our sense of what is beautiful and loving. Poorly developed, it is vulgar, tasteless and self-indulgent. But its ideal is the flame of spiritual love—Aphrodite, goddess of love, and the sweetness and power of personal beauty.

MARS

This is raw, crude energy. The planet next to Earth but outward from the Sun is a fiery red sphere that charges through the horoscope with force and fury. It represents the way you reach out for new adventure and new experience. It is energy and drive, initiative, courage and daring. The power to start something and see it through. It can be thoughtless, cruel and wild, angry and hostile, causing cuts, burns, scalds and wounds. It can stab its way through a chart, or it can be the symbol of healthy spirited adventure, well-channeled constructive power to begin and keep up the drive. If you have trouble starting things, if you lack the get-up-and-go to start the ball rolling, if you lack aggressiveness and self-confidence, chances are there's another planet influencing your Mars. Mars rules soldiers, butchers, surgeons, salesmen—any field that requires daring, bold skill, operational technique or self-promotion.

JUPITER

This is the largest planet of the Solar System. Scientists have recently learned that Jupiter reflects more light than it receives from the Sun. In a sense it is like a star itself. In astrology it rules good luck and good cheer, health, wealth, optimism, happiness, success and joy. It is the symbol of opportunity and always opens the way for new possibilities in your life. It rules exuberance, enthusiasm, wisdom, knowledge, generosity and all forms of expansion in general. It rules actors, statesmen, clerics, professional people, religion, publishing and the distribution of many people over large areas.

Sometimes Jupiter makes you think you deserve everything, and you become sloppy, wasteful, careless and rude, prodigal and lawless, in the illusion that nothing can ever go wrong. Then there is the danger of over-confidence, exaggeration, undependability and over-indulgence.

Jupiter is the minimization of limitation and the emphasis on spirituality and potential. It is the thirst for knowledge and higher learning.

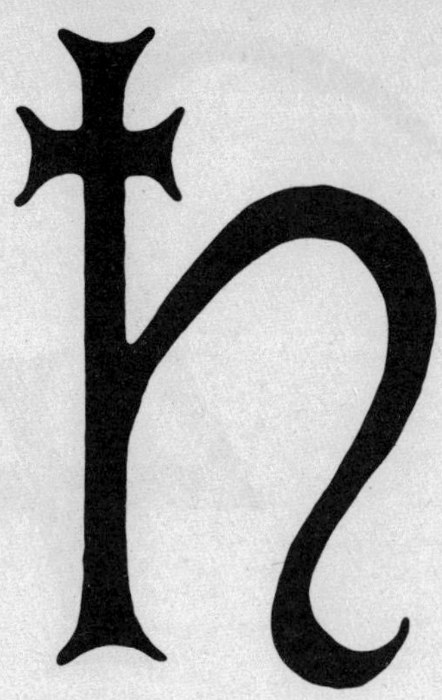

SATURN

Saturn circles our system in dark splendor with its mysterious rings, forcing us to be awakened to whatever we have neglected in the past. It will present real puzzles and problems to be solved, causing delays, obstacles and hindrances. By doing so, Saturn stirs our own sensitivity to those areas where we are laziest.

Here we must patiently develop *method,* and only through painstaking effort can our ends be achieved. It brings order to a horoscope and imposes reason just where we are feeling least reasonable. By creating limitations and boundary, Saturn shows the consequences of being human and demands that we accept the changing cycles inevitable in human life. Saturn rules time, old age and sobriety. It can bring depression, gloom, jealousy and greed, or serious acceptance of responsibilities out of which success will develop. With Saturn there is nothing to do but face facts. It rules laborers, stones, granite, rocks and crystals of all kinds.

The Outer Planets

The following three are the outer planets. They liberate human beings from cultural conditioning, and in that sense are the law breakers. In early times it was thought that Saturn was the last planet of the system—the outer limit beyond which we could never go. The discovery of the next three planets ushered in new phases of human history, revolution and technology.

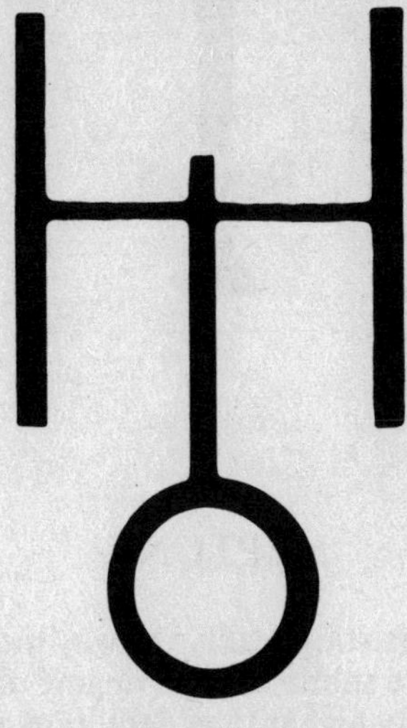

URANUS

Uranus rules unexpected change, upheaval, revolution. It is the symbol of total independence and asserts the freedom of an individual from all restriction and restraint. It is a breakthrough planet and indicates talent, originality and genius in a horoscope. It usually causes last-minute reversals and changes of plan, unwanted separations, accidents, catastrophes and eccentric behavior. It can add irrational rebelliousness and perverse bohemianism to a personality or a streak of unaffected brilliance in science and art. It rules technology, aviation and all forms of electrical and electronic advancement. It governs great leaps forward and topsy-turvy situations, and *always* turns things around at the last minute. Its effects are difficult to ever really predict, since it rules sudden last-minute decisions and events that come like lightning out of the blue.

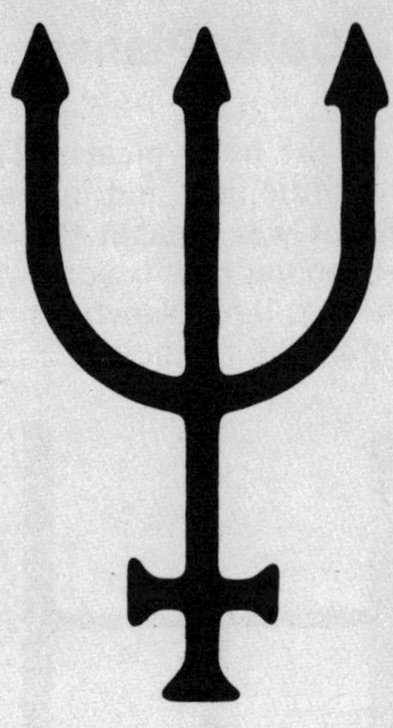

NEPTUNE

Neptune dissolves existing reality the way the sea erodes the cliffs beside it. Its effects are subtle like the ringing of a buoy's bell in the fog. It suggests a reality higher than definition can usually describe. It awakens a sense of higher responsibility often causing guilt, worry, anxieties or delusions. Neptune is associated with all forms of escape and can make things seem a certain way so convincingly that you are absolutely sure of something that eventually turns out to be quite different.

It is the planet of illusion and therefore governs the invisible realms that lie beyond our ordinary minds, beyond our simple factual ability to prove what is "real." Treachery, deceit, disillusionment and disappointment are linked to Neptune. It describes a vague reality that promises eternity and the divine, yet in a manner so complex that we cannot really fathom it at all. At its worst Neptune is a cheap intoxicant; at its best it is the poetry, music and inspiration of the higher planes of spiritual love. It has dominion over movies, photographs and much of the arts.

PLUTO

Pluto lies at the outpost of our system and therefore rules finality in a horoscope—the final closing of chapters in your life, the passing of major milestones and points of development from which there is no return. It is a final wipeout, a closeout, an evacuation. It is a distant, subtle but powerful catalyst in all transformations that occur. It creates, destroys, then recreates. Sometimes Pluto starts its influence with a minor event or insignificant incident that might even go unnoticed. Slowly but surely, little by little, everything changes, until at last there has been a total transformation in the area of your life where Pluto has been operating. It rules mass thinking and the trends that society first rejects, then adopts and finally outgrows.

Pluto rules the dead and the underworld—all the powerful forces of creation and destruction that go on all the time beneath, around and above us. It can bring a lust for power with strong obsessions.

It is the planet that rules the metamorphoses of the caterpillar into a butterfly, for it symbolizes the capacity to change totally and forever a person's life style, way of thought and behavior.

FAMOUS PERSONALITIES

ARIES: Hans Christian Andersen, Pearl Bailey, Marlon Brando, Wernher Von Braun, Charlie Chaplin, Joan Crawford, Da Vinci, Bette Davis, Doris Day, W. C. Fields, Alec Guinness, Adolf Hitler, William Holden, Thomas Jefferson, Nikita Khrushchev, Elton John, Arturo Toscanini, J. P. Morgan, Paul Robeson, Gloria Steinem, Lowell Thomas, Vincent van Gogh, Tennessee Williams

TAURUS: Fred Astaire, Charlote Brontë, Carol Burnett, Irving Berlin, Bing Crosby, Salvador Dali, Tchaikovsky, Queen Elizabeth II, Duke Ellington, Ella Fitzgerald, Henry Fonda, Sigmund Freud, Orson Welles, Joe Louis, Lenin, Karl Marx, Golda Meir, Eva Peron, Bertrand Russell, Shakespeare, Kate Smith, Benjamin Spock, Barbra Streisand, Shirley Temple, Harry Truman

GEMINI: Mikhail Baryshnikov, Boy George, Igor Stravinsky, Carlos Chavez, Walt Whitman, Bob Dylan, Ralph Waldo Emerson, Judy Garland, Paul Gauguin, Allen Ginsberg, Benny Goodman, Bob Hope, Burl Ives, John F. Kennedy, Peggy Lee, Marilyn Monroe, Joe Namath, Cole Porter, Laurence Olivier, Harriet Beecher Stowe, Queen Victoria, John Wayne, Frank Lloyd Wright

CANCER: "Dear Abby," David Brinkley, Yul Brynner, Pearl Buck, Marc Chagall, Jack Dempsey, Mildred (Babe) Zaharias, Mary Baker Eddy, Henry VIII, John Glenn, Ernest Hemingway, Lena Horne, Oscar Hammerstein, Helen Keller, Ann Landers, George Orwell, Nancy Reagan, Rembrandt, Richard Rodgers, Ginger Rogers, Rubens, Jean-Paul Sartre, O. J. Simpson

LEO: Neil Armstrong, Russell Baker, James Baldwin, Emily Brontë, Wilt Chamberlain, Julia Child, Cecil B. De Mille, Ogden Nash, Amelia Earhart, Edna Ferber, Arthur Goldberg, Dag Hammarskjöld, Alfred Hitchcock, Mick Jagger, George Meany, George Bernard Shaw, Napoleon, Jacqueline Onassis, Henry Ford, Francis Scott Key, Andy Warhol, Mae West, Orville Wright

VIRGO: Ingrid Bergman, Warren Burger, Maurice Chevalier, Agatha Christie, Sean Connery, Lafayette, Peter Falk, Greta Garbo, Althea Gibson, Arthur Godfrey, Goethe, Buddy Hackett, Michael Jackson, Lyndon Johnson, D. H. Lawrence, Sophia Loren, Grandma Moses, Arnold Palmer, Queen Elizabeth I, Walter Reuther, Peter Sellers, Lily Tomlin, George Wallace

LIBRA: Brigitte Bardot, Art Buchwald, Truman Capote, Dwight D. Eisenhower, William Faulkner, F. Scott Fitzgerald, Gandhi, George Gershwin, Micky Mantle, Helen Hayes, Vladimir Horowitz, Doris Lessing, Martina Navratalova, Eugene O'Neill, Luciano Pavarotti, Emily Post, Eleanor Roosevelt, Bruce Springsteen, Margaret Thatcher, Gore Vidal, Barbara Walters, Oscar Wilde

SCORPIO: Vivien Leigh, Richard Burton, Art Carney, Johnny Carson, Billy Graham, Grace Kelly, Walter Cronkite, Marie Curie, Charles de Gaulle, Linda Evans, Indira Gandhi, Theodore Roosevelt, Rock Hudson, Katherine Hepburn, Robert F. Kennedy, Billie Jean King, Martin Luther, Georgia O'Keeffe, Pablo Picasso, Jonas Salk, Alan Shepard, Robert Louis Stevenson

SAGITTARIUS: Jane Austen, Louisa May Alcott, Woody Allen, Beethoven, Willy Brandt, Mary Martin, William F. Buckley, Maria Callas, Winston Churchill, Noel Coward, Emily Dickinson, Walt Disney, Benjamin Disraeli, James Doolittle, Kirk Douglas, Chet Huntley, Jane Fonda, Chris Evert Lloyd, Margaret Mead, Charles Schulz, John Milton, Frank Sinatra, Steven Spielberg

CAPRICORN: Muhammad Ali, Isaac Asimov, Pablo Casals, Dizzy Dean, Marlene Dietrich, James Farmer, Ava Gardner, Barry Goldwater, Cary Grant, J. Edgar Hoover, Howard Hughes, Joan of Arc, Gypsy Rose Lee, Martin Luther King, Jr., Rudyard Kipling, Mao Tse-tung, Richard Nixon, Gamal Nasser, Louis Pasteur, Albert Schweitzer, Stalin, Benjamin Franklin, Elvis Presley

AQUARIUS: Marian Anderson, Susan B. Anthony, Jack Benny, Charles Darwin, Charles Dickens, Thomas Edison, John Barrymore, Clark Gable, Jascha Heifetz, Abraham Lincoln, John McEnroe, Yehudi Menuhin, Mozart, Jack Nicklaus, Ronald Reagan, Jackie Robinson, Norman Rockwell, Franklin D. Roosevelt, Gertrude Stein, Charles Lindbergh, Margaret Truman

PISCES: Edward Albee, Harry Belafonte, Alexander Graham Bell, Frank Borman, Chopin, Adelle Davis, Albert Einstein, Jackie Gleason, Winslow Homer, Edward M. Kennedy, Victor Hugo, Mike Mansfield, Michelangelo, Edna St. Vincent Millay, Liza Minelli, John Steinbeck, Linus Pauling, Ravel, Diana Ross, William Shirer, Elizabeth Taylor, George Washington

ARIES

CHARACTER ANALYSIS

People born under the astrological sign of Aries are often strong-willed and energetic. Ariens are seldom afraid of taking a risk, provided that it is well-calculated. They are people who dare; they are sometimes impulsive but almost never irrational. The Aries man or woman likes to keep busy. They are not a people who like to while away the time in an aimless fashion. Ariens are known for their drive and their boldness. They generally know how to make proper use of their energies; they are positive and productive people who seldom doubt themselves. They know what they want out of life and they go after it. They generally have a pioneering sort of spirit and are always anxious to begin something new. They know how to make use of opportunity when it appears. Many Ariens have no trouble in achieving success.

The strong and positive sort of Arien knows how to channel his energies properly so that he will get the most out of what life has to offer. He is a sensible, practical person, who does not only think about himself but does what he can to help those in less fortunate positions than himself. If a plan goes awry, he does not hesitate to see what he can do to fix it. The Arien is usually quick to initiate a change if it seems necessary to do so. He is an activist, generally, and does not believe in sitting about, waiting for good things to tumble into his lap. If good fortune does not appear, the positive Arien will go out and look for it; his search does not end until he has it. Obstacles do not frighten the Aries man or woman. In fact, contrary situations or people seem to spur him on. The Arien often thrives on adversity. He knows how to turn a disadvantage to an advantage in short order. Not easily discouraged, he will forge ahead on a plan or idea until it is exactly the way he wants it. The

Arien knows how to shift for himself. He won't wait for others to lend a helping hand, but starts himself, without assistance. Some find the Aries person a little too ruthless in his manner for getting what he wants. Patience is a virtue some Ariens lack; they are people who are usually interested in fast results. They want to see the fruits of their investments as quickly as possible.

The average Arien is a person who has many ideas; he is never at a loss for a new approach to an old or familiar situation. He is ever adaptable and knows how to make a profit out of a loss. In emergency situations, the Arien is always quick to act. When an accident occurs, he often knows the proper remedy. Decision-making does not frighten the strong Aries man or woman. They have the ability to think clearly and to direct their interests and energies toward their ultimate goal. Aries people are easily attracted to anything that is new and interesting. They have naturally inquiring minds.

Although Ariens are often alert and quick to act, they are sometimes easily distracted by side issues. Almost everything interests them and this can have its disadvantages, especially when a one-track mind is needed in order to solve a problem. Ariens can sometimes make a mess of things in their eagerness to get things done as soon as possible.

The weak or poorly directed Arien sometimes has a problem trying to put all of his eggs in one basket. He is easily distracted and often argumentative. He sometimes finds it difficult to see the forest for the trees. In trying to get many things accomplished at one time, he achieves nothing. In spite of his short-comings, he is apt to be quite caught up with what he fancies to be his virtues. He will underestimate the intelligence and abilities of others, especially if they seem to threaten his position in one way or another. The confused Arien is always ready for a quarrel. He will often refuse to see the other person's point of view and dismiss their opinions as so much poppy-cock. The Aries man or woman who does not know how to concentrate his or her energies effectively, easily jumps from one mistake to another, leaving things in an incomplete and jumbled state. The weak Arien will seldom admit his faults, although he will eagerly point out those of others . . . or what he imagines to be those of others.

The misdirected Arien more often than not misses his mark. He is too anxious to succeed. He wants success fast and is in too much of a hurry to prepare himself adequately. The weak Aries man or woman can be as stubborn as a mule. When intent on some illusory goal they will seldom take the time to listen to others. Not afraid of taking a risk, the ill-prepared Arien often finds himself leaping from one unsuccessful plan to the other. His optimism often makes a fool of him. He is the type of person who leaps before looking. Although he is easy to anger, his temper quickly cools off. When hurt, he can rant and rave for an hour but once he has defended himself, he will drop the matter altogether and move on to something else. The Arien seldom carries a grudge. In love, too, the Aries man or woman who has not learned how to curb impulsiveness, often finds him- or her- self in a pot of hot water. Love at first sight is not uncommon to this sort of Aries person; he is romantic for as long as the impulse carries him. He is not averse to fly-by-night romances, and is liable to throw caution to the winds when in love.

Because the Aries person has an enterprising nature, he never finds it difficult to keep busy. He is an extremely independent person —sometimes to a fault. Others sometimes find him rather haughty and arrogant. This weak sort of Aries finds it difficult to be objective in anything. He resents criticism even when it is due, yet he will not find it difficult to criticize others. He is the kind of person who takes any dare as an opportunity to prove his worth. Others are often annoyed by the manner in which he presses an issue. He is capable of becoming quite aggressive when the situation calls for tact and understanding. If the weak Arien made an attempt to see or understand both sides of one story, he could improve his own insight into problems. He should do what he can to develop a balanced sense of judgment. It is important for this sort of Aries person to prepare himself adequately before taking on a new project. He should avoid overdoing as that only ends in total exhaustion and very little actual progress is made.

Health

People born under the sign of Aries are generally quite healthy. Their physical condition tends to be good. Still, it is necessary that they take steps not to abuse their health by overdoing. The Arien is sometimes accident-prone because he is careless in his actions, particularly when intent on achieving a particular goal. The head and the face are areas of the body that are often injured. It is important that Ariens learn to relax. The Aries man or woman usually does fairly well in sports. Their bodies are generally well-developed and lithe. The Arien's constitution is almost always good. He is capable of great physical strength for short periods of time. This, or course, has its disadvantages as well as advantages. The Arien can achieve more if he learns how to apply his spurts of strength correctly. Sports where staying power is important are not likely to be ones in which he can excel. The sign of Aries governs the head; nerves, head, and stomach are apt to be the weak points under this sign.

Headaches and fevers are not uncommon complaints. As was mentioned before, it is essential that the person born under this first sign of the Zodiac learn how to relax. It is often the case that they wear out easily because they are impulsive and headstrong; they do not know how to channel their energies in a consistent manner. This can sometimes lead to a breakdown. The Arien is so intent on achieving his goal that he allows himself to overwork. Self-control must also be learned. Sometimes the Arien is too free in expressing himself—this can lead to emotional bankruptcy. He is a person who is quick to anger; he worries. Controlling negative emotions is vitally important as bad moods can often affect his health. People born under this sign should always get their proper rest. Adequate sleep can help an exhausted Arien to regain his strength. A sensible, well-balanced diet is also important. Overeating or immoderate drinking habits can, to some extent, incorrectly influence the general disposition of the Aries man or woman. The Arien does not like to be ill. Sickness makes him restless and impatient. He does not like to spend too much time recuperating from an illness. Because of his drive and enthusiasm, the Arien often recovers more quickly than others. An illness may strike him hard, but he is soon on his feet again. The person born under this sign is almost lively and enterprising. Ariens generally lead long and active lives; to some, they never seem to grow old. The Aries person who learns how to conserve his energies as well as to correctly channel them, can add years to his life-span. Good health habits should be continually observed.

Occupation

The Arien is an active, industrious person. He should find a career in which he can best put his talents to use. Although an Arien is apt to have many interests, he should try to find out which interest is the most suited to his actual means and abilities. He is a person who is sincerely interested in getting on in the world and making a success of himself.

The sign of Aries governs the head and the intellect. The person born during the period, March 21 to April 20, is usually quite ambitious and enterprising. He is not a person who can sit still when there is something to do. Some Ariens have an artistic bent and do well in creative work. Others have some trouble in making up their minds about what kind of work they should do because they are interested in so many things and can handle them all reasonably well. Generally speaking, whatever profession the Arien chooses to enter, he makes a good job of it. The Aries man or woman is never lacking in personality and charm. Quite often they do well in work that requires them to come in direct contact with the public. Quite often they are clever conversationalists. They know how to deal with people—how to amuse them, how to convince them. Others often turn to Aries for advice or counsel when in difficulty. The Aries person can usually handle a position that requires authoratative behavior without any problem at all. They make good leaders and advisors. Ariens are inventive and forward-looking. They have plenty of energy and drive; many have a talent for successfully realizing their plans and dreams.

Aries is a person of action. Quite often he does well in the military or in organized sports. Some Ariens make excellent doctors and nurses. Other do remarkably well as dentists and draftsmen. They are a resourceful people—men and women who often know what they want to achieve in life.

The person born under the sign of Aries is more often than not an individualist. He prefers giving orders to taking them. He is not a "group" sort of person. He enjoys working by himself more than working in a team. A modern person, he usually sees to it that he keeps abreast of the new developments in his field.

One fault often found in the underdeveloped Arien, is that he will undertake a project with much enthusiasm, then as his interest flags he will readily give it up for something new. In such cases, he will often pass the unfinished chore or project on to someone else. Some Ariens make a habit of starting things, then turning them over to others. The sort of Arien who falls into this habit often does it unknowingly. New plans and ideas attract people of this sign quickly. They are always off for new fields to conquer. The strong Arien, however, seldom has difficulties of this sort; he knows how to stick with one job until it is done. He will do his utmost to direct his efforts and energies toward one goal. This sort of Ram makes a success of his life without much effort.

The Aries man or woman is seldom a person who is only interested in work and material gain. He or she knows how to go about having a good time. Some are quite happy when they are able to combine business with pleasure. Ariens usually are not hard materialists, but they know well what money can do. They busy themselves earning money, but they sometimes spend it as soon as it comes into their pockets. The Aries man or woman is generally honest when it comes to money matters. If he or she directs him- or her- self to one goal, there is a good chance that it will be attained without too much effort. The Arien has a driving and courageous personality. In work, this often stands him in good stead.

People born under the sign of Aries generally like to be surrounded by fashionable furnishings and the like. Luxury makes them feel comfortable and successful and often has an important influence in making them positive and enterprising. Shabby or old surroundings are apt to depress the Aries person. He is modern and forward-looking; he must live in an environment that is suited to his general disposition.

Some Ariens tend to be rather careless with their money. Saving is something of a problem for them. They would rather spend what they earn instead of putting something aside for a rainy day. They know how to live for the moment. The weak Arien often invests unwisely or mismanages his joint finances without regard for his partner or mate. The wise Arien avoids impulsive spending and thinks of the future. He sees to it that he learns how to budget his expenses in an effective manner.

Home and Family

The Aries man or woman is a home-loving person by nature. Home means a lot to the Ram. Here he can relax at the end of a hard day and enjoy the comfort of his surroundings. Aries woman are generally excellent home-makers. They have a way with furnishings and color arrangement. They know how to make a home radiate harmony and comfort. Invariably, they have good taste. They can beautify a room or a home without much difficulty. The Aries home usually gives one the feeling of freedom and roominess. A guest is not apt to feel himself confined or uncomfortable.

The Arien enjoys entertaining his friends and family. Nothing pleases him more than people dropping in. He knows how to make the best of a social situation even if it occurs on the spur of the moment. They know how to please visitors and enjoy company. Friends generally respect them and their homes.

In family matters, the Aries man or woman is very emotional—in the good sense of the word. Affection and love between members of his or her immediate family are essential for getting along. The Arien is keenly interested in keeping his home peaceful and harmonious. If possible, the Aries husband or wife tries to exert a strong influence in household matters. The Arien feels that his guidance is important to others.

The person born under this sign of the Zodiac is usually quite fond of children. They understand children and children usually feel close to them. The Arien himself usually has something youthful about his nature. Children have no difficulty in getting along with them and generally enjoy having them join them in some of their activities. Ariens know the value of a good joke and children love them for this. A sense of humor that is rich and well-balanced makes them a favorite with children. Aries people seldom forget the joys of their own youth and enjoy living somewhat vicariously through the adventures and games of their own children.

Although the Aries man or woman is not much of a disciplinarian, they do become rather disappointed if their children do not live up to their expectations in later life. Aries generally thinks he knows what is best for his children and can become rather overbearing if his children are not inclined to agree. The Arien is a person who enjoys being popular and respected and he can be a proud parent.

Social Relationships

The Aries person usually has no trouble in making new friends. He is generally outgoing and generous. He enjoys having many friends. People are easily attracted to the Arien because of his bright and pleasant personality. He knows how to make people feel at ease and encourages them in their self-expression. People often turn to an Arien when they are in trouble. The Aries man or woman knows how to counsel a friend in trouble; he or she is sometimes willing to share the burden or responsibilities of a good friend.

On the other hand, Aries people often make a habit of jumping from one friend to another. As long as a person remains new, interesting, and somewhat mysterious, he remains a friend. As soon as an Arien becomes aware of this friend's limitations, he is apt to try to find someone new to replace him. This is the pattern an uncultivated Arien follows in work. As long as the project is new, it absorbs his interest. As soon as it becomes old hat, he turns it over to someone else and starts something new.

Ariens make friends quickly. If they are really impressed, they will place the new friend on a very high pedestal. Some Ariens become very possessive of their friends and if someone else shows an interest in them, they become rather jealous and resentful. If a friend becomes tiresome or dull, the tactless Arien will not hesitate to handle him in an inconsiderate manner.

Although Ariens generally have a talent for making friends quickly, they also are apt to lose them rather fast if they are not careful. Some Ariens tend to neglect their friends and acquaintances as soon as something new catches their fancies. The weak Arien is sometimes a bit of a gossip and finds it hard not to supply others with the secrets of their friends. This sort of Aries person generally takes people for what they appear to be and not for what they actually are.

LOVE AND MARRIAGE

Romance and the Aries Woman

The Aries woman is more often than not charming. The opposite sex generally find her attractive, even glamorous. She is a woman who is very interested in love and romance. The female Arien has plenty of affection to give to the right man—when she meets him. Women born under this sign are usually very active and vigorous; their intelligence and strong character are also qualities which make them attractive to men. The Aries woman has no trouble in communicating with a man on an intellectual plane; she can easily hold her own in any conversation. She should, however, try to curb her eagerness to talk; quite often she winds up dominating the conversation. The Arien who has cultivated the talent of being a good listener generally does not have any trouble in attracting the sort of man who might propose to her.

The Aries woman is not the sort to sit back and wait for the right man to come along. If she sees someone who interests her, she will more than likely take the lead. She can usually do this in such a charming fashion, that the object of her affection hardly notices that he is being coaxed into a romance.

The Aries woman has no trouble in being true to the man she loves. She is true to herself and believes in remaining faithful to the man she has chosen. She usually makes a thoughtful and considerate companion. When her man is in need of advice she is often able to give him wise counsel. Aries women are generally able to voice an intelligent opinion on just about any subject. Their range of knowledge—just as their range of interests—is quite broad. They are imaginative and know how to keep a relationship alive and interesting.

The woman born under the sign of the Ram makes an excellent wife. It is seldom that she will bother her mate or partner with matters that she can easily handle herself. She has a way of transforming almost any house or apartment into a very comfortable home. With household budgeting, she often turns out to be a mastermind. All in all, the Aries woman is very considerate and dependable; she has all the qualities it takes to make an excellent wife or partner. She knows how to bring up children correctly. She is fond of children and affectionate. She is often the kind of mother who enjoys a large family.

Romance and the Aries Man

The Aires man is often quite romantic and charming when courting the opposite sex. He knows how to win the heart of the woman he loves. The Arien in love is as persuasive and energetic as he is in anything else that interests him. He makes an attentive and considerate lover. A direct and positive person, he has no trouble in attracting women. They are often taken by his charming and dashing manner. The opposite sex feels very safe and confident when with an Aries man—for he knows how to make a woman feel wanted and appreciated. However, the Aries man is sometimes so sure of himself that he frightens the more sensitive woman away.

Although the man born under the sign of the Ram, is usually quite faithful when married, he does not mind "playing the field" as long as he remains single. He can be quite a flirt; sometimes the Aries man goes from one romance to the other until he finds the right girl. Making conquests on the battlefield of love is apt to give his ego quite a boost. The Aries man never has very much trouble with rivals. When he is intent on love he knows how to do away with all opposition—and in short order. The Arien is a man who is very much in need of love and affection; he is quite open about this and goes about attaining it in a very open way.

He may be quite adventurous in love while he is single, but once he settles down, he becomes a very reliable and responsible mate. The Aries man is really a family-type man. He enjoys the company of his immediate family; he appreciates the comforts of home. A well-furnished and inviting home is important to a man born under this sign. Some of the furnishings may be a little on the luxurious side; the Arien feels often inspired to do better if he is surrounded by a show of material comfort. Success-oriented, he likes his home to radiate success.

The Aries man often likes to putter around the house, making minor repairs and installing new household utensils. He is a man who does not mind being tied down as long as he does not really feel it. He will be the head of the house; he does not like the woman to wear the pants in the family. He wants to be the one who keeps things in order. He remains romantic, even after marriage. He is tremendously fond of children and is quite apt to spoil them a bit. He makes an affectionate father. Children make him happy when they make him feel proud of them.

Man—Woman

ARIES MAN
ARIES WOMAN

The Aries man will be contented with the Aries woman so long as she reflects his qualities and interests without trying to outshine him. Although he may be progressive and modern in many things, when it comes to pants-wearing, he's downright conventional: it's strictly male attire. The best position an Aries woman can take in the relationship is a supporting one. He's the boss and that's that. Once that is settled and thoroughly accepted by his Aries spouse, then it's clear sailing.

The Aries man, with his seemingly endless drive and energy, likes to relax in the comfort of his home at the end of an action-packed day, and the Aries wife who is a good homemaker can be sure of his undying affection. He's a lover of slippers and pipe and a comfortable armchair. The Aries wife who sees to it that everything in the house is where her man expects to find it—including herself—will have no difficulty keeping the relationship ship-shape.

When it comes to love, the Aries man is serious and constant, and the object of his affection should be likewise. He is generally not interested in a clinging-vine kind of wife; he justs wants someone who is there when he needs her; someone who listens and understands what he says; someone who can give advice if he should ever have to ask for it—which is not likely to be often. Although he can appreciate a woman who can intelligently discuss things that matter to him, he is not interested in a ranting chatterbox who, through her fondness for earbending, is liable to let the apple pie burn up in the oven.

The Aries man wants a woman who is a good companion and a good sport; someone who will look good on his arm without hanging on it too heavily. He is looking for a woman who has both feet on the ground and yet is mysterious and enticing . . . a kind of domestic Helen of Troy whose face or fine dinner can launch a thousand business deals if need be. The cultivated Aries woman should have no difficulty in filling such a role.

The Aries man and woman have similar tastes when it comes to family style: they both like large ones. The Aries woman is crazy about kids and the more she has, the more she feels like a wife. Children love and admire the affectionate Aries mother. She knows how to play with them and how to understand them. She's very anxious that they do well in life and reflect their good homelife and upbringing. However, both Aries parents should try not to smother their offspring with too much love. They should be urged to make their own decisions—especially as they grow older—and not rely unnecessarily on the advice of their partents.

**ARIES MAN
TAURUS WOMAN**

The woman born under Taurus may lack the sparkle or dazzle you often like your women to have. In many respects, she's very basic—never flighty—and puts great store in keeping her feet flat on the ground. She may fail to appreciate your willingness to jump here, then there, especially if she's under the impression that there's no profit in it. On the other hand, if you do manage to hit it off with a Taurus woman you won't be disappointed at all in the romance area. The Taurus woman is all woman and proud of it, too. She can be very devoted and loving once she decides that her relationship with you is no fly-by-night romance. She's pretty rugged, too, or can be, when the situation calls for a stiff upper lip. It's almost certain that if the going ever gets too rough she won't go running home to mother. She'll stick by you, talk it out, fight it out, or whatever. When bent on a particular point of view, she can be as hard as nails —without having it adversely affect her femininity. She'll stick by you through thick and thin. She can adjust to hard times just as graciously as she can to good times. You may lose your patience with her, though, if when trying to explain some new project or plan to her, she doesn't seem to want to understand or appreciate your enthusiasm and ambition. With your quick wit and itchy feet, you may find yourself miles ahead of your Taurus woman. At times, you are likely to find this distressing. But if you've developed a talent for patience, you won't mind waiting for her to catch up. Never try grabbing her hand and pulling her along at your normal speed—it is likely not to work. It could lead to flying pots and pans and a fireworks display that would put the Fourth of July to shame. The Taurus woman doesn't anger readily but when prodded often enough, she's capable of letting loose with a cyclone of illwill. If you treat her correctly, you'll have no cause for complaint. The Taurus woman loves doing things for her man. She's a whiz in the kitchen and can whip up feasts fit for a king if she thinks they will be royally appreciated. She may not fully understand you but she'll adore you and be faithful to you if she feels you're worthy of it. She won't see green, either, if you compliment another woman in her presence. When you come home late occasionally and claim that there were a lot of last-minute things to attend to at the office, she won't insinuate that one of those last-minute things was most likely your new, shapely secretary. Her mind doesn't run like that. She's not gullible, but she won't doubt your every word if she feels there is no reason to. The woman born under Taurus will make a wonderful mother for your children. She's a master at keeping children cuddled, well-loved, and warm. You may find, however, that when your offspring reach the adolescent stage you'll have to intervene: Taureans are not very sympathetic to the whims of ever-changing teenagers.

ARIES MAN
GEMINI WOMAN

You may find a romance with a woman born under the sign of the Twins, a many-splendored thing. In her you can find the intellectual companionship you often crave and so seldom find. A Gemini girl-friend can appreciate your aims and desires because she travels pretty much the same route as you do, intellectually . . . that is, at least part of the way. She may share your interests, but she will lack your stick-to-it-iveness. Her feet are much itchier than yours, and as a result, she can be here, there—all over the place, and all at the same time, or so it seems. It may make you dizzy. However, you'll enjoy and appreciate her liveliness and mental agility.

Geminians often have sparkling personalities; you'll be attracted by her warmth and grace. While she's on your arm, you'll probably notice that many male eyes are drawn to her—she may even return a gaze or two, but don't let that worry you. All women born under this sign have nothing against a harmless flirtation; they enjoy this sort of attention and, if they feel they're already spoken for, they'll never let it get out of hand.

Although she may not be as handy in the kitchen as you'd like, you'll never go hungry for a filling and tasty meal. She's in as much a hurry as you and won't feel like she's cheating by breaking out the instant mashed potatoes or the frozen vegetables. She may not be handy at the kitchen range but she can be clever—and with a dash of this and a suggestion of that, she can make an uninteresting TV dinner taste like something out of a Jim Beard cookbook. Then again, maybe you've struck it rich with your Gemini and have one who finds complicated recipes a challenge to her intellect. If so, you'll find every meal a tantalizing and mouth-watering surprise.

When you're exercizing your brain over the Sunday crossword puzzle and find yourself bamboozled over 23 Down and 11 Across, just ask your Gemini friend; she'll give you the right answers without batting an eye. Chances are she probably went through the crossword phase herself years ago and gave them up because she found them too easy.

She loves all kinds of people—just like you do. Still, you're apt to find that you're more particular than she. Often, all that a Gemini requires is that her friends be interesting—and stay interesting. One thing she's not able to abide is a dullard.

Leave the party-organizing to your Gemini sweetheart or mate and you'll never know what a dull moment is. She'll bring the swinger out in you if you give her half a chance.

With kids, woman born under Gemini seem to work wonders. Perhaps this is because they are like children themselves in a way:

restless, adventurous, and easily bored. At any rate, the Gemini mother is loving, gentle, and affectionate with her children.

ARIES MAN
CANCER WOMAN

Romancing a girl born under the sign of the Crab may occasionally give you a case of the jitters. It may leave you with one of those "Oh, brother . . . what did I get into now" feelings. In one hour she can unravel a whole gamut of emotions that will leave you in a tizzy. If you do fall in love with a Cancerian, be prepared for anything. She'll keep you guessing, that's for sure. You may find her a little too uncertain and sensitive for your tastes. You'll most likely have to spend a good deal of your time encouraging her, helping her to erase her foolish fears. Tell her she's a living doll a dozen times a day and you'll be well-loved in return. Be careful of the jokes you make when you are with her—and for heaven's sake don't let any of them revolve around her, her personal interests, or her relatives. Chances are if you do, you'll reduce her to tears. She can't stand being made fun of. It will take bushels of roses and tons of chocolates, not to mention the "I'm sorrys", to get you back in her good graces again.

In matters of money-managing, she may not easily come around to your way of thinking. Ariens are often apt to let money burn a hole in their pockets. Cancerians are just the opposite. You may think your Cancerian sweetheart or mate is a direct descendant of Scrooge. If she has it her way, she'll hang onto that first dollar you ever earned. She's not only that way with money, but with everything from bakery string right on to jelly jars. She's a saver and never discards anything no matter how trivial.

Once she returns your "I love you", you'll find that you have a very loving, self-sacrificing and devoted friend on your hands. Her love for you will never alter unless you want it to. She'll put you high up on a pedestal and will do everything—even if it's against your will—to see that you stay up there.

Cancer women make reputedly the best mothers of all the signs of the Zodiac. She'll consider every minor complaint of her child a major catastrophe. She's not the kind of mother who will do anything to get her children off her hands; with her, kids come first. You'll run a close second. You'll perhaps see her as too devoted and you may have a hard time convincing her that the length of her apron-strings is a little too long. When Junior or Sis is ready for that first date, you may have to lock your Cancer wife in the broom closet to keep her from going along. As an Arien you are apt to understand your children more as individuals than your wife. No matter how many times your Cancer wife insists that no man is good enough for your daughter, you'll know it's all nonsense. If you don't help her to curb her super-maternal tendencies, your Cancer wife may have a good chance of turning into a formidable mother-in-law.

ARIES MAN
LEO WOMAN

If you can manage a girl who likes to kick up her heels every once in a while, the Leo woman's your mate. You'll have to learn how to put away your jealous fears—or at least forget about them—when you take up with a woman born under this sign, because she's often the sort that makes heads turn and sometimes tongues wag. You don't necessarily have to believe any of what you hear; it's most likely just jealous gossip or wishful thinking. She's usually got more than a good share of grace and glamor. She knows it, generally, and knows how to put it to good use. Needless to say, other women in her vicinity turn green with envy and will try anything short of shoving her into the nearest lake in order to put her out of commission, especially if she appears to be cramping their style.

If she has captured your heart and fancy, woo her full-force if your intention is to eventually win her. Shower her with expensive gifts, take her regularly to Ciro's, and promise her the moon—if you're in a position to go that far—and you'll find that Miss Leo's resistance will begin to weaken. It's not that she's so difficult—she'll probably make a lot over you once she's decided you're the man for her—but she does enjoy a lot of attention. What's more, she feels she's entitled to it. Her mild arrogance, though, is becoming. The Leo woman knows how to transform the crime of excessive pride into a very charming misdemeanor. It sweeps most men right off their feet . . . in fact, all men. Those that do not succumb to her leonine charm are few and far between.

If you've got an important business deal to clinch and you have doubts as to whether it will go over well or not, bring your Leo wife along to that business luncheon or cocktail party and it will be a cinch that you'll have that contract in your pocket before the meeting is over. She won't have to say or do anything . . . just be there at your side. The grouchiest oil magnate can be transformed into a gushing, dutiful schoolboy if there's a Leo woman in the room.

If you're a rich Arien, you may have to see to it that your Leo wife doesn't become to heavy-handed with the charge accounts and credit cards. When it comes to spending, Leos tend to overdo. If you're a poor Arien, then you have nothing to fear—for Miss Leo, with her love of luxury, will most likely never give you the time of day, let alone exchange vows.

As a mother, she can be strict and easy-going at the same time. She can pal around with her children and still see to it that they know their places.

ARIES MAN
VIRGO WOMAN

The Virgo woman may be a little too difficult for you to understand at first. Her waters run deep. Even when you think that you do know her, don't take any bets on it: she's capable of keeping things hidden in the deep recesses of her womanly soul—things she'll only reveal when she is sure that you're the one she's been looking for. It may take her sometime to come around to this decision. Virgo women are finnicky about almost everything; everything has to be letter-perfect before they're satisfied. Many of them have the idea that the only people who can do things correctly are other Virgos. Nothing offends a Virgo woman more than sloppy dress, character, or careless display of affection. Make sure your tie's not crooked and your shoes sport a bright shine before you go calling on this lady. Keep your off-color jokes for the locker-room; she'll have none of that. Take her arm when crossing the street. Don't rush the romance. Trying to corner her in the back of a cab may be one way of striking out. Never criticize the way she looks—in fact, the best policy would be to agree with her as much as possible. The Arien, however, with his outspoken, direct, and sensible nature, may find a Virgo relationship too trying. All those Do's and Don't's you'll have to observe if you want to get to first base with a Virgo may be just a little too much to ask of you. After a few dates, you may come to the conclusion that she just isn't worth all that trouble. However, the Virgo woman is mysterious enough, generally, to keep her men running back for more. Chances are you'll be intrigued by her airs and graces.

Love means a lot to you and you may be disappointed at first in Virgo's cool ways. However, underneath that glacial facade lies a hot cauldron of seething excitement. If you're patient and artful in your romantic approach, you'll find that all that caution was well worth the trouble. When Virgos love, they don't stint. It's all or nothing as far as they're concerned. Once they're convinced that they love you, they go all the way right off the bat, tossing all cares to the wind. One thing a Virgo can't stand in love is hypocrisy. They don't give a hoot about what the neighbors might say as long as their hearts tell them "go ahead." They're very concerned with human truths. So much so that if their hearts stumble upon another fancy, they're liable to take up with that new heart-throb and leave you standing in the rain. She's that honest—to her own heart, at any rate. But if you are earnest about your interests in her, she'll know, and will respect and reciprocate your love. Do her wrong once, however, and you can be sure she'll come up with a pair of sharp scissors and cut the soiled ribbon of your relationship.

As a housewife, she'll be neat and orderly. With children, she can be tender and strict at the same time. She can be a devoted and loving wife—it all depends on you.

ARIES MAN
LIBRA WOMAN

That girl born under the sign of Libra is worth more than her weight in gold. She's a woman after your own heart. With her, you'll always come first, make no mistake about that. She'll always be behind you, no matter what you do. And when you ask her for advice about almost anything, you'll most likely get a very balanced and realistic opinion. She's good at thinking things out and never lets her emotions run away with her when clear logic is called for. As a homemaker, she's hard to beat. She is very concerned with harmony and balance; your home will be tastefully furnished and decorated. A Libran cannot stand filth or disarray—it gives her goose bumps. Anything that does not radiate harmony, in fact, runs against her orderly grain.

She's chock-full of charm and womanly ways; she can sweep just about any man off his feet with one winning smile. When it comes to using her brains, she can out-think anyone and sometimes with half the effort. She's diplomatic enough, though, never to let this become glaringly apparent. She may even turn the conversation so that you think that you were the one who did all the brain work. She couldn't care less, really, just as long as you wind up doing what is right. She's got you up there on a pretty high pedestal. You're her man and she's happy if you make all the decisions, big and small—with a little help from her if necessary. In spite of her masculine approach to reason, she remains all woman in her approach to love and affection. You'll literally be showered with hugs and kisses during your romance with a Libra woman. She doesn't believe in holding out. You shouldn't, either, if you want to hang on to her. She's the kind of girl who likes to snuggle up to you in front of the fire on chilly autumn nights. She'll bring you breakfast in bed Sundays then cuddle beside you and tuck a napkin under your chin so you won't get any crumbs on the blankets.

She's very thoughtful about anything that concerns you. If anyone dares suggest that you're not the grandest guy in the world, your Libran is bound to defend you. She'll defend you with her dying breath. When she makes those marriage vows she means every word. As an Arien who also has a tendency to place people you like on a pedestal, you won't be let down by a girl born under the sign of Libra. She'll be everything you believe she is . . . even more. As a mother of your children, she'll be very attentive and loving. However, you won't have to take the backseat when Junior comes along. You'll always come first with her—no matter if it's the kids, the dog, or her maiden aunt from Keokuk. Your children will be well-mannered and respectful. She'll do everything in her power to see that you're treated like a prince.

ARIES MAN
SCORPIO WOMAN

The Scorpio woman can be a whirlwind of passion—perhaps too much passion to suit you. When her temper flies, better lock up the family heirlooms and take cover. When she chooses to be sweet, you're apt to think that butter wouldn't melt in her mouth . . . but of course, it would. She can be as hot as a *tamale* or as cool as a cucumber, but whatever mood she is in, it's no pose. She doesn't believe in putting on airs.

Scoprio women are often quite seductive and sultry—their charm can pierce through the hardest of hearts like a laser ray. She doesn't have to look like Mata Hari (quite often Scorpio women resemble the tomboy next door) but once you've looked into those tantalizing eyes, you're a goner. Life with her won't be all smiles and smooth-sailing; when prompted she can unleash a gale of venom. Generally, she will have the good grace to keep family battles within the walls of your home; when company visits she's apt to give the impression that married life with you is one great big joy-ride. It's just one of her ways of expressing her loyalty to you—at least in front of others. She may fight you tooth and nail in the confines of your living room but at a ball or during an evening out, she'll hang on your arm and have stars in her eyes. She doesn't consider this hypocrisy; she just firmly believes that family quarrels should stay a private matter.

She's pretty good at keeping secrets. She may even keep a few hidden from you if she feels like it. This sort of attitude, of course, goes against the Arien's grain; you believe in being open and straight-from-the-shoulder.

Never cross her up, not even in little things; when it comes to revenge, she's an eye-for-an-eye woman. She's not keen on forgiveness if she feels she's been done wrong. You'd be well-advised not to give her cause to be jealous, either. When she sees green, your life will be made far from rosy. Once she's put you in the dog-house, you can be sure that you're going to stay there an awfully long time.

There's a good possibility that you may find your relationship with a Scorpio too draining. Although she may be full of the old paprika and bursting with dynamite, she still is not the girl you'd exactly like to spend the rest of your natural life with. You'd prefer someone gentler and more direct; someone who won't go throwing pots and pans at the mention of your secretary's name; someone who's flexible and understanding; someone who can take the highs along with the lows and not bellyache; someone who can ride with the punches. If you've got your sights set on a shapely Scorpio, you'd better forget that sweet girl of your dreams. True: a woman born under Scorpio can be heavenly, but she can also be the very devil when she chooses.

ARIES MAN
SAGITTARIUS WOMAN

You most likely won't come across a more good-natured girl than the one born under the sign of Sagittarius. Generally, they're full of bounce and good cheer. Their sunny dispositions seem almost permanent and can be relied upon even on the rainiest of days. No matter what she'll ever say or do, you'll know that she always means well. Women born under this sign are almost never malicious. If ever they seem to be, it is only superficial. Sagittarians are quite often a little short on tact and say literally anything that comes into their pretty little heads, no matter what the occasion. Sometimes the words that tumble out of their mouths seem downright cutting and cruel. They're quite capable of losing their friends—and perhaps even yours—through a careless slip of the lip. On the other hand, you're liable to appreciate their honesty and good intentions. To you, qualities of this sort play an important part in life. With a little patience and practice, you can probably help cure your Sagittarian of her loose tongue; in most cases, it will be worth the effort.

Chances are she'll be the outdoors-type of girlfriend; long hikes, fishing trips, and water skiing will most likely appeal to her. She's a busy person; she could never be called a slouch. She sets great store in being able to move about. She's like you in that respect: she has itchy feet. You won't mind taking her along on camping or hunting trips. She is great company most of the time and generally a lot of fun. Even if your buddies drop by for an evening of poker and beer, she'll manage to fit right in. In fact, they'll probably resent it if she doesn't join in the game. On the whole, she is a very kind and sympathetic woman. If she feels she's made a mistake she'll be the first to call your attention to it. She's not afraid of taking the blame for a foolish deed.

You might lose your patience with her once or twice, but after she's seen how upset you get over her short-sightedness, and her tendency to talk too much, chances are she'll do everything in her power not to do it again. She is not the kind of wife who will pry into your business affairs. But she'll always be there, ready to offer advice if you ask for it. If you come home from a night out with the boys and tell your Sagittarius wife that the red stains on your collar came from cranberry sauce, she'll believe you. She'll seldom be suspicious; your word will almost always be good enough for her.

Although she can be a good housewife, her interests are generally too far-reaching and broad to allow her to confine her activities to just taking care of the house. She's interested in what is going on everywhere.

As a mother, she'll be a wonderful and loving friend to her children. She's apt to spoil them if she is not careful.

ARIES MAN
CAPRICORN WOMAN

If you're not a successful businessman or at least on your way to success, it's quite possible that a Capricorn woman will have no interest in entering your life. She's generally a very security-minded female and will see to it that she only invests her time and interests in sure things. Men who whittle away their time and energy on one unsuccessful scheme or another, seldom attract a Capricorn. Men who are interested in getting somewhere in life and keep their noses close to the grindstone quite often have a Capricorn woman behind them, helping them to get ahead. Although she is a climber herself, she is not what one could call cruel or hard-hearted. Beneath that cool, seemingly calculating exterior there's a warm and desirable woman. She just happens to feel that it's just as easy to fall in love with a rich or ambitious man as it is with a poor or lazy one. She's practical. Although she is keenly interested in rising to the top, she's not aggressive about it. She'll seldom step on someone's feet or nudge competitors away with her elbows. She's quiet about her wishes. She sits, waits, and watches. When an opening or an opportunity does appear, she'll latch on to it, lickety-split. For an on-the-go Arien, an ambitious Capricorn wife or girlfriend can be quite an asset. She can probably give you some very good advice about your business affairs and when you invite the boss and his wife to dinner, she'll charm them both right off the ground. She's generally thorough in whatever she undertakes. She'll see to it that she is second to none in good housekeeping.

Capricorn women make excellent hostesses as well as guests. Generally, they are very well-mannered and gracious, no matter what their background is. They seem to have a built-in sense of what is right and proper. Crude behavior or a careless comment can offend them no end.

If you should marry a woman born under Capricorn you need never worry about her going on a wild shopping spree. Capricorns are very careful about every cent that comes into their hands. They understand the value of money better than most women and have no room in their lives for careless spending. If you turn over your paycheck to her at the end of the week, you can be sure that a good hunk of it will wind up in the bank.

Capricorn girls are generally very fond of family—their own, that is. With them, family ties run very deep. Never say a cross or sarcastic word about her mother. She won't stand for that sort of nonsense and will let you know by not speaking to you for days. In fact, you'd better check her family out before you decide to get down on bended knee, because after you've taken that trip down the aisle, you'll undoubtedly be seeing an awful lot of them.

With children, she's loving and correct. They'll be well brought up and polite.

ARIES MAN
AQUARIUS WOMAN

If you find that you've fallen head over heels for the woman born under the sign of the Water Bearer, better fasten your safety belt. It may take a while before you actually discover what she's like and even then you may have nothing to go on but a string of vague hunches. This girl is like the rainbow—full of all bright and shining hues; she's like no other girl you've known. There's something elusive about her, something delightfully mysterious—you'll most likely never be able to put your finger on it. It's nothing calculated, either; Aquarians don't believe in phoney charm. There will never be a dull moment in your romance with the Water Bearing woman. She seems to radiate adventure, magic, and without even half trying. She'll most likely be the most open-minded woman you've ever met. She—like you—has a strong dislike of injustice and prejudice. Narrow-mindedness runs against her grain.

She is very independent by nature and is quite capable of shifting for herself if necessary. She may receive many proposals for marriage and from all sorts of people. Marriage is one heck of a big step for her; she wants to be sure she knows what she's getting into. If she thinks that it will seriously curb her independence and her love of freedom, she's liable to shake her head and give you back your engagement ring—if she's let the romance get that far.

The line between friendship and romance is a pretty fuzzy one for an Aquarian. It's not difficult for her to remain buddy-buddy with someone with whom she's just broken off. She's tolerant, remember? So, if you should ever see her on the arm of an ex-lover, don't jump to any hasty conclusions.

She's not a jealous person, and doesn't expect you to be, either. You'll find her pretty much of a free spirit most of the time. Just when you think you know her inside-out, you'll discover that you don't really know her at all.

Very sympathetic and warm, she can be helpful to people in need of assistance and advice.

She's often like a chameleon and can fit in anywhere without looking like she doesn't belong.

She'll seldom be suspicious even if she has every right to be. If the man she loves slips and allows himself a little fling, chances are she'll just turn her head the other way and pretend not to notice that the gleam in his eyes is not meant for her. That's pretty understanding. Still, a man married to a woman born under Aquarius should never press his luck in hanky-panky. After all, she is a woman—and a very sensitive one at that.

She makes a fine mother, of course, and can easily transmit her positive and big-hearted qualities to her offspring.

ARIES MAN
PISCES WOMAN

Many a man dreams of a Piscean kind of a girl—and an Arien is no exception. She's soft and cuddly, and very domestic. She'll let you be the brains of the family; she's content to just lean on your shoulder and let you be master of the household. She can be very ladylike and proper; your business associates and friends will be dazzled by her warmth and femininity. She's a charmer, though, and there's much more to her, generally, than just her pretty exterior. There's a brain ticking away in that soft, womanly body. You may never become aware of it, that is, until you're married to her. It's no cause for alarm, however; she'll most likely never use it against you. Still, if she feels that you're botching up your marriage through inconsiderate behavior, or if she feels you could be earning more money than you do, she'll tell you about it. But, then, any wife would, really.

She'll never try to usurp your position as breadwinner of the family. She'll admire you for your ambition and drive. No one had better dare say one bad word about you in her presence. It's liable to cause her to break into tears. Pisces women are usually very sensitive beings and their reactions to adverse situations is sometimes nothing more than a plain, good, old-fashioned cry. They can weep buckets when inclined.

She'll have an extra-special dinner waiting for you to celebrate your landing a new and important account. Don't bother to go into the details, though, at the dinner table; she doesn't have much of a head for business matters, usually, and is only too happy to leave all that to you.

She can do wonders with a home. She's very fond of soft and beautiful things. There will always be a vase of fresh flowers on the hall table. She'll see to it that you always have plenty of socks and handkerchiefs in the top drawer of your dresser. You'll never have to shout downstairs, "Don't I have any clean shirts left?" She'll always see to it that you have. Treat her with tenderness and the relationship will be an enjoyable one.

She'll most likely be fond of chocolates. A bunch of beautiful flowers will make her eyes light up. See to it that you never forget her birthday or your anniversary. These things are very important to her. If you ever let them slip your mind, you can be sure of sending her off to the bedroom for an hour-long crying fit. An Arien with patience and tenderness can keep a Pisces woman happy for a lifetime.

She's not without faults herself, however, and after the glow of love-at-first-sight has faded away, you may find yourself standing in a tubful of hot water. You may find her lacking in imagination and zest. Her sensitivity is liable to get on your nerves after a while. You may even feel that she only uses tears in order to get her own way.

Pisces make strong, sacrificing mothers.

Woman—Man

ARIES WOMAN
ARIES MAN

The mating of Aries with Aries could lead to some pretty frantic fireworks, but it does not necessarily have to. As strong in her ways as he is in his, the Aries woman will make her Aries man happiest by supplementing his drives and dreams. An Aries woman can understand and respect a man born under the same sign if she puts her mind to it. He could be that knight in shining armor that Aries women are often in search of. Women born under the sign of the Ram are hard to please and are not interested in just getting a man. They know just what kind of a man he should be and usually do not settle for anything less than their ideal. They are particular. As far as love goes, neither of them shilly-shally with passion. They play for keeps. An Aries-Aries union could be something strong, secure, and romantic. If both of them have their sights fixed in the same direction and have mutual appreciation for each other, there is almost nothing they could not accomplish. It is a block-buster of a combination.

However, if the Aries wife chooses to place her own interests before those of her husband, she can be sure of rocking the boat . . . and perhaps eventually torpedoing it. The career-minded Aries woman, out to do better than her Aries husband, generally winds up doing herself in. He won't stand for it and your relationship won't stand the strain it will bring about. The Aries wife who devotes herself to teas and evenings of bridge will find that she's burned the one bridge she didn't intend to. The homeloving Aries man finds hastily scribbled notes on the dining-room table and TV dinners in the freezer equally indigestible. When you get home from that night out with the girls, he'll take his heartburn out on you instead of reaching for the Alka-Seltzer. If you want to avoid burps and bumps in your marriage, be on hand with his favorite meals, snacks, plus a generous amount of affection. The way to an Arien's stomach is through his heart.

Homemaking, though, should present no problems to the Aries wife. With her, it's second nature. With a pot of paint and some paper, she can transform the dreariest domicile into a place of beauty and snug comfort. The perfect hostess—even when friends just happen by—she knows how to make guests feel at home and this is what makes her Arien man beam with pride. Home is where some people hang their hat; for an Arien, it's where you hang your heart. It's his castle. Marriage can coast along royally for the Aries couple if the little woman keeps the home fires burning and wholeheartedly stands behind her man. This is no problem for the sensitive Aries wife.

ARIES WOMAN
TAURUS MAN

It is the Aries woman who has more than a pinch of patience and reserve who can find her dream-come-true in a man born under the sign of the Bull.

The steady and deliberate Taurean is a little slow on the draw; it may take him quite a while before he gets around to popping that question. For the Arien women who has learned the art of twiddling her thumbs and who doesn't care if her love life seems like a parody of "Waiting for Godot," the waiting and anticipating almost always pays off in the end. Taurus men take their time. Every slow step they take is a sure one—they see to that, especially when they feel that the path they're on could lead them to the altar.

Any Aries woman looking for a whirlwind romance had better cast her net in shallower waters. Moreover, most Taureans prefer to do the angling themselves. They're not keen on women taking the lead—once she does, he's liable to drop her like a dead fish. Once the Aries woman lets herself get caught on his terms, she'll find that her Taurean has fallen for her: hook, line and sinker.

The Taurus man is fond of comfortable homelife. It's as important to him as it is to the Aries woman. The Arien who centers her main activities on keeping those home fires burning will have no worries about keeping that flame in her hubby's heart aglow. The Aries woman, with her talent for homemaking and harmony, is sometimes the perfect match for the strong, steady, and protective bull. He can be the anchor for her dreams and plans, and can help her acquire a more balanced outlook and approach to her life and her goals. Not one for wild schemes, himself, the Taurean can constructively help her to curb her impulsiveness. He's the man who is always there when you need him. Taureans are rather fond of staying put, especially when it's near someone they love and cherish. When tying her knot with a Taurean, the Aries woman can put away all fears about creditors pounding on the front door. Taureans are practical about everything including bill-paying. When he carries you over that threshold, you can be certain that the entire house is paid for.

As a housewife, the Arien married to a Taurus man, need not worry about having to put aside her many interests for the sake of back-breaking house chores. He'll see to it that you have all the latest time-saving appliances and comforts.

The Aries mother can forget about acquiring premature gray hairs due to unruly, ruckus-raising children under her feet. Papa Taurus is a master at keeping offspring in line. He's crazy about his kids, but he also knows what's good for them. And although he may never resort to the rod, he'll never allow himself to spoil his child, either. Children respect Taurean authority and will usually do their best to make papa proud of them.

The Taurus spouse or lover is generous, patient, and easy-going. He's no slouch and it can lead to disaster if the ambitious Aries wife misinterprets his plodding ways for plain laziness. He knows where he's going. Make no bones about that. Stick with him even if sometimes he seems as slow as molasses on a cold day, and your marital life will be all sweetness and light.

The Taurus man is a steady-Eddy—the kind of man the Aries woman often needs. He appreciates her interest in his work, and pays heed to her helpful suggestions because they pay off. Taureans are faithful and never flirt. All his love and attention are riveted to the woman of his choice, as long as she shows that she's deserving.

ARIES WOMAN
GEMINI MAN

The Aries woman and the Gemini man are a twosome that can make beautiful music together. Perhaps that is due to the fact that they are alike in certain respects. Both are intelligent, witty, outgoing, and tend to be rather versatile. An Aries woman can be the Miss Right that Mr. Gemini has been looking for—his prospective better half, as it were. One thing that causes a Twin's mind and affection to wander is a bore, and it's highly unlikely that an Arien would ever be accused of that. He'll admire the Ram for her ideas and intellect—perhaps even more than her good cooking and flawless talent for homemaking. She needn't feel that once she's made that vow that she'll have to store her interests and ambition in the attic somewhere. He'll admire her for her zeal and liveliness. He's the kind of guy who won't pout and scowl if he has to shift for himself in the kitchen once in a while. In fact, he'll enjoy the challenge of wrestling with pots and pans himself for a change. Chances are, too, that he might turn out to be a better cook than his Mrs., that is, if he isn't already.

The man born under the sign of the Twins is like an intellectual mountain goat leaping from crag to crag. There aren't many women who have pep enought to keep up with him. But this doesn't fluster the spry Ram. In fact, she probably knows before he does which crag he's going to spring onto next. In many cases, she's always a couple of jumps ahead of him—and if she's the helpful wife Ariens usually are, she won't mind telling him when and how to jump. They're both dreamers, planners, and idealists. The woman born under the sign of the Ram, though, is more thorough and possesses more stick-to-it-iveness. She can easily fill the role of rudder for her Gemini's ship-without-a-sail. He won't mind it too much, either. If he's an intelligent Twin, he'll be well aware of his shortcomings and won't mind it if somebody gives him a shove in the right direction—when it's needed. The average Gemini does not have serious ego hangups and will even accept a well-deserved chewing out from his mate quite gracefully.

You'll probably always have a houseful of interesting people to entertain. Geminis find it hard to tolerate sluggish minds and dispositions. You'll never be at a loss for finding new faces in your living room. Geminis are great friend-collectors and sometimes go about it the same way kids go about collecting marbles—the more they sparkle and dazzle, the greater their value to him. But then in a day or two, it's not unusual to find that he has traded yesterday's favorites for still brighter and newer ones. The diplomatic Arien can bring her willy-nilly Gemini to reason and point out his folly in friendships in such a way that he'll think twice before considering an exchange of old lamps for new.

As far as children are concerned, it's quite likely that the Aries wife will have to fill the role of house disciplinarian. Geminis are pushovers for children, perhaps because they understand them so well and have that childlike side to their nature which keeps them youthful and optimistic. They have no interest in keeping a child's vigor in check.

Gemini men are always attractive to the opposite sex and vice-versa. The Aries woman with her proud nature will have to bend a little and allow her Gemini man an occassional harmless flirtation—it will seldom amount to more than that if she's a proper mate. It will help to keep his spirits up. An out-of-sorts Twin is capable of brewing up a whirlwind of trouble. Better to let him hanky-pank—within eyeshot, of course—than to lose your cool; it might cause you to lose your man.

ARIES WOMAN
CANCER MAN

It's quite possible that a man born under this sign of the Crab may be a little too crabby for the average Aries woman; but then, Cupid has been known to perform some pretty unlikely feats with his wayward bow and arrow. Again, it's the Arien with her wits about her who can make the most out of a relationship with the sensitive and occassionally moody Cancerian. He may not be altogether her cup of tea, but when it comes to security and faithfulness—qualities Aries women often value highly—she couldn't have made a better choice.

It's the perceptive Arien who will not mistake the Crab's quietness for sullenness, or his thriftiness for pennypinching. In some respects he can be like the wise old owl out on a limb; he may look like he's dozing but actually he hasn't missed a thing. Cancers often possess a storehouse of knowledge about human behavior; they can come across with some pretty helpful advice for those troubled and in need of an understanding shoulder to cry on. The Aries girl about to rush off for new fields to conquer had better turn to her Cancerian first. Chances are he can save her from making unwise investments in time and—especially—money. He may not say much, but he's capable of being on his toes even while his feet are flat on the ground.

The Crab may not be the match or catch for many a Ram; in

fact, he might seem downright dull to the ambitious, on-the-move Arien. True to his sign, he can be fairly cranky and crabby when handled in the wrong way. He's sensitive, perhaps more sensitive than is good for him. The talkative Arien who has a habit of saying what is on her mind had better think twice before letting loose with a personal criticism of any kind, particularly if she's got her heart set on a Cancerian. If she's smart as a whip, she'd better be careful that she never in any way conveys the idea that she considers her Crab a little short on brain power. Browbeating is a sure-fire way of sending the Crab angrily scurrying back to his shell, and it's quite possible that all of that ground lost might never be recovered.

Home is an area where the Aries woman and the Cancer man are in safe territory. Both have serious respect and deep interest in home life, and do their best to keep things running smoothly and harmoniously there. The Crab is most comfortable at home. Once settled in for the night or the weekend, wild horses couldn't drag him any further than the gate post—that is, unless those wild horses were dispatched by his mother. Cancerians are often Momma's boys. If his mate doesn't put her foot down, the Crab will see to it that his mother always comes first whenever possible. No self-respecting Arien would ever allow herself to play second fiddle, even if it is to her old gray-haired mother-in-law. If she's a tactful Ram, she may find that slipping into number-one position can be as easy as pie (that legendary apple pie that his mother used to make). She should agree with her Cancerian when he praises his mother's way with meat loaf, then go on to prove herself a master at making a super-delicious chocolate souffle. All Ariens are pretty much at home in the kitchen; no recipe is too complicated for them to handle to perfection. If she takes enough time to pamper her Cancerian with good-cooking and comfort, she'll find that "mother" turns up less often, both at the front door and in daily conversations.

Crabs make grand daddies. They're protective, patient, and proud of their children. They'll do everything to see that their upbringing is as it should be.

ARIES WOMAN
LEO MAN

For the Arien who doesn't mind being swept off her feet in a royal, head-over-heels, fashion, Leo is the sign of love. When the Lion puts his mind to romancing, he doesn't stint. It's all wining, dining, and dancing till the wee hours of the morning—or all poetry and flowers, if you prefer a more conservative kind of wooing. The Lion is all heart and knows how to make his woman feel like a woman. The Aries lass in constant search of a man whom she can admire, need go no farther: Leo's ten-feet tall—if not in stature, then in spirit. He's a man not only in full control of his faculties but of just about every situation he may find himself in, including of course, affairs of the heart. He may not look like Tarzan, but he knows how to roar and beat his chest if he has to. The Aries woman who has had her fill of weak-kneed men, at last finds in a Leo someone she can lean upon. He can support you not only physically, but also as far as your ideas and plans are concerned. Leos are direct and don't believe in wasting time or effort. They see to it that they seldom make poor investments; something that an Arien is not apt to always do. Many Leos often rise to the top of their profession and through their example, are a great inspiration to others.

Although he's a ladies' man, he's very particular about his ladies, just as the Arien is particular about her men. His standards are high when it comes to love interests. The idealistic Arien should have no trouble keeping her balance on the pedestal the Lion sets her on, so long as he keeps his balance on hers. Romance between these two signs is fair give-and-take. Neither stands for monkey business when involved in a love relationship. It's all or nothing. Aries and Leo are both frank, off-the-shoulder people. They generally say what is on their hearts and minds.

The Aries woman who does decide upon a Leo mate, must be prepared to stand behind her man with all her energies. He expects it, and usually deserves it. He's the head of the house and can handle that position without a hitch. He knows how to go about breadwinning and, if he has his way (and most Leos do have their way), he'll see to it that you'll have all the luxuries you crave and the comforts you need.

It's unlikely that the romance will ever die out of your marriage. Lions need love like flowers need sunshine. They're amorous and generally expect similar amounts of attention and affection from their mates. Fond of going out occasionally, and party-giving, the Lion is a very sociable being and will expect you to share his interest in this direction. Your home will be something to be proud of. The Joneses will have to worry about keeping up with you.

Leos are fond of their children but sometimes are a little too strict in handling them. The tactful Aries spouse, though, can step in and sooth her children's roughed-up feelings if need be.

ARIES WOMAN
VIRGO MAN

Quite often the Virgo man will seem like too much of a fuss-budget to wake up deep romantic interests in an Arien. Generally, he's cool, calm and very collected. Torrid romancing to him is just so much sentimental mush. He can do without it and can make that quite evident in short order. He's keen on chastity and if necessary can lead a sedentary, sexless life without caring too much about the fun others think he's missing. In short, the average Aries woman is quite likely to find him a first-class dud. His lack of imagination and dislike for flights of fancy can grate on an Arien's nerves no end. He's correct and likes to be handled correctly. Most things about him will be orderly. "There's a place for everything and everything in its place," is likely an adage he'll fall on quite regularly.

He does have a heart, however, and the Aries woman who finds herself attracted to his cool, feet-flat-on-the-ground ways, will find that his is a constant heart, not one that cares for flings or sordid affairs. Virgos take an awfully long time before they start trying to rhyme moon with spoon and June, but when and if they get around to it, they know what they're talking about.

The impulsive Arien had better not make the mistake of kissing her Virgo friend on the street—even if it's only a peck on the cheek. He's not at all demonstrative and hates public displays of affection. Love, according to him, should be kept within the confines of one's home, with the curtains drawn. Once he believes that you're on the level with him, as far as your love is concerned, you'll see how fast he can lose his cool. Virgos are considerate, gentle lovers. He'll spend a long time, though, getting to know you. He'll like you before he loves you.

An Aries-Virgo romance can be a life-time thing. If the bottom ever falls out, don't bother to reach for the Scotch tape. Nine times out of ten, he won't care about patching up. He's a once-burnt-twice-shy guy. When he crosses your telephone number out of his address book, he's crossing you out of his life for good.

Neat as a pin, he's thumbs-down on what he considers "sloppy" housekeeping. An ashtray with just one stubbed-out cigarette in it can be annoying to him, even if it's just two-seconds old. Glassware should always sparkle and shine. No smudges please.

If you marry a Virgo, keep your kids spic-and-span, at least by the time he gets home from work. Chocolate-coated kisses from Daddy's little girl go over like a lead balloon. He'll expect his children to observe their "thank yous" and "pleases."

ARIES WOMAN
LIBRA MAN

Although the Libran in your life may be very compatible, you may find this relationship lacking in some of the things you highly value.

You, who look for constancy in romance, may find him a puzzlement as a lover. One moment he comes on hard and strong with

"I love you," the next moment you find that he's left you like yesterday's mashed potatoes. It does no good to wonder "What did I do now?" You most likely haven't done anything. It's just one of Libra's ways.

On the other hand, you'll appreciate his admiration of harmony and beauty. If you're all decked out in your fanciest gown or have a tastefully arranged bouquet on the dining-room table, you'll get a ready compliment—and one that's really deserved. Librans don't pass out compliments indiscriminately and generally they're tactful enough to remain silent if they find something is distasteful or disagreeable.

Where you're a straight-off-the-shoulder, let's-put-our-cards-on-the-table person, Librans generally hate arguing. They'll go to great lengths just to maintain peace and harmony—even lie if necessary. The frank Aries woman is all for getting it off her chest and into the open, even if it does come out all wrong. To the Libran, making a clean breast of everything sometimes seems like sheer folly.

The Aries woman may find it difficult to understand a Libran's frequent indecisiveness—he weighs both sides carefully before committing himself to anything. To you, this may seem like just plain stalling.

Although you, too, greatly respect order and beauty, you would never let it stand in the way of "getting ahead." Not one who dilly-dallies, the Aries may find it difficult to accept a Libran's hestiation to act on what may seem like a very simple matter.

The Libra father is most always gentle and patient. They allow their children to develop naturally, still they see to it that they never become spoiled.

Money burns a hole in many a Libran's pocket; his Aries spouse will have to manage the budgeting and bookkeeping. You don't have to worry about him throwing his money around all over the place; most likely he'll spend it all on you—and lavishly.

Because he's quite interested in getting along harmoniously chances are he won't mind an Aries wife taking over the reins once in a while—so long as she doesn't make a habit of it.

ARIES WOMAN
SCORPIO MAN

Many find the Scorpio's sting a fate worse than death. The Aries woman quite often is no acception. When he comes on like "gangbusters," the average Aries woman had better clear out of the vicinity.

The Scorpio man may strike the Aries woman as being a brute

and a fiend. It's quite likely he'll ignore your respect for colorful arrangements and harmonious order. If you do anything to irritate him—just anything—you'll wish you hadn't. He'll give you a sounding out that would make you pack your bags and go back to mother —if you were that kind of a girl. Your deep interest in your home and the activities that take place there will most likely affect him indifferently. The Scorpio man hates being tied down to a home— no matter how comfortable his Aries wife has made it. He'd rather be out on the battlefield of life, belting away at what he feels is a just and worthy cause. Don't try to keep those homefires burning too brightly too long—you may just run out of firewood.

As passionate as he is in business affairs and politics, he's got plenty of pep and ginger stored away for romance. Most women are easily attracted to him, and the Aries woman is no acception. That is, at least before she knows what she might be getting into. Those who allow a man of this sign to sweep them off their feet, shortly find that they're dealing with a cauldron of seething excitement. He's passion with a capital P, make no bones about that. And he's capable of dishing out as much pain as pleasure. Damsels with fluttering hearts who, when in the embrace of a Scorpio, think "This is it," had better be in a position to realize "This isn't it," some moments later. Scorpio's are blunt. If there's not enough powder on your nose or you have just goofed with a sure-fire recipe for Beef Stroganoff (which is unlikely, you being an old hand with pots and pans) he'll let you know and in no uncertain terms. He might say that your *big* nose is shiny and that he wouldn't serve your Stroganoff to his worst enemy—even your mother. She might be sitting right beside him when he says this, too.

The Scorpio's love of power may cause you to be at his constant beck-and-call.

Scorpios often father large families and generally love their children even though they may not seem to give them the attention they should.

ARIES WOMAN
SAGITTARIUS MAN

The Aries woman who's set her cap for a man born under this sign of Sagittarius, may have to apply an awful amount of strategy before being able to make him say "I do." Although Sagittarians may be marriage-shy, they're not ones to shy away from romance. An Aries woman may find a relationship with a Sagittarian—whether a fling or "the real thing"—a very enjoyable experience. As a rule, Sagittarians are bright, happy, and healthy people and they can be a source of inspiration to the busy, bustling Aries woman. Their deep sense of fair play will please you, too. They're full of ideas and drive. You'll be taken by the Sagittarian's infectious grin and his light-hearted friendly attitude. If you do choose to be the woman in his life, you'll find that he's apt to treat you more like a buddy than like the woman he deeply loves. But it is not intentional; it's just the way he is. You'll admire his broadmindedness in most matters—including that of the heart. If, while you're dating, he claims he still wants to play the field, he'll expect you to do the same. The same holds true when you're both playing for keeps. However, once he's promised to love, honor, and obey, he does just that. Marriage for him, once he's taken that big step, is very serious business. The Aries woman with her keen imagination and love of freedom will not be disappointed if she does tie up with a Sagittarian. They're quick-witted, generally, and they have a genuine interest in equality. If he insists on a night out with the boys once a week, he won't scowl if you decide to let him shift for himself in the kitchen once a week while you go out with the girls.

You'll find he's not much of a homebody. Quite often he's occupied with far away places either in daydreams or reality. He enjoys —just as you do—being on the go or on the move. He's got ants in his pants and refuses to sit still for long stretches at a time. Humdrum routine—especially at home—bores him. At the drop of a hat, he may ask you to whip off your apron and dine out for a change instead. He'll take great pride in showing you off to his friends; he'll always be a considerate mate and never embarrass or disappoint you intentionally. His friendly, sun-shiny nature is capable of attracting many people. Like you, he's very tolerant when it comes to friends and you'll most likely spend a great deal of time entertaining people. He'll expect his friends to be your friends, too, and vice-versa. The Aries woman who often prefers male company to that of her own sex, will not be shunted aside when the fellows are deep in "man talk." Her Sagittarian will see to it that she's made to feel like one of the gang and treated equally.

When it comes to children, you may find that you've been left to handle that area of your marriage single-handedly. Sagittarians are all thumbs when it comes to tots.

ARIES WOMAN
CAPRICORN MAN

Chances are the Aries woman will find a relationship with a Capricorn man a bit of a drag. He can be quite opposite to the things you stand for and value. Where you are generally frank and open, you'll find the man born under the sign of the Goat, closed or difficult to get to know—or not very interesting once you've gotten to know him. He may be quite rusty in the romance department, too, and may take quite a bit of drawing out. You may find his seemingly plodding manner irritating, and his conservative, traditional ways downright maddening. He's not one to take chances on anything. "If it was good enough for my father, it's good enough for me" may be his motto. He follows a way that is tried and true.

Whenever adventure rears its tantalizing head, the Goat will ring up a No Sale sign; he's just not interested. He may be just as ambitious as you are—perhaps even more so—but his ways of accomplishing his aims are more subterranean or at least, seem so. He operates from the background a good deal of the time. At a gathering you may never even notice him, but he's there taking everything in and sizing everyone up, planning his next careful move. Although Capricorns may be intellectual, it is generally not the kind of intelligence an Arien appreciates. You may find they're not quick-witted and are a little slow to understand a simple joke. The Aries woman who finds herself involved with a Capricorn may find that she has to be pretty good in the "cheering up" department, as the man in her love life may act as though he's constantly being followed by a cloud of gloom. If the Arien and the Capricorn do decide to tie the knot, the area of their greatest compatibility will most likely be in the home and decisions centered around the home. You'll find that your spouse is most himself when under the roof of home sweet home. Just being there, comfortable and secure, will make him a happy man. He'll spend as much time there as he can and if he finds he has to work overtime, he'll bring his work home rather than stay in the office.

You'll most likely find yourself frequently confronted by his relatives—family is very important to the Capricorn, *his* family, that is—and they had better take a pretty important place in your life, too, if you want to keep your home a happy one.

Although his caution in most matters may all but drive you up the wall, you'll find his concerned way with money justified most of the time. He is no squanderer. Everything is planned right down to the last red penny. He'll see to it that you never want.

As far as children are concerned, you may find that you have to step in from time to time when he scolds. Although he generally knows what is good for his children, he can overdo somewhat when it comes to taking them to the woodshed.

ARIES WOMAN
AQUARIUS MAN

The Arien is likely to find the man born under Aquarius dazzling. As a rule, Aquarians are extremely friendly and open; of all the signs, they are perhaps the most tolerant. In the thinking department they are often miles ahead of others, and with very little effort, it seems. The Aries woman will most likely not only find her Aquarian friend intriguing and interesting, but will find the relationship challenging as well. Your high respect for intelligence and fair play may be reason enough for you to settle your heart on a Water Bearer. There's an awful lot to be learned from him, if you're quick enough. Aquarians love everybody—even their worst enemies, sometimes. Through your relationship with the Aquarian you'll find yourself running into all sorts of people, ranging from near-genius to downright insane—and they're all freinds of his.

In the holding hands stage of your romance you may find that your Water Bearing friend has cold feet that may take quite a bit of warming up before he gets around to that first goodnight kiss. More than likely he'll just want to be your pal in the beginning. For him, that's an important step in any relationship—even love. The "poetry and flowers" stage will come later, perhaps many years later. The Aquarian is all heart, still when it comes to tying himself down to one person and for keeps, he is liable to hesitate. He may even try to get out of it if you breath too hard down his neck. He's no Valentino and wouldn't want to be. The Aries woman is likely to be more attracted by his broadmindedness and high moral standards than by his abilities to romance. She won't find it difficult to look up to a man born under the sign of the Water Bearer—but she may find the challenge of trying to keep up with him dizzying. He can pierce through the most complicated problem as if it were a matter of $2 + 2$. You may find him a little too lofty and high-minded, however. But don't judge him too harshly if that's the case; he's way ahead of his time; your time, too, most likely.

In marriage you need never be afraid that his affection will wander. It stays put once he's hitched. He'll certainly admire you for your intelligence and drive; don't think that once you're in the kitchen you have to stay there. He'll want you to go on and pursue whatever you want in your quest for knowledge. He's understanding on that point. You'll most likely have a minor squabble with him now and again, but never anything serious.

You may find his forgetfulness a little bothersome. His head is so full of ideas and plans that sometimes he seems like the Absent-Minded Professor incarnate. Kids love him and vice-versa. He's tolerant and open-minded with everybody, from the very young to the very old.

ARIES WOMAN
PISCES MAN

The man born under the sign of Pisces, may be a little too sluggish for the average Aries woman. He's often wrapped up in his dreams and difficult to reach at times. He's an idealist like you, but unlike you, he will not jump up on a soapbox and champion a cause he feels is just. Difficult for you to understand at times, he may seem like a weakling to you. He'll entertain all kinds of views and opinions from just about anyone, nodding or smiling vaguely, giving the impression that he's with them one hundred percent. In reality, that may not be the case at all. His attitude may be "why bother" to tell someone he's wrong when he so strongly believes that he's right. This kind of attitude can make an Arien furious. You speak your mind; he'll seldom speak his unless he thinks there'll be no opposition. He's oversensitive at times—rather afraid of getting his feelings hurt. He'll sometimes imagine a personal injury when none is intended. Chances are you'll find this sort of behavior maddening and may feel like giving your Pisces friend a swift kick where it hurts the most. It won't do any good, though. It may just add fire to his persecution complex.

One thing you'll admire about this man is his concern and understanding of people who are sickly or who have serious (often emotional) problems. It's his nature to make his shoulder available to anyone in the mood for a good cry. He can listen to one hard-luck story after another without seeming to tire and if his advice is asked he's capable of coming across with some very well-balanced common sense. He often knows what is bugging a person before that person knows it himself. It's amost intuitive with a Pisces, it seems. Still, at the end of the day, he'll want some peace and quiet and if his Aries friend has some problem or project on her mind that she would like to unload in his lap, she's liable to find him rather short-tempered. He's a good listener but he can only take so much.

Pisces are not aimless, although they may often appear to be when viewed through Arien eyes. The positive sort of Pisces man is quite often successful in his profession and is likely to wind up rich and influential—even though material gain is never a direct goal for a man born under this sign.

The weaker Pisces are usually content to stay put on the level they find themselves. They won't complain too much if the roof leaks and the fence is in need of repair. He's capable of shrugging his shoulders and sighing "that's life."

Because of their seemingly free-and-easy manner, people under this sign, needless to say, are immensely popular with children. For tots they play the double role of confidant and playmate.

ARIES

LUCKY NUMBERS: 1996

Lucky numbers and astrology can be linked through the movements of the Moon. Each phase of the thirteen Moon cycles vibrates with a sequence of numbers for your Sign of the Zodiac over the course of the year. Using your lucky numbers is a fun system that connects you with tradition.

New Moon	First Quarter	Full Moon	Last Quarter
Dec. 21 ('95) 5 2 6 0	Dec. 28 ('95) 8 0 9 7	Jan. 5 1 2 9 4	Jan. 13 5 8 2 7
Jan. 20 1 6 1 4	Jan. 27 2 2 9 9	Feb. 4 5 5 7 8	Feb. 12 8 3 9 6
Feb. 18 0 4 7 5	Feb. 25 5 3 3 8	March 5 1 3 2 6	March 12 6 3 9 4
March 19 4 3 2 2	March 26 5 5 1 0	April 3 3 9 4 8	April 10 5 2 6 0
April 17 9 7 4 2	April 25 2 7 9 1	May 3 4 5 2 8	May 10 3 6 6 4
May 17 4 4 2 1	May 25 6 8 9 4	June 1 8 1 7 2	June 8 2 5 3 3
June 15 3 1 7 3	June 24 5 6 1 0	June 30 5 4 8 2	July 7 2 9 9 7
July 15 7 7 3 5	July 23 4 5 9 6	July 30 2 7 1 8	August 6 8 8 6 6
August 14 6 2 4 5	August 21 9 4 1 7	August 28 6 5 3 3	Sept. 4 3 1 1 6
Sept. 12 6 8 9 4	Sept. 20 1 7 8 3	Sept. 26 0 9 4 4	Oct. 4 2 2 7 9
Oct. 12 9 1 5 2	Oct. 19 8 3 6 0	Oct. 26 7 7 5 5	Nov. 3 5 1 3 4
Nov. 10 4 8 5 2	Nov. 17 6 0 9 3	Nov. 24 7 8 8 4	Dec. 3 4 6 7 2
Dec. 10 2 8 5 9	Dec. 17 3 1 0 6	Dec. 24 5 4 9 2	Jan. 2 ('97) 8 3 7 4

ARIES

YEARLY FORECAST: 1996

Forecast for 1996 Concerning Business
and Financial Matters, Job Prospects,
Travel, Health, Romance and Marriage
for Those Born with the Sun
in the Zodiacal Sign of Aries.
March 21–April 20

For those born under the influence of the Sun in the zodiacal sign of Aries, which is ruled by Mars, planet of vitality, initiative, and action, 1996 is likely to bring greater stability, fulfillment, and rewards. Your labors and efforts over the past few years now achieve results beyond your hopes. Personal difficulties will be easier to resolve, with the help of patience and determination. Feelings of inner frustration or conflict are likely to vanish in the face of greater success and achievement. Health problems will tend to improve, and may even disappear altogether. As a whole, this year can bring you rapidly closer to the fulfillment of your most secret hopes and dreams, provided you are willing to discipline yourself and, above all, trust in your own abilities. Diplomacy will be the key to success. Some extra manipulating will almost certainly be necessary in order to counterbalance the deviousness of competitors. Do not put all your cards on the table; keep a few tricks up your sleeve. And be on guard against underhanded dealings which might land you on the wrong side of the law. Financially, this year may be slightly less secure than last. Do some advance thinking to plan the best long-term strategies. Guard against overspending, especially if you have to live on a tight budget. Occupationally, this is a year when you start to see the light at the end of the tunnel. Feelings of job frustration will probably give way to a stronger sense of motivation than you have experienced in a long time. This tends to be a better year for travel, both over long and shorter distances. After what has been a rather uncommunicative and even solitary period, 1996 is likely to bring more romantic opportunities for entering into a permanent relationship. Understanding which you have gained through experience and even through suffering over the past few years makes you more capable than ever of entering into a truly mature, responsible, and meaningful partnership. This is also a favorable year for married Aries, and indeed for taking the plunge if you are ready to settle down. However, you need to be a little more flexible and less dominant in the relationship. The strong, silent type can easily intimidate a current or potential mate. All in all, this year promises excellent opportunities both personally and professionally. Show the world that you mean business and you will come to be respected, trusted, and valued more than ever.

There is little point trying to deny that this can be a confusing year for business and professional affairs. One of the greatest weaknesses of Aries people is a tendency to make snap judgments based simply on appearances and first impressions. This year business and career affairs will not be exactly what they seem. People who appear hostile to you can in fact have your best interests at heart. Do not reject their criticisms; take what they say very seriously. And people who try to ingratiate themselves with you through flattery or sweet talking may be secretly plotting your downfall. Be prepared to learn a few tricks in the art of being streetwise. Do not imagine that confrontations and showdowns will allow you to get to the truth or expose the double-dealing of unscrupulous people; they are much too clever for that. Avoid making too much of an issue of personal honor. It is important to you, but people will not be very impressed by qualities such as ethical integrity, so there is little to be gained from trying to capitalize on them. Emphasize what you can do for others but not how you intend to do it. On the positive side, there are many factors working in your favor throughout 1996. Early in the new year you are likely to find business affairs in general starting to stabilize and move forward on a more even keel. A calmer economic climate will prove helpful in this respect. This can be an auspicious year for entering into a new business partnership, especially where the other party will be able to supply some much-needed funding. Arrangements of this kind can allow you to diversify dramatically and put into action new plans which you have reluctantly had to keep shelved. Distant travel continues to be helpful as a means of establishing new contacts and also overseeing current business ventures. Between June 12 and July 24 can be good for diverting extra funding into advertising or other media campaigns. Between July 25 and September 8 is favorable for taking more initiative in matters relating to the purchase, lease, or transfer of property. In all such matters you will need to be on guard against the risk of deception. Between October 30 and the end of the year favors all staff-related matters, including hiring additional employees. Set a personal example to those who are working under you. Come down heavily on laziness or carelessness, but also be prepared to reward hard work and initiative with bonuses, promotions, and extra incentives.

Where finances are concerned, this is a year where patience and long-term planning are likely to pay off. The chances of making a quick buck tend to be fewer and farther between, except between May 2 and June 11. At that time a new job could prove especially lucrative. Between September 9 and October 29 a gamble may well pay off. Otherwise, concentrate on securing your major sources of income and taking extra measures to protect savings and investments. Additional precautions to guard against inflation can be an especially wise idea. If a particular investment in which you have a stake starts to shake at its foundations, do not panic and make hasty decisions. Unfortunately, this is a year when friends or would-be friends can become a major financial liability if you allow yourself to be too trusting and generous. The chances are good that money you lend to a casual acquaintance is money you will never see again. This is true above all for the period between January 8 and February 14.

Many Aries men and women have not had an easy time during the last two years where work and occupational matters are concerned. It may have seemed that you were incapable of getting ahead and that your contributions were passing unnoticed and unrewarded. This year, however, you are likely to find that this scenario has become a thing of the past. The sooner you realize that your future is in your own hands, the better. You have the power and the ability to make things happen for yourself. This can be a good year for entering into the world of self-employment, even if only on a modest scale to begin with; small beginnings are often the best. Wait until the first week of April before making any major moves or commitments. After that time you can be surprised by the offers and opportunities that come your way without your even needing to solicit or invite them. Do not undervalue your skills or sell yourself short. For those of you who are temporarily unemployed, between October 30 and the end of the year can be an ideal time for making an energetic comeback.

Certain limiting conditions, possibly related to domestic matters or to your own health or the illness of someone close to you, may have prevented you from traveling as much as you would have liked during the past few years. From April of this year onward, you will find your opportunities and horizons broadening once again. Travel can be an ideal way of learning and of accumulating valuable experience. This may even be a year when you take serious steps toward deciding to relocate or even live in a foreign country, at least for a while. Be resourceful. Traveling can give you that exhilarating sense of getting back to basics which makes life seem so much more meaningful and worthwhile.

Health matters will tend to see a significant improvement this year. You may even find that a period of illness or debility in the recent past has in a subtle way transformed you and made you more aware of your capabilities. Learn to listen more to your body. One of your greatest weaknesses, which can also be your strength, is your ability to keep pushing yourself regardless of the discomfort and inconvenience until your body finally gives up. This is no longer the right approach for you. Heed your body's warning signals. Take things easier toward the end of the year, particularly from October 30 onward. Get extra rest at the first sign of a cold or any illness. There is nothing to be gained from pushing yourself too hard.

This is a year when many Aries people will find that friendship is just as important as love and romance, if not more so. Your easygoing nature makes you inclined to value the kind of relationship that is comparatively free of the emotional attachments a romance almost invariably includes. At the same time, however, be honest with yourself. Aries singles are apt to be eager for a lasting, meaningful relationship with a partner whom you can trust and respect as well as share your most intimate feelings. If the opportunity for such a relationship arises, do not put up an independent, know-it-all wall of defense. Let down your guard, or you may never know how much you have missed.

In all areas, be more open and responsive to what is new and therefore somewhat frightening. You have the self-confidence to succeed by standing on your own two feet and relying on your excellent Aries intuition.

DAILY FORECAST

January–December 1996

JANUARY

1. MONDAY. Tricky. This may not be a restful start to the New Year. Aries could be experiencing some anxiety when it comes to making career decisions. It may be clear to you that it is time to move on, but which direction to take can leave you feeling confused. Make a point of seeking some help and advice from a family member or an older friend. This can be a good day for shopping in the stores which have started their New Year sales or for combing through advertisements for upcoming sales. Try not to get carried away. Some items may not be the bargains they appear to be; hold on to all receipts in case you have to make returns.

2. TUESDAY. Calm. Aries people who go to business this morning should be able to ease back into work mode according to your own timetable. Dealing with paperwork from the end of last year, or with mail which has amassed over the vacation period, could take up the best part of the day. If you are at home, this is a good time for writing thank-you letters for gifts or hospitality received over Christmas. A telephone call from someone who has been away can brighten up the afternoon. For unemployed Aries people, this is a good time for a fresh start. Check out the job advertisements in your local newspaper; there could be several possibilities tailored for your training and interests.

3. WEDNESDAY. Variable. Guard against speaking out of turn. You could realize too late that you are supposed to keep certain information to yourself. But try not to be too hard on yourself; just resolve not to be the keeper of other people's secrets in the future. This can be a productive day for group work of all kinds. Business meetings are likely to go well, especially if you are making a presentation to new clients or to a superior. Be ready for tricky questions that can keep you on your toes. Address a personal problem this evening. A loved one is now willing to talk openly so that you can clear the air and reach a mutually acceptable compromise.

4. THURSDAY. Frustrating. Aries people who are in the process of house or job hunting may have to cope with some frustrating delays. You may feel that you have expended a lot of energy only to find yourself back at square one. Try to be patient. There is nothing to be gained from settling for what you do not really want. At work a certain individual who has been promoted recently could be giving you a hard time. Realize that they are just trying out their new power, but do not allow yourself to be bullied. Attending to routine home chores this evening can be boring but unavoidable. Write additional thank-you notes for gifts before it becomes embarrassingly late to do so.

5. FRIDAY. Tense. The end of the first working week this year may leave you feeling as if you have not been away or had a break. Someone in a position of authority could be piling on the pressure. The best policy is to stay calm. Although Aries are more than adept at getting things done quickly, you might have to point out that you only have two hands. Guard against passing on pressure to a colleague; working together is likely to get the best results. This evening could be sensitive. Avoid criticizing your mate or date over minor issues. A tiny spark could light the fuse for a major disagreement that leaves you out in the cold.

6. SATURDAY. Disconcerting. Arguments about housework are foreseen. Try to be democratic. For instance, establish a rotating schedule for regular chores. Shopping for household items could turn out to be fruitless. Consider phoning likely stores to see if they have what you want; this way you could save a lot of time and energy. There is a greater risk of an accident at home. Take extra care when handling sharp instruments such as kitchen knives or anything that might crack in your hands. Social arrangements for this evening need to be double-checked; someone may have forgotten the time or place or the entire plan. If unsure what to wear when you go out tonight, opt for the more formal choice.

7. SUNDAY. Stressful. Being at home with children can be more stressful than usual. Falling into the trap of laying down the law or losing your temper is almost certain to make matters worse. Bad behavior is often related to boredom; concentrate on finding things for them to do. Join in on games yourself; household chores may just have to wait. Friction between you and an older member of your family may come to a head. You might have to accept that you are never going to see eye-to-eye on certain issues. If you show that you are willing to respect their values, they are more likely to do the same for you and you can agree to disagree.

8. MONDAY. Difficult. For Aries parents there is a greater risk of a child begging off school this morning. You might suspect that they are exaggerating their ill feelings, but it would probably be best to give them the benefit of the doubt even if this means you have to take a day off work yourself. Business meetings can be difficult to handle. There is a greater risk of being outvoted or outmaneuvered on a matter which is close to your heart. Try not to give in to the pressure of changing your mind in order for other people to feel more comfortable. A new romance could be put to the test this evening. Keep in mind that one disagreement does not necessarily spell the end.

9. TUESDAY. Changeable. For Aries business people this day is likely to be a mixed bag. Meetings should go well on the whole, but someone who is at odds with you may be difficult to win over. Try to meet them halfway. Doing business with overseas contacts can be time consuming. It may prove impossible to track down the person with whom you need to talk. Your boss is likely to be in a generous mood. This is a good time for making special requests, such as asking for a pay raise or a day off. You may have to attend a social event alone this evening because your partner is delayed elsewhere. There should be no reason for you to cancel, however.

10. WEDNESDAY. Fortunate. You are more physically energetic than usual. A health worry which has been nagging at you for some time may spontaneously clear up. If you are at home you should be able to race through your regular chores and have the afternoon to yourself. At work this is a good day for meetings of a confidential nature. A higher-up is more willing to respect your request for an off-the-record discussion. Aries salespeople should not hesitate to be bold. Go straight to the top decision maker. A formal occasion this evening combining work with pleasure should prove to be both fun and successful.

11. THURSDAY. Energetic. For Aries people involved in charity work, this should be a good day for fund-raising efforts of all kinds. Approaching large corporations rather than individuals could be most productive. If you are out of work at the moment, consider offering your services to a charitable cause. This may be on a voluntary basis or for minimum pay, but it could eventually open up other opportunities for you. If you need an intellectual challenge, this is a good time for finding out about evening classes. Take up something completely new, or return to a subject you once enjoyed when you were regularly enrolled in school.

12. FRIDAY. Good. This can be a starred day if you are at work. You are unlikely to be under pressure, which means that you can whip through the smaller tasks that get put aside during busier times. It is important to joke and laugh with colleagues; a cheerful atmosphere can be beneficial to everyone. For unattached Aries people, this could be a lucky day for romance. Someone you met recently may make it obvious that they would like something more than friendship. If you are married, this evening favors socializing with mutual friends, perhaps at a favorite restaurant. Your good spirits will rub off on all who are around you.

13. SATURDAY. Demanding. Aries business people may have divided loyalties between work and family commitments. If you have brought work home with you this weekend, be prepared for some objections from loved ones. Try not to feel defensive; remind yourself that they have a right to some of your undivided attention. A friend could also make demands on your time today. If they are going through a personal crisis they may turn to you for some moral support. Just listening is probably all that is needed at the moment. A night out with a group of friends can be fun, but keep debate over political issues as lighthearted and congenial as possible.

14. SUNDAY. Variable. This is a good day for attending to joint financial matters. If you share a bank account with your mate or another partner, you might have to come to a new agreement regarding how much you should be spending on your social life; one of you may have been too extravagant recently. Consider updating your insurance policies; the coverage you have now may not be adequate. If you are thinking of purchasing life insurance or getting an additional amount, seek advice from an independent adviser. Visiting family later in the day could be stressful. Try to steer away from making observations about youngsters that may be taken as criticism of their parents.

15. MONDAY. Confusing.   This is unlikely to be a satisfactory start to the working week. There is a greater possibility of having to cover for a colleague; trying to make sense of what has to be done can waste a lot of time. Do what you can, but realize that there is no point in letting your own work suffer in the process. Do not hesitate to ask for help. If you are interviewing, you could find that the job bears little resemblance to the original advertisement; you may have to decide if you are still interested. Refrain from committing yourself to any new financial investment. Allow more time to investigate options that are potentially less profitable but also less risky.

16. TUESDAY. Fair.   Aries people involved in litigation may be able to make some progress with the case. Written reports are likely to be in your favor. However, your opponent could be keeping certain information up their sleeve. If a friend comes to you for personal advice, remind yourself that being a true friend does not mean saying just what they want to hear. You might have to refuse to be drawn into one of their romantic schemes. Give your honest opinion. If you are in a long-term relationship, this is a time to guard against keeping secrets. There is a greater risk that your partner could jump to the wrong conclusions.

17. WEDNESDAY. Challenging.   This could be a taxing day if you are taking a training course. Aries usually like to see instant results, but it will take time to digest all the new information that is being thrown at you. Remember that practice comes before perfection. If you have been experiencing problems at work lately, this is a good day for making a fresh start. Take the initiative; request to meet with those who can help you. Try not to dwell on mistakes you have made in the past; they were almost certainly good lessons. There could be someone at work who is interested in you as more than a colleague. If you are also interested, it is up to you to give them some encouraging signals. Protect yourself from gossip by being especially discreet.

18. THURSDAY. Pleasant.   This is an excellent day for entertaining current or potential clients. Getting to know someone on a more personal level can work wonders for your professional relationship. This is also a propitious day if you are thinking about going into business for yourself. You should be able to tie up loose ends and forge ahead. Browsing in an antique shop or used-book store can lead to some beautiful items at rock-bottom bargain prices. Make an effort to cheer up your place of work with fresh flowers or some colorful stationery. A call this evening from an old flame can bring back a rush of happy memories.

19. FRIDAY. Productive. If you are at work today, make an extra effort to bring administrative matters up to date so that you can start the next working week with a clear desk. For Aries in a managerial capacity, this should be a good day for individual meetings with staff members. Someone who has been thinking of resigning could be persuaded to stay once you identify what their grievances really are. If you are unemployed or eager for a job change, news of a suitable opening could come your way through word of mouth. Do not delay calling for more information. At home this should be a good time for a major clean-out of closets and drawers. Donate still usable items to a charitable cause.

20. SATURDAY. Unpredictable. Plans are subject to last-minute changes or may even be canceled. If a friend is making a habit of letting you down in this way, it may be time for you to say something. Let them know that you are not going to make further arrangements unless they promise to honor them. If you are looking for part-time work you may hear of a weekend job in your area that is worth following up. Take gossip with a grain of salt and some healthy skepticism. Try not to get hooked into someone else's feud. A new romantic relationship can be put on a firmer footing if you find out exactly where you stand. Do not play second fiddle to anyone. You should be the one calling the tune.

21. SUNDAY. Unsettling. You have recently spent a lot of time listening to other people's problems. Trying to be a good friend to everyone can mean that you are overlooking your own needs. You have a right to say no when someone wants to offload on you. This is a good day for looking up an old friend or work colleague. Someone may be able to provide you with new addresses or telephone numbers for those people with whom you have lost touch. An invitation out is worth rearranging your plans for. In a new group you could meet several people with whom you have a lot in common. Someone unconventional can capture your imagination and spark your creativity.

22. MONDAY. Fair. This morning is a good time for working in privacy. You are likely to get far more done if you can remove yourself from the distractions of the office. Consider working from home if your job allows this. Aries who work as part of a large department may have to deal with other people trying to impose unreasonable demands. Be clear in your own mind as to where your responsibilities begin and where they end. If you are returning merchandise to a store, be certain that you know your rights. In this way you are far more likely to avoid unnecessary arguments. This evening is a good time for relaxing at home with the phone off the hook.

23. TUESDAY. Important. Gear up for a lot of hard work today. You may have no choice but to buckle down to a two-person job which simply has to be done by you alone. You should enjoy a great sense of achievement once it is finished. Someone in authority who does not normally dish out praise may let you know just how much your efforts are valued. This can be a productive day for Aries students. Group work can be particularly helpful; an exchange of views and ideas could be just what you need to get yourself started on a difficult project. This evening could bring a telephone call from someone you had given up on hearing from without first making an apology.

24. WEDNESDAY. Good. Aries people are usually happiest when allowed to take the lead. This is a day when others seem content to let you do just that. At work do not hesitate to speak your mind, even in a large meeting. Your powers of persuasion are at full strength. This is a good day for public speaking in any forum. Your own confidence and enthusiasm can be easily transmitted to others. Interviews should go well; you may even be given a job offer on the spot rather than having to wait for further consideration of other applicants. This is a favorable day for shopping for clothes or personal accessories, such as jewelry or a new wallet.

25. THURSDAY. Variable. Go through official documents with a fine-tooth comb. Guard against signing anything which is even slightly unclear; seek professional advice if you have any doubts. If you are at home, catch up with personal letter writing. Do not put off thank-you letters from Christmas any longer. An older relative would be especially delighted to hear from you. Social invitations should be in good supply at the moment, although not all of them will appeal to you. But something which sounds boring could turn out to be good fun and a way to become involved with a different group of people.

26. FRIDAY. Unsettling. There is a greater risk of oversleeping this morning. Someone in authority may choose to make an issue out of your being late to work. Since you are usually on time, you are bound to feel the injustice of this; politely point out that this is not a regular habit of yours. If you are thinking of having your hair cut or colored, avoid a drastic change; stick to what you know suits you, or you could end up being disappointed. If you go shopping later in the day guard against impulse spending. Try to pay cash for what you buy rather than using credit cards. This can help you be realistic in making your selections.

27. SATURDAY. Inactive. After this hectic workweek you might opt to sleep late this morning. Aries with young children who wake up early may be able to persuade their partner to take over for the morning. You can always do the same for them on another occasion. A friend may urge you to go shopping with them. If the last thing you feel like tackling is a busy shopping mall, do not feel obliged to say yes. Instead, make arrangements to get together another time. This afternoon is good for doing some housework at a leisurely pace; listening to music as you work can be pleasant. Socialize at home this evening. You might decide to cook a meal for your partner or a few close friends, then watch TV or rent an upbeat video.

28. SUNDAY. Rewarding. You may need to buy some new furniture or just have an urge to redecorate. This is an excellent day for hunting locally after checking newspaper ads. There is a good chance of picking up quality goods at a fraction of department store prices. A relative may donate some items that they no longer need. Find out about auctions in your area as well. This is a starred day for lending your support to a local community event. Helping to raise money for a worthwhile cause can be fun as well as giving you a sense of achievement. Eating out with a few friends can be a pleasant way to top off the weekend. Get to bed earlier than usual.

29. MONDAY. Cautious. Allow extra time for your commute to work this morning. Traffic is likely to be heavy, and public transportation can be subject to unusually long delays. You cannot afford to take any risks when parking your car. It is better to spend time finding a proper parking space rather than chance a ticket or being towed away. Mail which you were expecting may not be delivered; it might be a wise move to find out if it is delayed or has gone astray. If mailing a package, be sure to insure it for full value. A brother or sister can be good company this evening; they can help you put a problem in proper perspective.

30. TUESDAY. Fortunate. If you have never learned to drive or use a computer, this can be a good day for booking some lessons. No matter what your age, remind yourself that it is never too late to learn. This is a propitious day for Aries who are taking any type of test; your powers of concentration are at their best. A colleague who has been difficult to work with in the past may respond to a more friendly approach. Invite them to lunch so that you have the chance for an informal chat. You might realize that the problem is rooted in their insecurity or shyness and is not based on personal dislike. Do more listening than talking when relatives gather at your home.

31. WEDNESDAY. Quiet. This should be an easygoing day. Take the opportunity to chase up outstanding money that is owed to you. Getting repaid now could make all the difference to your cash flow in the coming month. If you are looking for new living accommodations, this can be a good time for registering with local agencies. Make sure that you check whether they charge fees; these could vary considerably. Someone you work with may let you know of a place which will soon be vacant; you may be able to get a foot in the door before it is advertised. This evening is the perfect time for a quiet family dinner at home. Catch up with the events and news in each other's lives.

FEBRUARY

1. THURSDAY. Buoyant. Luck is on your side. Taking a calculated risk in your professional dealings can be more productive than sitting on the fence. Opportunties to improve your prospects are present; it is up to you to grab them. Your home life is likely to be especially harmonious. A loved one may be spontaneously generous to you, perhaps with a surprise gift or just letting you know how much you matter. A new romance can be a special joy as you find that you have more and more in common. This could be an excellent evening for introducing a new partner to your family. The interaction should be better than you dared hope.

2. FRIDAY. Disappointing. Trying to find the balance between work and home duties can be difficult. It may seem as if others are making increasingly unreasonable demands on you. Try not to let yourself be pulled in all directions. Divide up your time carefully; let family members as well as co-workers know that you are doing your best. A business transaction which you were hoping to complete today can present unforeseen problems. You may have no choice but to go back to the negotiating table. Patience is needed if you are going to get to the bottom of the matter. Do not be tempted to ignore small details in the hope that they will get sorted out by themselves. Follow through on suggestions from a well-off friend.

3. SATURDAY. Varied. Looking after children today can be taxing; you may wonder where they get their energy from. If you are going out, keep a close eye on a toddler. There is a greater risk of a child, or a pet, wandering off when your back is turned, especially on a busy street. If you are competing in a sport later in the day, guard against unnecessary risks that could lead to an injury such as a twisted ankle or even a small fracture. Aries people are natural competitors, but do not overlook playing for fun rather than only to win. A new hobby can put you in contact with like-minded people, and one could become a close friend or even a collaborator with you.

4. SUNDAY. Difficult. For Aries parents with teenage children, this could be a day of confrontation. Although some rebellious behavior is par for the course, they need to be reminded that there is a limit to what you will put up with. This might mean having to put your foot down about homework, staying out late, or the number of telephone calls. A romantic relationship may be causing you anxiety. If you have been making excuses for a person in your life instead of facing facts, this can be a good time for deciding what you really want. Choose between further commitment or a clean break. There is no point continuing if you are basically incompatible or just cannot communicate.

5. MONDAY. Starred. If you have been waiting to hear about a promotion or pay raise you could receive good news this morning. If further advancement depends on additional on-the-job or classroom training, this should be a good time for a discussion with your employer, who may be willing to pay course fees or at least help toward them. Find out a definite date when you can start. Aries salespeople who work on a commission basis can be especially productive. A deal which has been in the pipeline for a long time could be finalized in a rush. This evening favors sorting through old photographs and other memorabilia; preserve your favorites in an album.

6. TUESDAY. Useful.   If you have a spare room at home consider taking in a lodger. The extra cash is sure to come in handy. Someone at work may be looking for a place to rent. An arrangement with this person may work out better than taking in a complete stranger. Do not forget to ask for a deposit as security against breakage or unpaid bills. If you are unemployed at the moment, an offer of a temporary job could come your way. This could be a lucky move; the contacts you make can lead to better things. Tackle the larger domestic jobs at home, such as shampooing carpets or taking down curtains to be dry-cleaned.

7. WEDNESDAY. Rewarding.   A health problem may not be responding to conventional treatment. Consider seeing a practitioner in an alternative field of medicine such as a homeopath or acupuncturist. Although this can be expensive, it should be worthwhile paying at least for a consultation. Make an appointment with someone who comes highly recommended rather than picking a name out of the telephone book. This is a lucky day for interviews of all sorts. For Aries employers, this can be a good time to advertise for new staff. A publication that you do not read regularly could open your eyes to new possibilities both here and abroad. Look ahead.

8. THURSDAY. Tricky.   It would probably be wise not to take a gamble, especially of a financial nature. Impulsive decisions could turn out to be costly and are almost certain to be regretted later. Working closely with a certain individual can be stressful; you may feel that your views are incompatible. Consider whether you are being too demanding. Be prepared to work at reaching an acceptable compromise. If you are going through the painful process of separation of any sort, try to put personal feelings aside today and concentrate on the practical details. If there is even a glimmer of hope for reconciliation, give it a chance.

9. FRIDAY. Good.   This is a fun end to the working week. A colleague can be particularly supportive and may even offer to take a difficult task off your hands altogether. Business functions should be successful; you may get a chance to put a professional relationship on a much firmer footing. Close friends may announce their engagement or even a wedding date; an invitation to join in on the celebrations should be on the way. Do not wait until tomorrow to make social arrangements for the weekend. Consider inviting a group of friends over for a meal, or suggest an outing to a new restaurant featuring food and entertainment with an ethnic flair.

10. SATURDAY. Cautious. Keeping a personal worry bottled up inside you can leave you feeling stressed. You may worry about burdening others with your problem, but remind yourself that confiding in someone close to you could be a relief. Open discussion can help put a matter in its true perspective. This is a favorable time for treating yourself to a haircut and a manicure. A facial or a massage could be the additional pampering you need to combat the stress of daily life. This is also a good day for buying new clothes; you might pick something right off the fashion pages of a magazine. Your confidence zooms when you feel confident about the way you look.

11. SUNDAY. Disquieting. A social occasion today may fall short of your expectations. This might be because you feel out of your depth or simply because you have nothing in common with the other guests. Your best policy is to make your excuses after a respectable length of time. You will probably be happiest in your own company. Having some time to yourself is a necessity. This can be a good time for starting a personal journal. Committing your feelings and ideas to paper can be revealing, even therapeutic. But keep your writing hidden away from prying eyes. Someone may feel tempted to take a look if you leave it out and available. Some secrets are better never revealed.

12. MONDAY. Fair. This morning is a good time for concentrating on financial matters. An insurance claim or an application for a loan could be speeded up with a telephone call to the right person. Do not be put off with lame excuses. If you are self-employed, this morning can also be a good time to make an appointment with your accountant. A financial adviser may be able to help you make some savings on your income tax. Be ready for some problems at work this afternoon. You do not have to battle on alone; a colleague is sure to come to the rescue if you ask for help. Keep a low profile when the boss is around, or you could wind up with an assignment you do not want.

13. TUESDAY. Unsettling. If you are traveling a long distance, be prepared for some frustrating delays. Make sure that you have a good book or some work with you in order to make the waiting time more bearable. Taking an examination of any kind may be more of an ordeal than you anticipated. Your best policy is not to panic; be methodical, and allot your time as evenly as possible among the questions. You may do better than you think. An older relative may give you cause for concern. If they have been unwell or feeling lonely they are sure to welcome an invitation to visit. You may also want to begin planning a family reunion.

14. WEDNESDAY. Good. The day gets off to a cheerful start with good news in the mail or in a phone conversation. A letter from a loved one who now lives far away, perhaps abroad, may include an invitation to visit later in the year. Do not delay making vacation plans. If finances are tight, consider putting aside a certain amount each month for your transportation costs. This can be a propitious day for dealing with legal matters. Be guided by an expert who knows all the ins and outs and shortcuts. Do not try to take the law into your own hands. This evening favors such cultural pursuits as a trip to the theater or a concert featuring the work of a classical composer.

15. THURSDAY. Easygoing. Try not to overreact to problems or annoyances. A lighthearted approach can be more productive than entering into heated exchanges. Someone is more likely to come around to your way of thinking if you avoid putting them under pressure to do so. For Aries students, this can be an especially enjoyable day. A tutor with an informal touch can become an ally and offer valuable guidance with a current project. A fellow student may be romantically interested in you, although you may only have thought of them as a friend. Consider whether a romance would work or not. It may not be worth risking your current easygoing friendship.

16. FRIDAY. Exciting. For Aries whose work involves creativity, this morning is a starred time for presenting your ideas to a new client. If you are a freelancer you might consider signing up with a few agencies; you may soon have a steady flow of contracts. Ask for references from current or former satisfied employers if you are planning to move on. You should get glowing reports, which are certain to be a positive selling point. An opportunity for romance can come out of the blue. Someone is determined to win you over. Enjoy the attention, but keep your head out of the clouds. Aries can also be stellar matchmakers for a couple of old friends, whom you bring together.

17. SATURDAY. Productive. This is a busy back-and-forth day. If you have planned a shopping trip it would be wise to get an early start. This way you should be able to avoid the worst of the crowds and get around more quickly. If you are looking for a special outfit, take along a friend as an adviser. They may find just the right style by picking out something which you would normally pass over. A long-distance telephone call can be a pleasant surprise this afternoon. You may hear from an old school friend or someone you met on vacation last year. A party this evening is sure to swing. You are almost certain to meet someone new whom you would like to get to know better.

18. SUNDAY. Frustrating. Morning hours are the best part of the day. If you are trying to organize a social event or a get-together for next week, you should be able to contact most people before noon. A friend who has been going through a personal crisis should now be through the worst and will let you know how much your support has been appreciated. If you are cooking the Sunday meal you may feel as if your efforts are being taken for granted. Someone may turn up late and offer no apology. Do not let this go without comment; you have a right to be annoyed and to expect more consideration. It is all too easy to be taken for granted among your own family members.

19. MONDAY. Upsetting. Be wary of harboring grievances in any of your personal relationships. Letting yourself stew over a remark or an incident is not the way to get it resolved. Be clear in your own mind exactly what you are upset about; this way you are more likely to state your case logically and be taken seriously. Try not to let little problems escalate to become big ones; deal with them immediately and you could save yourself a lot of stress. If you are waiting for a medical appointment or test results to come through, it may be worth making a fuss. Your doctor may be able to hurry things along if you make it clear that you are genuinely concerned. Shy away from controversial conversation this evening.

20. TUESDAY. Variable. Taking on extra responsibilities is unavoidable. This may be due to the absence of a superior or to a colleague being home sick. Aries higher-ups may be worrying over a certain staff member who is not pulling his or her weight. This can be a good time for finding out if a personal problem is the cause. This way you will know if you need to offer help or mete out discipline. Either way, try to avoid coming across as an unyielding authority figure. Someone at work may announce their imminent retirement, which will probably be sad news for you. A quiet evening at home can be most appealing tonight; relax to some music or watch a television special.

21. WEDNESDAY. Fair. You may have forgotten that you made a loan to a friend some time ago. But the day could start off well when it is unexpectedly repaid. This is a good time for chasing down money owed to you. It would be a wise move to ask for a substantial deposit for new contracts exceeding a certain sum. Aries salespeople can get the best results by working on the telephone. An appointment which was hard won could be canceled at the last minute; reschedule it for as soon as possible. A business meeting or a first date this evening can be successful, but avoid overdressing for the occasion.

22. THURSDAY. Deceptive. If you are applying for a job, your best bet is to be highly selective and realistic. There is no point in going after positions which demand qualifications or experience that you do not have. This way you can save yourself a lot of time and energy. Someone in authority can be difficult to deal with. It may help to realize that they are being deliberately vague regarding certain issues for reasons which are known only to them. Although a personal relationship may be giving you cause for concern, you may not be able to put your finger on exactly what is wrong. Rather than making a big issue out of a small matter, wait and see what develops.

23. FRIDAY. Satisfactory. This is a good day for applying for a refund or certain benefits. If an expected payment is not in today's mail, make some phone calls to find out why. There is a greater risk of an administrative error holding things up. If you are off work due to ill health you may be entitled to additional benefits; do not hesitate to claim what is rightfully yours. Planning a surprise party for a friend can be fun, but make sure that you impress upon invited guests the need for secrecy. A night out with friends can prove to be more expensive than you had bargained for. Check newspaper ads for two-for-one offers for restaurant meals or theater tickets.

24. SATURDAY. Calm. This is a good day for shopping for items for your home. Look for bargains in soft furnishings, such as curtains, cushions, or throw rugs. A sofa bed could be a good investment, especially if your living accommodations are small. If you are paid at the end of the month, now is a prime time to assess your financial position. Work out exactly what you have left to spend, and try to stick to a budget. If you have never made a point of saving, start now; even a small amount banked each month can soon mount up. You may have planned to stay home this evening, but someone special might want to treat you to dinner or a movie. You may quickly go from no plans to conflicting invitations for the evening.

25. SUNDAY. Variable. If you have an elderly neighbor, make a point of calling, especially if you have not seen them out and about much lately. They would probably appreciate some company or an offer to help with chores around the house. A brother or sister could need some moral support, perhaps because they have come to the end of a relationship and are feeling adrift in the world. Try to include them in your own plans for the day. This afternoon is a time for unexpected visitors. Friends who are passing through your neighborhood may call on the off chance that you are home and not busy. This could develop into quite a party; be prepared to be up later than usual.

26. MONDAY. Good. This is a lucky day if you are looking to buy a secondhand car or make some other major purchase. A friend or someone at work may be selling or know of just what you want through a sale. Either way you are likely to come across some genuine bargains. This can be a good time for looking at the advantages of leasing a vehicle or renting furniture instead of buying. At work, meetings should be productive. Even if you are not in a position of authority you should be able to make your voice heard. Higher-ups will let you know that your opinions matter. Socializing with friends tops off the day in a happy fashion.

27. TUESDAY. Slow. Getting to work this morning can be more difficult than usual. There is a greater risk of a traffic jam due to an accident or road repairs. If you are a commuter, your usual train or bus may be canceled. There is no point getting uptight in situations over which you have no control. Today's mail could include a bill that is considerably higher than you had expected. If individual purchases are not listed, request an itemized bill; that way you can determine if any mistake was made. If you are mailing an important document, be sure to insure or register it for extra safety.

28. WEDNESDAY. Changeable. If you are at home you will enjoy the chance of some solitude. A personal problem can gradually come into focus during the day as you busy yourself with housework or other tasks. Family members mean well, especially a parent. But you could find yourself being bombarded with a lot of conflicting advice. Your best policy right now is to follow your own good intuition. Aries people can be overly impulsive at times. If you are married or engaged, resist the temptation of a romantic flirtation no matter how innocent. What may be innocent fun to you could be viewed seriously by the other person; do not take the risk.

29. THURSDAY. Sensitive. Although you may be thinking about renovating or redecorating your home, this is not a time for instant decisions. Careful research of contractors and building companies can be well worth the trouble. Think carefully about the look you want to achieve before you make a start. This can be a good day for overhauling your wardrobe. However, guard against throwing away garments which could be given a new lease on life with some minor alterations or perhaps by dyeing them a more fashionable color. This evening is a good time for entertaining at home, but keep your plans simple so you can enjoy the get-together.

MARCH

1. FRIDAY. Variable. Aries parents and Aries considering returning to the classroom themselves should begin investigating the choice of area schools. If you plan well in advance you have a greater chance of a place in the school of your choice. Child care arrangements for working parents can be a headache at the moment. Someone who appeared reliable can let you down with very short notice. You may need to devote some time to looking into other options, such as a nursery. This is a good time for suggesting that your employer provide such facilities. For single Aries, a party this evening can lead to new romance with someone from a different ethnic or cultural origin.

2. SATURDAY. Rewarding. This is likely to be an enjoyable day if you are at work. For once the more boring tasks can fall to somebody else while your own workload should be more stimulating. Being creative in your thinking can work wonders. A recent error on your part can be put to rights today; this can serve as a valuable learning experience for the future. This afternoon favors sporting activities of all kinds. If you are worried about not getting enough physical exercise, now is the time for new resolutions. If you dislike team sports consider joining a local gymnasium or health club. Swimming or yoga can also appeal.

3. SUNDAY. Tricky. A family get-together might not be the happy occasion you had hoped for. Friction between certain members of the family can be too obvious to ignore. Try not to get involved. You cannot fight other people's battles for them, no matter how strongly you may feel. Chances are you will only be accused of taking sides if you do attempt to intervene or mediate. If there are small children around, you might decide to spend time with them; entering into their world can be rewarding. A new romance may be cooling as you realize that you were infatuated, not in love. Try to keep all of your options open for a little while longer.

4. MONDAY. Productive. This is likely to be a hectic day. Someone in authority may be under extreme pressure, forcing them to delegate even more work to you. Your best tactic is to be methodical; list all the jobs to be done, then check them off as you go. This way you should feel as if you are getting somewhere despite the mountains yet to climb. Even if your efforts go uncongratulated they are sure to be noticed by those who matter. A sick animal may need some attention; a trip to the vet may be costly but unavoidable. The problem is unlikely to be too serious and should respond rapidly to treatment. If you are due for a physical or dental exam, make an appointment now.

5. TUESDAY. Demanding. This is another good day for attending to routine health matters, both for yourself and for other members of your household. If you are seeing a consultant today, be prepared for a longer wait than usual. It may be helpful to write down beforehand all the questions you want to ask. Working in privacy may be impossible; too many other matters demand your attention. Putting in some overtime may be inevitable to catch up with outstanding paperwork. Read between the lines of a letter from a friend. They may be asking for help or advice without actually putting their need in words.

6. WEDNESDAY. Good. Aries who are unattached may be thinking a lot about a recent acquaintance, perhaps someone you met last weekend. This is a propitious time for taking the initiative. It will probably be easier than you think to get a telephone number or address where you can contact them. An invitation to go to a movie or out for a drink is unlikely to be rejected. For married Aries, this is a good evening for devoting time to your partner. You should now be able to talk about a recent problem and clear the air. Begin to make plans for a vacation with a group of friends or family, maybe during the Easter break. A change of locale can be a breath of fresh air for you.

7. THURSDAY. Manageable. Be on your best behavior. An authority figure could be on the warpath, and you do not want to be in the line of fire. Even if you are burning to discuss an important issue, this is not the appropriate time; wait until you can be more certain of a fair hearing. For Aries who are planning to go into business, this is a time to weigh the pros and cons of taking on a partner. Be sure that you both have the same aims and goals; this way you can avoid friction. Do not overlook the importance of having a partnership agreement drawn up by a professional. Know your rights in any deal where your money will be thrown into the pot with other people's.

8. FRIDAY. Mixed. Those in positions of authority may not be as trustworthy as you believe. Be alert to the possibility of an ulterior motive when a certain individual turns their charm on you. They may think that they have you under their thumb, but do not allow yourself to be seduced. Standing up to someone might be difficult, but in doing so you could win their respect. This is a good day for teamwork of all kinds. Someone else's input is needed to get certain a project up and running. This evening is a good time for a night out with a group of friends. Be careful not to accept a ride home from someone who has clearly partied too much. Even if you go out alone, you may soon be part of a twosome.

9. SATURDAY. Important. Your mate or business partner could receive some good news on the financial front. This may be confirmation of a new job with a higher salary or a new contract. If you are waiting for a check for work done earlier this year, there is a good chance that this could turn up in today's mail. This can be a good time for discussing your long-term financial aims with those who share your assets. If you have not already drawn up a will, consider doing so now; do not shy away from the subject. This afternoon is a good time for visiting an art gallery or museum. If you are planning to go to the movies or theater, get your tickets in advance so that you have the best choice of seats.

10. SUNDAY. Helpful. An older friend or family member can be especially supportive in helping you resolve a personal problem. You may be surprised at how they empathize with you, even if you were fearful of being criticized or judged too harshly. A friend who has not been around for a while could put in a surprise appearance at your door. You could find yourselves enjoying the nostalgia of talking over old times. If you have recently argued with a neighbor, this should be a propitious day for making the peace. The secret to resolving difficulties lies in showing that you are prepared to discuss the problem without getting riled up. Your fiery side can be intimidating unless you keep it under tight control.

11. MONDAY. Disquieting. Legal matters can be a worry. There is a greater risk of not being in complete possession of all the facts. Someone may be deliberately withholding information. Your best policy is to delay any major decision until you feel sure that you are fully in the know. Avoid signing any official or legally binding document until you have read and understood the small print. A loved one is apt to be withdrawn. Stay away for the time being; they need time to resolve some sadness by themselves first. Keeping a secret from your partner might be a mistake. Once they learn of it they may leap to the wrong conclusions.

12. TUESDAY. Unsettling. There could be bad news regarding a friend's health. There is a chance that they could be admitted to a hospital for further tests and observation. You are unlikely to get any definite information about them today, but some encouraging news should soon be on the way. Vacation plans may have to be altered or even rescheduled. If you are planning a long weekend away, be extra thorough when it comes to travel arrangements. Book train or air tickets well in advance, and keep the paperwork in a safe place. If your passport has expired, renew it now for future use. Aries students may have to skip a night out if you want to keep on top of your homework.

13. WEDNESDAY. Good. Your financial situation may take a turn for the better. If you are self-employed, this could come in the form of a rush of extra work. This could be due to recent advertising which has proved effective, or referrals from other satisfied customers. For professional Aries people, this can be a good day for meetings with those in the higher echelons, such as shareholders or the board of directors. Presentations need to be planned carefully with extra attention to the small details. You need to know as much background information as possible so that you are not stumped by any tricky questions. This evening is a good time for a cozy dinner at home with that special someone in your life.

14. THURSDAY. Variable. This is a good day for conducting interviews or applying for a new job yourself. The high quality of applicants can make it difficult to choose between them. It would not be wise to rely just on your intuition; follow up references before making a decision. There is a chance that someone or some company does not have quite the glowing record that they have led you to believe. If you have spare time on your hands, find out about volunteer work within your community. Aries people are idealistic when it comes to helping those who are less well off, but be realistic about how much time and energy you can really afford to commit.

15. FRIDAY. Rewarding. A friend may ask to borrow some money. Use your discretion; if they are in desperate financial straits you probably should help out. But if this same person is making a habit of borrowing and not paying back, it may be wiser to refuse. Do not allow anyone to take advantage of your good nature. Dealings with a foreign contact are likely to be lucrative, but be prepared for some lengthy and detailed negotiations first. This is a day when your patience is going to be put to the test. Trying to rush a deal to completion could be costly in the long run. Keep your goals in sight; determination can be your best strategy.

16. SATURDAY. Quiet. You may decide to sit back and take it easy. If you must do some shopping, at least aim to get it done by lunchtime so that you have the rest of the day to relax. Find time for a creative hobby or for reading up on a subject which is of great interest to you. Later in the day can be good for meeting up with a close friend or inviting someone special over for a meal. You are unlikely to be in the mood to be part of a large gathering. Steer conversation to a discussion of current events and issues which affect the world as a whole. Someone else's opinion may give you a different angle on your own political beliefs.

17. SUNDAY. Difficult. A disturbing dream may leave you troubled when you wake up this morning. Do not feel tempted to dismiss it out of hand; think about what it might mean. This analyzing may lead to helpful insight into a personal problem. A close relationship can be heavy going today. You may feel as if someone is determined to blame you or make you feel guilty about a disagreement. Point out that you both need to examine your own behavior before you start laying fault at each other's feet. However, do not let pride prevent you from offering an apology if you are clearly in the wrong. Getting to bed earlier than usual will be beneficial to your well-being But first prepare for the hectic workweek ahead.

18. MONDAY. Productive.   This is a busy start to the working week. Most of the morning may have to be spent on the telephone dealing with inquiries or arranging meetings for later in the week. If your work involves dealing directly with the public, this is a day when you especially need to call upon your powers of diplomacy. Someone with a complaint can turn into an ugly customer. By not taking their aggression personally you should be able to avoid inflaming the situation further. A loved one may try to pick a fight with you over a matter which seems trivial to you. Avoid rising to the bait by politely laughing it off.

19. TUESDAY. Promising.   You may have low expectations for the outcome of a meeting scheduled for this morning. It should come as a pleasant surprise to find that others have done their homework and are prepared to support your recommendations. A certain individual who has often been a thorn in your side can now resolve to be more flexible. This may not be stated openly, but you should soon notice their efforts at compromise. Later in the day is propitious for Aries people who work in education or child care. A larger budget could be approved so that you can take on an assistant. A loved one is likely to be more indulgent toward you than usual.

20. WEDNESDAY. Risky.   If you are attending an interview of any kind it would be wise to dress conventionally. First impressions can count for a lot; you cannot afford to risk appearing nonconformist even if you are a rebel at heart. Bite your tongue in the presence of superiors; your outspokenness could be mistaken for impertinence. The start of the Aries birthday period today is a good time for reassessing your goals for the next few months. You might have to accept that certain projects are overly ambitious in the current economic climate. Proceed slowly if you are involved in a new romance; being too insistent or possessive could scare somebody away.

21. THURSDAY. Sensitive. Covering for an absent colleague can be time consuming. You need to prioritize tasks if you are going to make any headway. Someone else can delegate work to you without explaining what is really needed. Do not hesitate to point out that clear instructions would get the job done more quickly and more efficiently. If you are at home you may be tired of the sight of your own four walls. Make a point of going out this afternoon, perhaps to visit a friend or just to window shop. Keep a close watch on your personal belongings when you are in public places; there is a risk of being pickpocketed in a crowd.

22. FRIDAY. Starred. Some material possession may be too costly for your budget at the moment. This is a good time for working out a savings plan; you may be able to reach your target quicker than you think. Consider treating yourself now by using a credit card, but apply some restraint if you are already close to your spending limit. At work you could be on the receiving end of compliments; enjoy the recognition even if they reach you secondhand. Being secretly attracted to someone connected with your work can be exhilarating. However, find out more about their personal status before you set out to make your interest known. They may already be involved with someone else, perhaps a person you also know quite well.

23. SATURDAY. Fair. If you are shopping for furniture or other household items, consider driving some distance to get rock-bottom prices. A little tucked-away place could have exactly what you want at significant savings. For Aries people who are diet and health conscious, this can be a good time for buying organically grown produce direct from a market or farm. Prices can be better than what a supermarket charges. For Aries chefs, this can be a good time to experiment with exotic recipes, especially those that call for fresh herbs and spices. Whatever you cook should be appreciated by your guests if you are entertaining at home.

24. SUNDAY. Relaxing. The hectic pace of the past few weeks may have kept you out of touch with loved ones. This morning is a good time for telephoning them to catch up on the general news and maybe arrange some social dates. Do not forget to take into consideration time zone differences if you are making long-distance calls. Otherwise you may unwittingly wake someone up. A brother or sister can be pleasant company. You will enjoy being with someone who allows comfortable silences. If you are cooking for your own household consider inviting a neighbor or work colleague who lives alone; they could prove to be great admirers of your kitchen skills.

25. MONDAY. Easygoing. This is a propitious day for Aries people embarking on a new venture such as a first-time job or formal training. A special teacher or an educational course on a subject which has always fascinated you could be available. Do not put off signing up or you could be left out in the cold. Joining a club can also be an excellent move if you are seeking to widen your existing social circle. Business functions should go well. If you are hosting a get-together you should find that your guests mingle spontaneously rather than waiting for you to make formal introductions. Relax and enjoy yourself as well.

26. TUESDAY. Disquieting. This morning keep in mind the maxim of more haste, less speed. If you are running late it might be better just to accept that you are behind schedule. Rushing will probably only make you more flustered or impatient. Consider ways in which you can be better organized in the mornings, especially if you have to get children ready as well as yourself. House hunting can be stressful. There is a greater risk of your offer on a property being turned down; this may be due to the fact that another buyer has offered slightly more. Try to gracefully accept this setback.

27. WEDNESDAY. Disconcerting. There is a greater risk of a household mishap this morning. A pipe may burst, or the bathtub overflow. You might have to take the morning off work in order to wait for a repair person. Plans for home decorating may be on your mind, but this is not a good time for making a start because you are putting in long hours at work. The danger at the moment is that you could start off with good intentions, only to find yourself living in the midst of chaos for the next month or so. Devote time and attention to your partner this evening; reassurance from you that they are number one may be overdue. Children may need extra guidance from you.

28. THURSDAY. Fair. Looking for business supplies or equipment can take up a lot of valuable time. The price may be right, but do not let this sway you if the quality or color is not what you had in mind. Consider working through an agent; their fees could be worthwhile if they can come up with the package you are looking for. This is a good day for working from home, but guard against wasting too much time allowing yourself to daydream. If finding the motivation to get down to a tough task is difficult, try setting time limits for yourself on each job. Aim for a relaxing evening at home with no talk about work or other tension-producing subjects. Also, avoid stressful physical activities.

29. FRIDAY. Satisfactory. A creative approach can pay dividends. If you are putting together a written report, think carefully about the way you want to present the information. A touch of colorful artistry can make even a factual document easier on the eye and more inviting to read. Being at home with small children can be rewarding, although you are unlikely to get much else done. But housework is unimportant when compared with investing quality time with children. If a friend offers to babysit, take advantage of the chance for a night out. Try a new restaurant, or splurge on last-minute tickets for a theatrical performance.

30. SATURDAY. Disappointing. Shopping for clothes or other personal items can be frustrating. Something you intended to buy may now be sold out in your size. Guard against buying an inferior substitute; it will turn out to be a disappointment. A social invitation received today is likely to appeal greatly, but you have to take a realistic look at your financial position before you accept. There is a chance that it is beyond your means because of the new clothes you would need or the gift you would have to buy. Comfort yourself with the fact that there will always be other social opportunities. Getting together with a group of people you have never met can make you nervous. Remind yourself that they are probably just as unsure as you are.

31. SUNDAY. Sensitive. Because of the busy week just past you probably have a backlog of domestic chores to attend to today. Make sure that you are not constantly tidying up after other people or doing far more than your fair share of housework. If everyone pitches in, the jobs can be done in record time. It might be worth offering incentives to your children in order to encourage them to do their share. An outing to the movies later in the day can be special family fun. You might decide to make an evening of it and go on to a restaurant afterward. Break with tradition and try out somewhere new; it could be a good find and become a family favorite.

APRIL

1. MONDAY. Fortunate. This is an excellent day for Aries people who are starting something new. Friends and colleagues are likely to be both congenial and helpful. If traveling, you should soon feel at home wherever you are. If you feel unchallenged by your present job, this can be a good time for seeking advancement through promotion or a career change. A final interview for a new position should go even better than you had hoped. After all of the recent stress, you may feel ready to make some health resolutions. This is a good time for giving up something which you know is bad for you, such as smoking or snacking too much. A diet started today could produce quick results to help you get in shape for the summer season.

2. TUESDAY. Fair. This morning is the best part of the day for dealing with routine chores, either at home or at your place of work. You may have to put a hold on certain tasks until other people provide you with the information you need. Aries who work in direct sales may have difficulty getting hold of decision makers this morning, but several of your telephone calls could be returned this afternoon. Make sure that you are dealing with the person who wields power; this way you can avoid wasting a lot of time. If you are single a new romance could start up unexpectedly, perhaps with someone you have known as a friend or co-worker for quite a while.

3. WEDNESDAY. Disappointing. For Aries people who have been battling a difficult relationship, this is a day when problems can come to a head. If you have been holding back your anger for too long you may not be able to keep it to yourself any longer. A full-fledged argument may be what is needed to clear the air. Showing your real feelings is usually the healthiest option. At work you could be under a lot of pressure to give in to other people's needs. Getting your own way over certain issues may be impossible at the moment. Dealing with red tape can be frustrating. Your best policy is to be positively assertive without being aggressive.

4. THURSDAY. Deceptive. Take what people say to you today with a pinch of salt. You cannot afford to assume that you are being told the truth. A certain individual is not beneath distorting the facts to suit their own ends. Be especially vigilant in your professional dealings. It would be wise to follow up all verbal agreements with written confirmation. This can be a frustrating day for Aries people who make a living from any type of writing. The notorious writer's block can strike just when you hoped to get something finished. Double-check new information before acting on it or talking about it. You could wind up spreading false news.

5. FRIDAY. Variable. Aries people who work in the caring professions, such as counseling or teaching, can look forward to an especially successful day. There is a greater chance of a breakthrough with a client who has been working through a problem. A personal concern which has been weighing on your mind may be difficult to discuss with anyone close to you. Consider seeking advice from a trained, objective person who could provide the guidance you need. Be cautious in all financial dealings, especially if you are planning to invest a lump sum. Take the time to investigate all the options; do not allow yourself to be hustled into a quick decision.

6. SATURDAY. Tricky. Trying to plan a vacation for later in the year can be a complicated process. If you are going away with a group, the difficulty may lie in coordinating a time when you can all take time off. It may even get to the stage where your original plans have to be scrapped or some members of the original group have to be dropped. Take your time buying any type of equipment. What looks good may not necessarily be good. Make sure that you file the guarantee away in a safe place; the receipt alone may not be sufficient for repairs. Keep evening social plans flexible. There is a greater risk of someone being late or not turning up at all. Be sure to bring some extra cash in case your plans become more expensive.

7. SUNDAY. Fair. Drop by to visit in-laws or other family members. This can turn out to be a pleasant occasion as long as you make an effort to be sociable. You may sometimes feel that you do not have a lot in common; turning the conversation to less conventional subjects can have surprisingly good results. You could discover that their views are not as rigid as you had supposed. A sporting event can be fun, either as a competitor or a spectator. If you make a bet on the outcome, be prepared to pay up. There is a possibility of meeting someone new at a social gathering. This introduction through a brother or sister can give you a special reason to thank them.

8. MONDAY. Good. Long-distance traveling is likely to be a breeze. Do not hesitate to enter into conversation with a fellow passenger; they can prove to be entertaining company. You may even consider exchanging telephone numbers on the offchance of meeting up again. This is an excellent day for seeking legal advice; you could receive information which can be of great value to you. If you are taking any sort of an examination there is a good chance that you will do even better than you had hoped. This is a good day for seeking career guidance from someone who has on-the-job direct experience. Steer clear of employment agencies that charge a fee.

9. TUESDAY. Mixed. Aries may be in for a frustrating start to the day. An important meeting for which you had prepared diligently may be postponed at the last moment. Although you may suspect that a certain individual is deliberately employing delaying tactics, there is probably very little that you can do to change the situation at the moment. This is a good time for conducting business over the telephone. You should be able to sew up a lot of loose ends in comparatively little time. If you are unemployed, this is a good day to apply for benefits. If you are waiting to receive payment for prior work, do not accept the excuse that the check is in the mail.

10. WEDNESDAY. Disquieting. You may be inclined to daydream a little too much. Try to concentrate more on what you are doing. A moment's inattention could result in an accident due to carelessness, such as cutting yourself or breaking an object. Try not to be too impatient; let things proceed under their own steam in their own timeframe. Remind yourself that trying to impose too tight a schedule can leave you feeling stressed. This is not a day for impulsive decisions. Avoid taking risks wherever possible. Guard against making decisions on someone else's behalf; you will almost certainly be accused of being bossy or of trying to take over despite your good intentions.

11. THURSDAY. Changeable. Today's mail could include a final demand for an unpaid bill. If this is a genuine oversight on your part, make sure that you bring everything up to date immediately. Even if you are currently suffering financial hardship do not ignore these demands. Immediately contact the people or companies concerned; you should be able to reach an alternative arrangement, such as staggered payments. Teamwork can be tricky. There could be fierce debate between some of your colleagues. If you are not directly involved, try to keep a low profile; let them fight it out for themselves. A surprise telephone call from someone you have been thinking about can brighten up the evening and lead to new plans.

12. FRIDAY. Outstanding. This is a good day for getting your own way with issues that matter to you. Others seem more willing to give in to your demands. Someone who has opposed you in the past has now come around to your way of thinking. For Aries who are trying to drum up financial support or get signatures on a petition, this can be an excellent day for canvassing; you may be able to win some new recruits. Consider giving your time or money to an organization which deals with concerns close to your heart, such as human rights or historic preservation. Even if you do not want to be an active campaigner, your membership fee can help a worthwhile cause. A nonviolent march or demonstration can have a positive effect in raising public consciousness.

13. SATURDAY. Frustrating. You are unlikely to start the day in a particularly good mood. Not having gotten a good night's sleep could account for feeling irritable with those around you. Aries may find it difficult to work or study at home. Constant interruptions can break your train of thought. Consider going off to the local library to find the peace and quiet you need. Disagreements with your mate or partner are likely to stem from different values. Make an extra effort to be tolerant. There is little point in trying to force someone to change. You will only create resentment unless you let them proceed at their own pace.

14. SUNDAY. Helpful. Check clothing pockets before you put anything into the washing machine. There is a good chance that you had forgotten about some money or some other small item. A local organization asking for donations of food or furniture could prompt you to turn out drawers and closets. You may be amazed at how much storage space you really have once you have turned out all the accumulated junk. This afternoon is a good time for a leisurely get-together at home with only family members or close friends. The conversation may soon turn to the past. Someone who has an excellent memory can recall stories that you had forgotten. You are apt to laugh and cry over these shared memories.

15. MONDAY. Difficult. The morning favors meetings of a confidential nature. Take advantage of the opportunity to spell out the nature of a problem to your boss. Hold out for the assurances you need in terms of extra manpower or money. Later in the day can be hard going. So much work may be coming in that you cannot comfortably cope with it. There is a good chance that you will have to put in some overtime if you are going to stay on schedule for the rest of the week. A loved one may be preoccupied with their own problems relating to work or the social scene. As a result they can monopolize the conversation this evening. It may be worth pointing out that you have your own share of troubles and stress.

16. TUESDAY. Demanding. Aries people usually come across with great confidence, but this is a day when you need to remind yourself of your strengths and capabilities. A certain individual seems intent on undermining your self-esteem. Realize that this is probably rooted in jealousy or their own insecurity. Although tackling problems head-on can be productive, keep other people's feelings in mind. There is nothing that cannot be dealt with successfully as long as you are tactful. This can be a good day for buying clothes, especially casual wear. A brother or sister may pass on to you some garments which are still in excellent condition. Do not refuse their generosity.

17. WEDNESDAY. Mixed. Aries may suffer from a lack of motivation today. Ask yourself if this is just temporary boredom or are you simply in the wrong job. Try to take the long-term view. Be guided by the element of job satisfaction rather than just financial incentives. Try not to worry too much about a drop in salary; doing something you really enjoy can be compensation enough. Single Aries in a long-standing relationship may be thinking about making it permanent. But some hard-to-shake doubts may be stopping you from making a commitment. Talk these over with your partner or a close friend whose judgment you trust.

18. THURSDAY. Disquieting. Avoid carrying a large amount of cash. There is a greater chance of losing it or having it stolen. If you are depositing a check into your account, be sure to wait until it has cleared before drawing out cash based on that sum. Lending possessions to a friend can be risky; they may not treat them with the necessary care and respect. Remind yourself that you have a right to say no, or to insist that any damage be mended. It is best not to rely too much on other people. If you want something done right, find time to do it yourself. Even a friend who is normally reliable can let you down for reasons which may be hard to understand at the moment.

19. FRIDAY. Good. This is a lucky day for creative Aries aspiring to become better known. A commission or booking can come your way which makes all the difference in your cash flow situation. In the long term, being in the public eye can do wonders for improving your image. This should also be a productive day if you work in sales. Knowing when to talk and when to listen is the key to closing a major deal. Today is also a favorable time for entering a competition or buying a raffle ticket, especially if there is a cash prize. An idea for making extra money that is presented to you is worth investigating further. Find out first if it is genuine or merely a get-rich-quick scheme intended to make someone else rich at your expense.

20. SATURDAY. Fair. Your telephone is likely to be busy this morning. Conversations can last a long time, especially with a member of your family. If you are calling long distance, keep an eye on the clock; there is a greater risk of running up a high bill with idle chitchat. Overseas mail could go astray; make sure that your letters or parcels are clearly and correctly addressed. If you are driving, try to keep away from heavily traveled thoroughfares. You could waste a lot of time just sitting in a traffic jam. An old car could be on its last legs. Decide if it is worth spending more money to keep it on the road a little while longer.

21. SUNDAY. Excellent. This morning is a favorable time to visit a local garden center. Consider planting an assortment of flowers so that your garden will be a blaze of color in the summer. If you do not have an outdoor garden, some new houseplants may appeal to you. A windowbox can also add a touch of hospitality. Objects of beauty are likely to be found in secondhand stores or through a classified advertisement in the Sunday newspaper. Do not pass up an ornate picture frame at a bargain price. A recent rift with a loved one may not be as serious as you fear. Their silence is probably more because they are sulking rather than angry. A thoughtful card could break the ice and restore harmony to your relationship.

22. MONDAY. Demanding. If you are having major remodeling or redecorating done at home you can expect a few days of chaos. Stay out of the way as much as possible until the worst is over. Working from home can prove difficult today. Outside noise is likely to be of a higher level than usual, especially road repairs or a barking dog. If you go to a friend for advice about a personal matter, be prepared to hear the unvarnished truth. There is no point in getting angry just because they do not say what you had hoped to hear. Remind yourself that this is a hallmark of a real friendship. Try to deal with criticism in a constructive manner.

23. TUESDAY. Quiet. If you have leave owed to you at work, this can be a good time for taking a day off. At home alone you will probably enjoy the peace and quiet. Avoid scheduling any strenuous tasks; take the day at a leisurely pace. Aries employees are likely to have a pleasant day; the boss should be content to let you get on with your own work in your own way. You may be able to finish slightly earlier than usual and beat the rush-hour commute. This evening can be a favorable time for entertaining close friends or famly at home. You will enjoy an informal supper rather than an elaborate dinner. You might even consider buying take-out food if you prefer not to cook.

24. WEDNESDAY. Stressful. News of a burglary in your area can be worrisome. This is a good time for assessing your own home security measures. Determine just how difficult it would be for someone to break in. Advice from your local police department could be of great value if you are unsure of what steps to take. Also check the battery in your smoke detector. Consider purchasing another smoke detector, especially if you have young children or an elderly relative living with you. A friend whose marriage is on the rocks may come to you for comfort later in the day. Although there is probably little that you can say to make them feel better, listening and giving moral support mean a lot.

25. THURSDAY. Disquieting. Aries parents could be in a dilemma this morning regarding child care arrangements. Try to avoid taking little ones to work or other appointments; you cannot afford to assume that they will be on their best behavior. If you have to leave an older child home alone, be sure they have your phone number or a nearby relative's. It may be best to take the day off yourself if there is no clear or safe alternative. A friend may be totally absorbed in a new romantic relationship. Try to be understanding if they do not have time for you at the moment. Or it may be that you need to distance yourself from someone who has been nothing but trouble; do not allow them to drain your energy and put a damper on your spirits.

26. FRIDAY. Good. Someone in your immediate circle could have news of a baby on the way, a sure cause for celebration. This can be a favorable day for creative endeavors of all kinds, and especially artwork or learning to play a musical instrument. Aries parents should encourage children who seem bogged down with academic work to take up a physical sport or an artistic hobby. For Aries who are unattached, this can be a propitious day for romance. Someone who has recently moved into your neighborhood or transferred to your office could be showing more than a passing interest. Give them some encouragement if you suspect that they are naturally shy.

27. SATURDAY. Changeable. This is a favorable day for sports activities. A friend who is at loose ends may be willing to play a round of golf or a tennis match with you. If you know that you are not as physically fit as you would like, now is a good time for resolving to get in shape. Consider joining a local health club or gym so that you have the benefit of a professional assessment at the outset. A loved one can be in an irritable mood this morning; try not to overreact if they snap at you for no apparent reason. They may not want to go out this evening, but you should insist. Do not underestimate the psychological benefit of having some fun and relaxation.

28. SUNDAY. Positive. If you have been in a cash crunch lately you may be in for a pleasant surprise today. A relative could offer to help out without being asked. Do not feel guilty about accepting money as a gift; there is probably no need to regard it as a loan. Aries tend to be animal lovers, and today you may be asked to give an animal a home. Think carefully about the responsibilities involved before you say yes. A new pet could bring you a lot of pleasure along with extra expense and scheduling. A younger relative could be experiencing an emotional crisis which you recognize only too well. Now is your chance to pass on some understanding words of wisdom to show that you empathize with them.

29. MONDAY. Tricky. This morning is apt to be taken up with small and seemingly unnecessary tasks. You might fail to understand the importance of what the boss tells you to do. Your superior's priorities are probably somewhat different from your own. Do not push jobs aside in the belief that they do not matter; accept that sometimes you should not reason why. Avoid impulsive decisions in all of your dealings; for once your immediate reaction may be unreliable. Discipline yourself to put your personal feelings out of mind so that you can look objectively at the hard facts. This way you could save yourself the trouble of expensive mistakes or embarrassing social blunders.

30. TUESDAY. Rewarding. Someone you have recently started to work with can be developing into a firm friend and ally. This can make being at work feel more like pleasure than drudgery. A friendly approach should work wonders; this could be the key to breaking through someone's natural reserve. You can afford to be less conventional in your professional line of duty. For Aries people who are unattached, a romantic opportunity may crop up when you least expect it. Do not let this chance pass you by. If you are married, this evening favors a night out with your mate or a cozy dinner in the relaxing comfort of your home.

MAY

1. WEDNESDAY. Fair. A letter or phone call from a loved one this morning gets the day off to a cheerful start. Working closely with colleagues can produce the best results. They may be able to shed light on a problem which has you baffled. Advice from a superior should be taken to heart even if you find it difficult to understand the way their mind is working. Give new ideas a chance rather than just sticking to the tried and trusted. If you work from home, this can be a good day for bringing paperwork up to date. Consider reorganizing to make your life less stressful. A better filing system will help you find what you want without having to pull your hair out searching. This can be a good time for investing in an answering machine or a faster computer.

2. THURSDAY. Unsettling. Aries people going through a painful legal process, such as a divorce, separation, or inheritance battle, could be in for a rough ride today. It may be impossible to resolve practical details without tempers running high on all sides. If your ability to communicate with the person who has become your opponent has completely broken down, it may be worth leaving all negotiations in the hands of your lawyer. All personal relationships need to be handled with care and sensitivity. Especially guard against being too possessive. If you are on the receiving end of obsessive behavior, resolve the problems or cut loose altogether.

3. FRIDAY. Stressful. For Aries who play the stock market this can be a nail-biting day. If you can keep your nerve you are likely to make a profit by the close of business today. This can be a good time for enrolling in an investment plan, such as an endowment policy or signing up to put an additional sum in your employee benefit plan. If your employer does not provide you with a pension, now is a good time for starting one of your own. Be careful, however, not to overstretch when it comes to deciding on the amount of monthly contributions. It is better to start small; you can always put in more at a later date. If you are struggling with debt, try not to let the situation get any worse; work out a recovery strategy.

4. SATURDAY. Variable. Confiding a personal problem to someone close to you could turn out to be a mistake. They may not be able to identify with the situation or your feelings on the matter. This means that you are unlikely to get the sympathy you need. But this does not mean that your problem is unimportant; do not allow yourself to feel put down. Try to get away from housework or other chores this afternoon. Consider going out into the countryside; a long drive or walk can blow away the cobwebs. If you are staying in town, visit a local museum or art gallery. You may prefer to go alone so that you can walk around at your own pace.

5. SUNDAY. Quiet. For full-time Aries students, this can be an excellent day for devoting time to your studies. It may be difficult to get started, but keep in mind how good you will feel if you can finish up current projects. If you are not studying, reading or writing for pleasure can pleasantly occupy a good part of the day. A documentary on television may be of special interest. A loved one who now lives far away is apt to be in your thoughts. This is a good day for making a telephone call or writing a long letter to air your feelings. Cultural activities may be on the agenda this evening. A concert or stage play should be memorable.

6. MONDAY. Changeable. This is a demanding start to the working week. If you are facing a deadline, you may have no choice but to take on extra responsibilities personally. A superior may be relying on your initiative more than you realize. Extra efforts may not be rewarded immediately, but you could be in line for a bonus or even a pay raise if you sustain your current level of effort. If you are looking for a new job, hold out for the salary you want and deserve; knowing your own worth can win the respect of a potential employer. A new romance may flourish best if you play a little hard to get. A hard-won prize is often most highly valued, and this holds true in personal relationships as in other areas of your life.

7. TUESDAY. Outstanding. This can be a propitious day for business meetings of all kinds. If you are self-employed, a new contract signed now is likely to be a lucrative source of revenue both currently and in the future. Your cash flow can receive a welcome boost from an unexpected quarter. Aries who work in sales should be in excellent form. Go after clients who have been difficult to pin down in the past. There is a greater chance of getting a positive response, but do not waste any more time with those individuals who cannot make up their minds. Change into more formal clothes if you are going out to dinner or the theater this evening.

8. WEDNESDAY. Challenging. A business meeting scheduled for this morning is likely to run on longer than intended. Someone who likes the sound of their own voice can be hard to silence. You will have to listen closely in order to sort facts from opinion. Aries employees are apt to be deluged with work. You might have to forfeit a lunch break; a sandwich on the go is probably all you will have time for during the workday. Try to avoid canceling a social arrangement with a friend this evening; they may not think that work pressures are a good enough excuse. Be cautious when it comes to airing your political beliefs in a roomful of strangers; a fierce argument could result.

9. THURSDAY. Disquieting. The day could start on a disappointing note. Plans to celebrate a special occasion or to go away on a trip might have to be abandoned due to financial difficulties. Avoid accepting the offer of a loan from a friend unless you are absolutely sure that there are no strings attached. Do not take the risk of sending cash or valuable items through the mail; there is a greater danger of it never reaching its destination. Going out with someone who has expensive tastes could be awkward this evening unless you anticipate potential problems. Point out beforehand that you are living on a limited entertainment budget. You may be able to get last-minute theater tickets at a significant discount.

10. FRIDAY. Disconcerting. If you work as part of a large company it can sometimes be impossible to ignore the inevitable office politics. But this is a day when you cannot afford to be implicated in gossip of any nature. It is best to keep your opinions to yourself, no matter how hard a certain individual may press you. Although you might be accused of sitting on the fence, this can be the safest perch for the moment. Teamwork can be successful if you do not allow someone to impose their own ideas at the expense of everyone else's. Dealing with a family problem can be stressful but nevertheless necessary if you are going to put it into perspective and find a solution.

11. SATURDAY. Good. This is a favorable day for taking part in fund-raising efforts for a local charity. You might offer to help with a collection of money or of food or used clothing from the general public. If you are physically fit, a sponsored sports event for charity, such as walking or swimming, could be a fun way to raise money. Someone close to you who has been ill could take a decided turn for the better today; a full recovery should now be in sight. Make a point of finding time to call or drop by to visit this afternoon. This evening favors entertaining at home. Candlelight can provide the perfect atmosphere for intimate conversation with that special person in your life.

12. SUNDAY. Fair. Browsing around consignment stores or antique shops can be a pleasant way to spend the day. Some genuine bargains could be found if you have a discerning eye. But secondhand machinery or automobiles are likely to be a disappointment. Noise from neighbors may be a problem. Try to be tolerant if this happens infrequently; an objection may not be unreasonable if your peace is continually being invaded. If you are pleasant and diplomatic you should get an apologetic response. There is no need to return telephone calls from someone you do not want to see. Sometimes an indirect way of getting the message across can be the least distressing.

13. MONDAY. Rewarding. Aries people who have been job hunting for a while should be ready for a fresh onslaught on the jobs market. Do not hesitate to ask around; friends may have suggestions that are worth following up. Someone might even know of an opening at their own place of work. If you are calling unannounced on potential employers, make sure that you look well-groomed. This is a day when first impressions can be more important than usual. Obtaining vital information should be easier. Find sources by making good use of your imagination to figure out connections. Numerous social invitations can come your way, for now and the future. Do not postpone replying to them.

14. TUESDAY. Calm. Push your own needs forward. Those in authority are more kindly disposed toward helping. You are likely to get your own way with comparatively little effort. For Aries enjoying a day off, this is a good time for shopping for personal items. With the summer coming, you might decide to treat yourself to some light casual clothes or beachwear. A new hair style or a manicure or massage can give you a sense of well-being. Do not be coerced into a night out if you would really prefer to stay home. This evening is a favorable time for enjoying your own company. Get absorbed in a hobby or game.

15. WEDNESDAY. Disquieting. Aries who live with a partner need to be extra careful regarding money matters. Joint finances are under more strain than usual. This is the time when your different priorities may clash. There is a risk that you could be accused of extravagance. Consider whether there is any truth in this before you fly off the handle. Guard against going on the attack; hurtful words can prove difficult or impossible to retract. Aries employees may feel overworked and underpaid. If you belong to a union, take grievances to your official representative. This is not a good time for taking matters into your own hands in direct confrontation with higher-ups.

16. THURSDAY. Favorable. If you are self-employed, this can be a good day for a meeting with your accountant. Your business could be in a healthier state than you had realized. Offsetting expenses against tax demands can save a lot of money. Spending more on advertising at this time could be productive. If you are about to go into business for yourself, do not put off finalizing financial details. An attorney can offer a wealth of valuable information. This is a good time for making advance reservations for a special occasion. Find out about forthcoming plays or concerts. Tickets to a sports event could be a special treat for children.

17. FRIDAY. Fair. This can be a favorable day for investing in art and entertainment. Shares in a movie or musical production could soon go up in value. Collect money owed to you. Insurance claims submitted at this time should be processed more quickly than usual. For Aries drivers, this is a good time for taking out membership with a road service company. Check your fuel tank before setting out on a trip; there is a greater risk of running out of gas in a most inconvenient place. Aries business people should consider investing in a car telephone or a beeper to help stay in touch when away from the office.

18. SATURDAY. Starred.   Your mail could include a letter or card from someone special, just when you had given up hope of hearing from them. This can be a heartwarming part of the day. Single Aries with a passion for someone new should take positive steps to get better acquainted. Be bold and make a telephone call; you will be glad that you did. Pick up photographs just developed from a recent vacation or special occasion. Some of the snapshots are sure to make you smile. Consider having enlargements made of your favorites. Indulge the romantic side of your nature this evening. Dinner with your loved one will be only the beginning of a memorable night.

19. SUNDAY. Important.   This is an excellent day for celebrating a special occasion within your family or immediate social circle. An anniversary or engagement party is sure to be enjoyable. Make the most of the opportunity to spend time with those you do not get to see frequently. A heart-to-heart talk with your mate or another family member regarding long-term plans can be lengthy but productive. This may include taking on new responsibilities, such as buying a home together or deciding to start a family. Commitments today should not be made lightly or with a frivolous attitude. Do not mistake a parent's words of wisdom for interference; they have your best interests at heart.

20. MONDAY. Relaxing.   Try to arrange to work from home. This way you can set your own pace and eliminate interference from colleagues as well as superiors. Not having to join the usual Monday morning rush of traffic should be a delight. If you must go into your place of work, arrange a slightly later start than usual. Concentrate on making your home more comfortable and eye-appealing. A fresh coat of paint or slipcovers in a warm color could transform a room. Do not overlook the effect of little touches, such as fresh flowers or potted plants. This evening is perfect for good conversation around the dinner table with your family.

21. TUESDAY. Variable.   If you are in the process of house hunting you could be shown more than one suitable place. One which is much bigger than you had originally contemplated could be available at an affordable price. Look for a property where the price has been reduced for a quick sale, or where the sellers are open to negotiation. Keep your wits at work today. A superior could be on the warpath, but with some quick thinking you can talk yourself out of a corner. If money is tight, remember that you do not have to spend to have a good time. Make plans to visit relatives at a distance as part of your summer traveling. You will enjoy their hospitality and save money at the same time.

22. WEDNESDAY. Stressful. Something which has been preying on your mind can interfere with your concentration this morning. This is a time when keeping a problem to yourself is unwise because you are likely to let worries grow out of all proportion. Someone whose advice you trust may be ready and willing to talk with you later in the day. Do not hesitate to confide in them. Working with children can be fun, although you have to be ingenious when it comes to drawing out a child who is shy. Be alert to problems of bullying; you may have no choice but to come down heavily on the ringleader. Do not forget to mail off a birthday or anniversary card even if it contains belated good wishes.

23. THURSDAY. Disquieting. A new romance may have had a promising start, but there is a risk of some disillusionment today. If you sense a cooling off, try to keep busy with your own personal plans. Do not make the mistake of sitting at home and waiting for the telephone to ring or of refusing to take no for an answer. Avoid participating in any dangerous activity; there is a greater risk of injury. Guard against overspending, especially on leisure pursuits or luxury items which could easily be postponed until another time. An unexpected expense could be just around the corner. If you are paid at the end of the month, you need to budget carefully to stretch cash on hand for this last week.

24. FRIDAY. Good. Artistic activities of all kinds are favored, whether they are connected with work or for your own personal pleasure. If you have never learned to type, now is a good time to do so. You do not have to invest in lessons; first try teaching yourself with the aid of a self-learning instruction book. Learning to use a word processor can also be rewarding and may save you a lot of time with administrative matters. For Aries parents, this afternoon is a good time for a children's get-together. A neighbor or friend may welcome the chance to leave a toddler with you for a few hours. The fun could go on into the evening as the parents later join in. Instead of cooking tonight, order a pizza or pick up some take-out food on your way home.

25. SATURDAY. Fortunate. For Aries who work on weekends, this can be an especially lucky day. Be alert for an opportunity to improve your prospects in the near future. This may be just a question of being in the right place at the right time. If you are looking for part-time work, an offer could be made today through the friend of a friend. A social invitation for this evening could come out of the blue. This is likely to be a rare opportunity for Aries who are looking for a wider social circle. New friendships made at this time could be lasting. If you are involved in a new romance, this is a good time for meeting your partner's friends or even your potential in-laws.

26. SUNDAY. Pleasant. Catching up on general household chores such as washing and ironing should not take as long as you fear. If you set a certain time limit you may be surprised at how quickly you can get things done. Try to make time for some physical exercise. This could be anything from a workout at the health club to a long walk in the park. Invite guests to your home for a leisurely meal. Be prepared for the numbers to escalate; your partner may suddenly want to include some friends from work. Opt for the sort of menu which can easily be stretched to feed extra mouths. Keep entertaining informal so that you have time to enjoy your company.

27. MONDAY. Fair. If you are part of a large household other people may make you late this morning. You may have to wait your turn for the bathroom or wait for someone to give you a lift. If you end up missing an important meeting, make sure that you get the information from someone else. Colleagues tend to be helpful today. Aries people are often so eager to be independent that you neglect to ask for assistance when you need it. Do not let pride stand in the way of bowing to someone else's better judgment. A romantic relationship could benefit from a more lighthearted approach; concentrate on having fun together without making elaborate plans.

28. TUESDAY. Disconcerting. You may suspect that you have somehow made an enemy of a person at work. If your efforts to get ahead are being blocked, your best policy is probably to let the situation ride for a while. Matters should improve by themselves given time. This is not a favorable time for lodging an official complaint. An interview or test today might be tougher than you had expected. You may be up against a surprising number of other candidates. If you are looking for work, try to steer clear of positions where you know the competition is fierce. A parent may make unreasonable demands on your time this evening, but be gracious and go along.

29. WEDNESDAY. Tedious. Single Aries need to guard against a tendency to idolize someone to whom you are attracted. You run the risk of being blinded to their natural human failings, which could result in sudden disillusionment. Campaigning for someone else's cause could prove to be a thankless task. You cannot afford to give away your time and energy too freely, especially for those who are more than capable of looking after themselves. Do not allow anyone to exploit your willingness to come to the rescue. Money matters can be stressful. A meeting with a financial advisor can leave you feeling angry or misunderstood.

30. THURSDAY. Good. This is an excellent day for making financial commitments such as taking on a mortgage or increasing your insurance coverage. Buying property with a partner or friend could prove to be a sound investment. An interest-free loan from a family member may be the answer for buying goods which would normally be out of your price bracket. However, do not let repayment put your finances under too great a pressure. Anxiety over a loved one can be laid to rest today; they are more likely to find a solution to a problem which they had confided in you. Advice from a counselor or newspaper columnist should not be ignored; there could be some truth in what they say even though you do not want to hear it.

31. FRIDAY. Sensitive. Handle professional relationships with kid gloves. Someone is not going to be acting as their usual robust self. There is a chance that they are dealing with a personal problem which you know nothing about. Make an extra effort to be understanding if they appear irritable or withdrawn. Later in the day a loved one could be leaving on a long trip. A farewell at the front door or at the airport can be a tearful occasion for all concerned, but remind yourself that making progress means that nothing stays the same forever. Plans to attend a show or concert this evening may be canceled; have an alternative suggestion in mind just in case.

JUNE

1. SATURDAY. Mixed.   If you have not already made plans for a summer vacation, this is a good day to drop by your local travel agency. There may be some package deal bargains if you are able to go away at short notice. Check newspaper advertisements too. Friends who are staying with you for the weekend may urge you to play the role of tourist guide around town. This may sound like a boring prospect, but if you enter into the spirit of the day you could have more fun than you had expected. Aries in a new relationship may discover that you differ when it comes to deciding on a night out; remind yourself that successful romance needs more than a little compromise.

2. SUNDAY. Inactive.   This is a day when your energy level is not at its highest. Opt for leisurely, intellectual pursuits as opposed to physical ones; read the newspapers or a novel. A crossword puzzle can soon have you engrossed. A telephone call from a loved one far away can be a treat, but there is a greater risk of feeling somewhat letdown afterward. Although it may be hard to get enthusiastic about life without them around, try not to give in to the blues. Avoid parking your car in a rough area; it could be at risk from a thief or vandal. Driving is subject to tedious delays or, more likely, waiting to pick up a passenger.

3. MONDAY. Variable.   For Aries business men and women this is a day when you may feel you are taking one step forward and two steps back. You need to cultivate patience in order to finalize a complicated deal. You cannot afford to rely too much on the element of luck. If you have recently applied for a transfer or promotion, you may have to take disappointment in stride today. But another opportunity could be nearer than you realize, so try not to feel downhearted. Avoid taking on too many commitments for the rest of the week, both professionally and socially. Keep in mind that even the fiery Aries energy cannot burn indefinitely. A good night's sleep will restore your vitality.

4. TUESDAY. Manageable.   This morning is a propitious time for training aimed at improving your career prospects. Much of the information which comes your way today may be new and possibly confusing, but a studious approach should pay dividends. For Aries with a business dream, this is a favorable time for turning it into a reality. If you are involved in a lawsuit or work in the legal profession, this promises to be a productive day. There is a better chance of a ruling being made in your favor. Group activities of all kinds are worthwhile, especially in a learning environment. Social invitations should be plentiful; enjoy the boost to your sense of popularity.

5. WEDNESDAY. Starred. Doing your bit to help the world at large can be satisfying. Consider taking a more active role in a political or charitable organization. A donation to an appeal, no matter how small, is sure to be welcomed. People will be impressed by a show of social conscience, and they are almost certain to follow your example. Also think about how you can contribute to ecology efforts. Start at home by using the proper facilities for disposing of bottles and newspapers. Do not overlook obligations which are close to home. The person most in need of your compassion and understanding could be someone from whom you have recently become estranged.

6. THURSDAY. Disquieting. Guard against being misled by false information. Check out facts for yourself, especially gossip regarding a friend. A certain individual is capable of stirring up trouble just for the sake of it; it is up to you not to fall victim to someone else's mind games. Finances are under considerable strain, with money going out much faster than it is coming in. Think of ways to economize over the next few days. Bringing a bag lunch to work instead of eating out can save a lot. Arguments over money matters with your partner can be distressing. However, there is no point creating a scene when the damage is already done.

7. FRIDAY. Quiet. This is not a busy end to the working week. If you have any vacation time due you, this can be a favorable day for taking a long weekend, especially if you are planning to go away. Medical appointments should run on schedule; a consultant can put your mind at rest concerning a recent health worry. Putting the final touches to a project can be rewarding. Preparation for an important meeting next week is sure to pay off. Someone from your past is apt to be in your thoughts. If you have been meaning to get back in touch for a while, do not hesitate any longer; they will probably be delighted to hear from you.

8. SATURDAY. Fair. A wake-up telephone call could turn out to be a wrong number. But you are likely to be awake earlier than usual this morning anyway, probably because of outside noise or a disturbing dream. There should be a mixed bag of news from family members, but a hint of encouraging financial developments could be whispered as well. If you are looking for new musical equipment this can be a good day for checking out what is available in a specialty store. This can also be a favorable time for buying evening wear for a forthcoming special occasion. If you have been invited to a friend's place for dinner this evening, a vintage bottle of wine, or even champagne, could be the perfect present for your host or hostess.

9. SUNDAY. Mixed.   Enjoy a leisurely start to the day. If you live with your partner, you might be able to cajole them into bringing you breakfast in bed. Younger children can be kept happily occupied if you set specific tasks; otherwise there could be complaints of being bored. Later in the day favors social activities. You might decide to join friends at a local restaurant rather than cooking at home. Unattached Aries can make new friends today through your existing social circle. Romance may not be on the immediate agenda, but take the time to get to know someone new and then sit back and see what develops.

10. MONDAY. Pleasant.   A superior at work may be in a difficult mood this morning, but it is unlikely that you are being singled out for rough treatment. They are apt to take out their displeasure on anyone who happens to be in the line of fire. The support and friendship of your colleagues can make this a fun day overall. Someone's quick wit should keep you smiling. If you are at home, make a point of calling on a neighbor. Having lunch or going shopping together gives you a chance to catch up on local news. A thoughtful gift from a brother or sister can be a pleasant surprise. This may be their way of thanking you for a recent favor when you went out of your way for them.

11. TUESDAY. Unpredictable.   On the financial front Aries should expect both gains and losses, but you are likely to finish up on the plus side. An intriguing money-making idea presented to you is worth investigating. It may not be as off the wall as it first appears. Creative endeavors of all kinds are favored. Do not hesitate to break with tradition or try something new. Keep in mind that all innovation is deemed odd until it is shown to be a flash of genius. For Aries involved in charitable work such as community projects, this can be an exciting day. Funding from an unexpected source, perhaps an anonymous benefactor, can be a lifesaver.

12. WEDNESDAY. Lucky. If you are in line for a promotion at work you may be wondering if someone else has been selected. But news today should confirm that you are still very much in the running. For Aries employers, this is a favorable time for introducing a bonus system as an extra incentive for your staff; the increase in productivity should more than cover the costs. Also investigate the merits of opening a branch office. This is a propitious day for officially opening a new business or launching a major project. A parent can come to the rescue, finding money so that you can take advantage of a special opportunity.

13. THURSDAY. Changeable. This morning favors business dealings of all kinds. Someone who has been elusive in the past may now be ready to sign on the dotted line. This could turn out to be a contract which was worth waiting for. Unexpected praise from a superior can leave you glowing with pride. However, there is a danger that a colleague can feel that your success has been at their expense. Be prepared for some bad feeling to be aimed in your direction later in the day. A busy schedule this afternoon could undo the calm of the morning and leave you feeling harassed. Set your own pace and refuse to be rushed into uncertain decisions or unthinking mistakes.

14. FRIDAY. Demanding. Aim for an earlier start than usual to the day if you hope to get everything done. Concentrate on being methodical; rushing jobs is likely to get you into trouble. Make an extra effort to prioritize; some tasks can easily be postponed until the beginning of next week. Administrative work can prove to be a headache and may take much longer than you thought. If you are using a word processor or computer, it would be a wise move to make a backup disc; there is a greater risk of losing your work on a vital document. Social arrangements for this evening may be canceled, but you will relish the prospect of a night at home with no commitments.

15. SATURDAY. Misleading. An ongoing dispute with a neighbor can be stressful. There is a greater risk that your tolerance could snap this morning. But at some point in a heated exchange you might be able to resolve the problem. If you are purchasing tickets of any kind by telephone, arrange to pick them up in person; documents sent by mail or messenger may arrive too late or not at all. If your work involves serving the general public, it could be hard to remember that the customer is always right, even when wrong. Try not to react to rudeness, although you are right to object to abusive language or behavior.

16. SUNDAY. Exciting. A backlog of household chores may keep you at home this morning, but you should be able to get through these quickly. A radio show can be good company as you work. Afternoon is a time to go all out to have fun; do what you enjoy and put worries on the back burner. You may want to spend time with close friends who share your special interests. Someone who knows just how to touch your sense of humor can be a real tonic. If you are planning to go to the movies, choose a comedy or a lighthearted musical. Discussions about world issues can challenge some of your own views and may put you on the defensive. Getting others to see things your way requires logic and patience.

17. MONDAY. Challenging. Aries business people may have to devote almost all available time to work matters. If you are single this is probably more manageable. But for married Aries, a few storm clouds could be gathering in the shape of objections from your spouse. Your best policy is to keep them fully informed; try to make a commitment to be home early at least once this week. If you are considering buying a car, a bargain could come your way today; this may be a lead from a friend or colleague. A surprise telephone call can change plans for tonight. You could find yourself at a concert or sports match instead of staying home.

18. TUESDAY. Fair. This morning is not a favorable time for finalizing a contract of any kind. A nagging doubt in the back of your mind should not be ignored. You probably need more time and information before entering into a binding decision. For Aries with little spare time, this can be a good day for buying what you need through a catalog. Clothes for children may be among the best bargains. An option to spread payments over the next few months could come in handy. If you are planning to return to work or to change jobs, this is time for discussing the move with family members, especially if you might have to relocate or to travel frequently.

19. WEDNESDAY. Satisfactory. Fears that your current relationship could be on the rocks are likely to be unfounded. You have negotiated a rough patch more successfully than you realized. Remind yourself that a partner's bad moods are not necessarily linked to you; there could be other pressures with which they do not want to burden you. For Aries parents, a child's school report can surpass expectations. A new teacher may be to thank for a dramatic improvement in certain subjects. If you are attending a parent-teacher conference, make sure that you discuss any anxieties, such as the options available for next year or the pros and cons of attending summer school or obtaining the services of a private tutor.

20. THURSDAY. Relaxing. For Aries who are looking for a new job, the field of arts and entertainment is likely to have excellent possibilities. Temporary summer work may be offered to you; this could turn out to be a great learning experience as well as a source of income until something more permanent comes along. If life seems to have been all work and no play recently, now is a favorable time for taking up a new hobby. Opt for one which is completely unrelated to the work you do during the day. If you are single, this can be a lucky evening for romance. You could be introduced to someone fascinating at a function.

21. FRIDAY. Good. This is an especially productive day for Aries who work from home. You should be able to thoroughly complete a list of outstanding tasks which have been waiting for your attention. Try to keep long-distance telephone calls to a minimum; there is a greater risk of running up an unacceptably high bill. If you need to hire a professional, make sure that you employ a reputable person who comes highly recommended. Do not overlook a friend's birthday or let the occasion go unmarked. They might say that it is not important, but they are sure to appreciate and enjoy your efforts to host a celebration. Choose their gift with extra care.

22. SATURDAY. Disquieting. There is a chance that you may not feel in the best of health. A minor ailment, such as a sore throat or stubborn headache, can leave you feeling under the weather. This is probably your body's way of telling you to take it easy for a while. Aries can often suffer from the effects of living life at too fast a pace. If you have been involved in an on-again, off-again feud with a neighbor, there could be an altercation today. It is likely to be over some detail such as wash hung on the line or excessive noise from a pet. Be prepared to reach a compromise. If you are about to move, make your terms absolutely clear in advance to your real estate agent.

23. SUNDAY. Fair. This is a good morning for getting some physical exercise. Playing a sport with a partner is likely to be more enjoyable than working out alone. If you have children, consider a family outing to a nearby swimming pool or lake. Having guests over can be hard work; ask for some help with basic tasks, such as peeling vegetables or setting the table. Conversation should be animated. A certain individual may not need much encouragement to go on and on about their favorite subject, but at the same time they can be responsive to intelligent questions. Talking late into the night could be an eye-opener for you.

24. MONDAY. Variable. You cannot afford to assume that you will get your own way, especially regarding options at work. You may not have given other people's viewpoints nearly enough consideration. When you do so, their opposition will come as less of a shock. Concentrate on giving a fair hearing to all opinions if you want to be listened to yourself. This is a good day for dealing with practical details, such as insurance and licensing. Guard against a tendency to impose your way of doing things on your partner; ask for their opinions rather than just giving your own and expecting them to comply with your wishes. Reason with a reluctant child instead of threatening.

25. TUESDAY. Deceptive. Trying to understand all that is going on at work can tax your energies, especially if you are new to the job. The absence of a superior or a colleague means that certain decisions fall to you. Be alert to the fact that a certain individual may try to take advantage of your inexperience. Your best policy is to wait for advice regarding issues which are unclear to you. A romantic relationship which started off as infatuation may be assuming more realistic proportions. At worst there is a danger that you are now finding out things about your partner which do not please you. Do not be afraid to admit that you may have been led on under false pretenses.

26. WEDNESDAY. Difficult. For Aries in the process of negotiations, this can be a day of unexpected complications. You might have to accept that you are not going to complete a deal as quickly as you had hoped. A bounced check can cause some embarrassment; it may be wise to make the repayment in cash. Insurance policies on your home or car may need to be renewed or updated. Consider including a clause to cover you for accidental damage to valuables. Family life can seem to close in on you. You may feel that you never get a moment to yourself. Try to plan to stay home alone the next time everyone is going out.

27. THURSDAY. Calm. A friend who has recently gone through a difficult time may be back in contact with you today. They are likely to be over the worst but may still need some time before they are ready to make a social comeback. An invitation for a quiet dinner is sure to be appreciated. This can be a good day for listening to your own inner voice. There is a greater chance that your first reactions are accurate. If someone asks you out or requests a favor, you should know instinctively if it is a good idea to go along or not. This evening favors enjoying your own company. A solution to a problem can suddenly dawn on you after some intense reflection.

28. FRIDAY. Fair. If you are traveling call before you set off; there is a greater risk of long delays or even a canceled flight. Doing business with foreign clients can be lucrative, although a language barrier could cause some initial difficulties in your negotiations. Having an interpreter on hand can save a lot of time and misunderstanding. Planning a summer vacation may be uppermost in your mind. Aries who are unattached may decide to take off with a friend for a couple of weeks. You could land a great vacation bargain by making last-minute arrangements or agreeing to travel on a standby basis.

29. SATURDAY. Frustrating. For Aries who work on the weekend, this is one of those mornings when it is particularly difficult to get out of bed. You might feel tempted to call in sick, but this is unlikely to be taken well by your boss. You cannot afford to risk being fired. Plans for a day out could be thwarted by somebody else's mix-up. Your companion for the day may suddenly realize that they have made two dates. Try to be gracious when it comes to accepting their apology; remind yourself that you have done the same sort of thing in the past. Cultural activities this evening should be more enjoyable than bland television entertainment.

30. SUNDAY. Demanding. Someone with whom you do not have much in common may press you into getting together. This may be the last thing you feel like doing, but they will probably only pester you again if you cancel now. In the future you need to take a firmer stand when it comes to your personal relationships. Mull over why you continue to see someone who always leaves you feeling exhausted or emotionally drained. An argument with an older relative can leave you struggling with guilt or resentment. The best policy is to state your own opinions without getting upset. Do not allow yourself to be blackmailed into going along with the plans of others because you do not have a ready excuse.

JULY

1. MONDAY. Quiet. This is unlikely to be a demanding start to the working week. You should be able to catch up with minor projects or take the opportunity to spend more time one-to-one with colleagues and friends. If you are unemployed, this can be an excellent day for sending off job applications or going on interviews. Think carefully about the references you can supply. Functions of a formal nature should go smoothly. If you are beginning a training course of any kind you can expect a relatively easy start; the pressure is likely to increase by the end of the week. Cultivate the company of those who have the power to improve your prospects.

2. TUESDAY. Unpredictable. Try not to rely too much on other people. Someone may be quick to make a promise to you, but they are likely to get caught up with their own affairs and forget all about it. If you want something done, do it yourself. This can be a good day for organizing a group event, both professionally and socially. Guard against paying up front for too much yourself; at least ask others for a deposit, or you could end up out of pocket. If you are trying to pin down a friend with regard to vacation plans, you may have to deliver an ultimatum. If they cannot give you a firm answer, go ahead with alternative arrangements with someone else.

3. WEDNESDAY. Good. The emphasis is on social activities. Avoid keeping a project close to your chest; working with others can be highly beneficial. If you are willing to pool your ideas with colleagues they are almost sure to follow suit. Local travel should be straightforward; you can afford to run on a tight schedule yet not be late. If you use public transportation regularly, this could be a favorable time for investing in a season ticket or a weekly pass; either is sure to save you both money and time. A friend's birthday can be the reason for a get-together this evening, maybe with people you have not seen for a while. Enjoy the role of guest rather than host.

4. THURSDAY. Frustrating. If you are expecting news from a distant friend you may have to wait a few more days. For Aries involved in lawsuits, this can be a day of frustrating setbacks; decisions might not be made in your favor. Think carefully about the stress you could be letting yourself in for if you decide to appeal; it may be better just to cut your losses. If you own an old property, this can be a favorable time for planning some home improvements. Guard against being overly ambitious; it could be helpful to obtain a professional opinion regarding your ideas for improvements. An independent survey for a new property should be well worth the cost.

5. FRIDAY. Disconcerting.   Finding out people's secrets is not always pleasant. You may discover that someone close to you has deliberately kept you in the dark with regard to current plans. Their reasons for doing so are unlikely to make sense to you. There is probably nothing to be gained from pushing for further explanations. Think carefully before buying a secondhand car or other machinery. If your mechanical knowledge is limited, take along someone who can give you advice. They may be able to spot faults which you would miss. Arguments with a loved one can spoil an evening at home; it may be one of those times when you feel that no matter what you do you cannot win.

6. SATURDAY. Fair.   This can be a good day for Aries who are setting off on a summer vacation. Make an extra effort to be systematic in your packing so that you are less likely to forget something essential. Long-distance travel should be easygoing. You may even find that you are running ahead of schedule. This is not a good day to shop for clothes. Finding what you want could be difficult; you may realize that you have also underestimated costs. Conditions favor looking for new living accommodations. However, avoid taking a place where the landlord lives near you; your freedom could be restricted by their prying into your affairs.

7. SUNDAY. Stressful.   A telephone call this morning could be from a friend determined to pin you down to a social arrangement for later in the day. Do not give in to pressure if you have already made other plans. Someone may not forgive you for letting them down at short notice because of what you view as a better offer. A recent argument with a loved one could still be on your mind. Although you may be tempted to send a letter saying exactly how you feel, putting pen to paper just now could be unwise. Wait until you are in a calmer frame of mind. Guard against airing your opinions too freely at a social gathering. Try not to mistake an older person's well-meaning advice for interference in your affairs.

8. MONDAY. Unsettling. You may have to accept that not everyone shares the same values as you. There is probably no point trying to convert a certain individual to your way of thinking; you may only end up antagonizing them or being accused of being hardheaded. Make an extra effort to abide by the maxim of live and let live. Business meetings are unlikely to be productive; there is a greater risk of being at cross-purposes. Instead, try to clarify the information you already have. You may be able to isolate an area of misunderstanding. An upcoming social event can prove to be foolishly expensive unless you make do with clothes you have worn on another occasion.

9. TUESDAY. Fortunate. There is a greater chance of some luck with regard to money matters. A bonus at work could be larger than you had been expecting, or you may win a small prize in a lottery. A request for a pay hike is likely to be taken seriously, especially if you back it up with solid reasons. For Aries people who are in the process of buying property, this can be a favorable time for finalizing such financial details as a mortgage offer or building insurance. Buying furnishings for your home can be fun. Consider using an interest-free offer to purchase larger items, such as furniture or new windows. Renting a video to watch at home can be an ideal way of relaxing this evening.

10. WEDNESDAY. Pleasant. This should be a productive day for Aries people who work in a job requiring creativity. For aspiring actors or writers, a new agent could be invaluable in helping to get your career off the ground. Do not underestimate the importance of landing a job that you really enjoy. You might even want to consider a drop in salary in order to make changes in your professional life. Do not let other people pour cold water on your dreams. Cultivate the company of those whose own outlook is positive and who can give you the encouragement you need. A dinner party this evening could set the stage for a romantic encounter.

11. THURSDAY. Good. You are likely to receive more mail than usual. A package which has been delayed could finally arrive intact. This should be a productive day for Aries people who make a living from writing or researching of all kinds. Snap up an unexpected offer that could stabilize your cash flow situation as well as having the potential of leading to other things. Personalized stationery can make the perfect gift for a friend who recently moved. If you are considering becoming self-employed, now is a good time for designing a logo and an advertising campaign. Do not hesitate to form a joint partnership. All forms of teamwork are favored over independent activity.

12. FRIDAY. Disquieting. You may get out of bed on the wrong side this morning. A difficult commute to work will do nothing to improve your general mood. Guard against taking out your irritation on those who are only trying to help. The best policy for the day is to attack your work with renewed vigor. If you direct your energy into something specific, you should be able to make great strides forward. Paperwork or other administrative duties could be a good placc to start. Strive to check off everything on your to-do list before quitting time. Being able to start next week with an uncluttered desk will give you an added lift. Take extra care when driving today; you could be stopped for speeding or for running a red light.

13. SATURDAY. Calm. This morning favors an early start in order to do your weekly grocery shopping or check out an advertised sale at a shopping mall. This way you can miss the crowds and have more time to devote to your own interests. Make a point of returning telephone calls from earlier in the week. If you are out frequently, consider investing in an answering machine. This afternoon is good for attending to odd jobs around the house. You may not feel in the mood to go too far afield this evening. An invitation to a friend's house for supper, or inviting others to visit you, can be more fun than a large or formal social event in a roomful of strangers.

14. SUNDAY. Deceptive. Someone you have trusted in the past may prove unreliable today. You might get the feeling that you are not quite as important to them as you used to be. Examine your own behavior; ask yourself if you have done or said anything which could have upset them. You cannot afford to rely on others being upfront with you now. Married Aries may find their spouse in an uncommunicative mood. An untruth which you considered to be a harmless exaggeration at the time you said it now comes to light. If you are challenged, your best policy is honesty. Make a clean breast of things or you may find yourself getting in even deeper.

15. MONDAY. Tricky. Aries business people need to handle new ventures with a healthy dash of skepticism. Do not be afraid to ask direct and probing questions. Your sharpness could deter someone from trying to take you for a ride. This is a day when you need to separate fact from fiction; do not take someone else's word as gospel. An offer that seems too good to be true is probably exactly that. If you have recently set up home with your partner you could be experiencing some problems because you need private space. Remind yourself that it takes time to adjust to each other's habits. Guard against the temptation to nag or criticize. Fragile items sent through the mail could be damaged unless you pack them with special care.

16. TUESDAY. Fair. If your work involves training others, you need to remind yourself of the power of positive feedback. Giving praise, even for little things, could prove to be the best motivator. Business dealings with distant contacts are likely to be lucrative. This can be a favorable time for learning another language, either for pleasure or to improve your job possibilities. If you are looking for a conversation class, be sure to choose one with a small number of students. A romantic relationship can benefit from an in-depth discussion this evening. Do not shy away from talking about the future, although this is not the time to make any promises.

17. WEDNESDAY. Happy. Working with children can be a special joy. Activities centered around writing or painting are likely to be the most successful. Innocent words from a child can suddenly shed light on a personal problem. The lesson may be to look at the world more simply. You might realize that you have unwittingly made something more complicated than was really necessary. If you are at home with youngsters, this afternoon favors a trip to a park or zoo. Keep them in your sight at all times, especially if you are in a crowd. You are in demand socially at the moment. An invitation to celebrate an anniversary or other landmark event could be fun.

18. THURSDAY. Uncertain. A business trip may have to be canceled due to pressures in your home office. You may need to make a quick decision with regard to which is more important. A busy schedule needs to be carefully thought out in advance; some clever planning of your itinerary could conserve both energy and time. Aries employees may have an uphill battle whipping up enthusiasm for work. This could be because of a lack of adequate sleep. If you have been burning the candle at both ends recently make a point of getting to bed early or at least spending a quiet evening at home. This is a good day for boosting your immune system with the extra nutrients found in leafy vegetables and whole grains.

19. FRIDAY. Productive. Certain routine jobs must not be put off any longer. It may be easier if you do your least favorite tasks first thing this morning. Knowing that they are out of the way can make for a pleasanter day ahead. A new colleague may come to you for advice or assistance; this means having to put some of your own work aside for a while. Look into moving to larger accommodations, but be careful not to overcommit yourself with regard to the rent or mortgage payment. Relocating somewhere near work could save on traveling costs. Your partner is the best person to help you sort out your feelings about a dispute with a parent or other older family member with whom you were once very close.

20. SATURDAY. Variable. Get everyone to pitch in with housework duties this morning. If everyone pulls their own weight a lot can be accomplished in a short span of time. Minor repairs or decorating jobs around the home should not be postponed. Be careful not to leave sharp tools lying around, especially if young children are running in and out. A new pet can soon become an established household member. This evening favors a social gathering at home. If the weather is fine you might opt for a barbeque. Warn your neighbors if you anticipate a late finish or a lot of noise. Be sure to have plenty of food and drink on hand.

21. SUNDAY. Disquieting. For Aries in permanent relationships, this is a day when you may have to battle with feelings of restriction. One part of you may be hankering after the freedom of being single. Do not be afraid to admit these feelings to yourself. Let your partner know if you need some time alone, or if you would prefer to see your own friends unaccompanied. A new romance should be going well, although there is a risk that one of you is investing far more hope in it for the future than the other. Be careful not to make statements which may be misleading. If you are dieting your discipline may crack today; resolve to make a fresh start tomorrow.

22. MONDAY. Fortunate. Recognition for past efforts is coming your way. This may be from a superior at work, and you may secretly feel that their praise is long overdue. Enjoy your moment of glory to the fullest. Aries are entering into a new phase on the creative front. There is a chance that you can discover talents which you never knew you possessed just by being prepared to try something new and challenging. News of a baby on the way for someone who had all but given up is cause for celebration. A teenager in your family circle can shine academically; this may come in the shape of a special award. Results from an examination or job interview should be excellent.

23. TUESDAY. Changeable.   The morning is the better part of the day. Business meetings before lunch can go surprisingly smoothly. This may come as a relief if you had anticipated having a fight on your hands. Decisive action pays off; this is not a time for straddling the fence. This afternoon becomes increasingly stressful at work. Meetings could put all your powers of diplomacy to the test. A certain individual may insist on dragging up old issues which you thought were dead and buried. Do not bother trying to get a word in edgewise; just wait until they have run out of steam. Resentments in a romantic relationship need to be addressed openly and honestly.

24. WEDNESDAY. Stressful.   You are likely to be preoccupied with a personal issue. You may be at a loss to know where to start when it comes to talking to your partner about the state of your relationship. If you fear being ridiculed, remind yourself that anything which is important enough to dominate your thoughts is worthy of serious discussion. Money is apt to be tight. Guard against frittering away cash on spur-of-the-moment purchases which you could really do without. Launching an economy drive for the remainder of the month could dig you out of a financial hole. A friend you have outgrown may try to make you feel guilty; it is up to you not to fall for the trap they are laying.

25. THURSDAY. Unsettling.   This is the sort of day when you seem to lurch from one crisis to the next. Work matters are apt to be in a state of confusion. Assistance is conspicuous by its absence. Remind yourself that all you can be expected to do is your best. You could find out who your real friends are when you need to discuss a problem. Someone you want to get close to may not be there when it counts. Guard against chasing after a person who is clearly unable or unwilling to give you what you need. If you are unattached at the moment, try not to enter into a new relationship merely because you feel lonely. You do not have to settle for anything less than the best.

26. FRIDAY. Relaxing.   Finalize plans for your summer vacation today. If you are looking for a last-minute bargain you should be able to find something which is comfortably within your budget. For Aries students on a summer break, this can be a good day for doing some school work at your leisure. Making a start now means that you can avoid a mad scramble at the last moment. A seasonal job could be the answer when it comes to earning some extra cash. This evening is ideal for eating out with some close friends. Try a new restaurant with an ethnic flair rather than choosing an old haunt. Ask the waiter for recommendations before making your menu selections.

27. SATURDAY. Fair. Long-distance travel can be subject to delays or rescheduling, possibly as a result of a strike or slowdown. For Aries who are politically minded, this can be a good day for joining a march or peaceful demonstration. Exchanging views with those who are opposed to your views can lead to harsh dispute. Remind yourself that you are not going to change their opinions by getting angry yourself. Rational, factual arguments are much more likely to make an impact. A friend from another culture may be the victim of discrimination today; be ready with both practical and emotional support.

28. SUNDAY. Starred. This is not a day for sitting around at home. Make an extra effort to find out about events in your community, such as an exhibition or an open-air concert. You are usually more than adept at using your natural Aries initiative. If you suggest an outing you are sure to find that others are willing to go along with your plans. A recent business proposition can stir your imagination. Your enthusiasm for a new challenge could be just what is needed to turn an idea into profitable reality. A parent or older relative can be a storehouse of wisdom. Their generosity of spirit in sharing their experiences with you can be heartwarming. Do not neglect to let them know how much they are appreciated.

29. MONDAY. Easygoing. The day gets off to a rather slow start, but your energy level should increase as the day progresses. Problems which you encounter at work this morning should be easily resolved later in the afternoon. A colleague can be especially helpful in relieving you of some of your routine work or taking over a difficult task. Someone you have worked closely with may make an unexpected announcement; this could be a new job or early retirement. For Aries parents who have been struggling with the problems of an adolescent, this can be a productive day. A teenager is likely to respond to a show of love and concern as one adult to another.

30. TUESDAY. Disconcerting. You may be more susceptible than usual to other people's moods. Pressure at work makes for a stressful day. A colleague's display of temper is probably the last thing you feel like dealing with. Keep in mind that you are not responsible for other people's problems. Concentrate on getting through your own work first before getting involved in helping others. Make an extra effort to put the day's problems behind you when evening comes. Your partner or other family members are unlikely to be sympathetic to a catalog of the day's woes and may need some ego bolstering themselves. Take the phone off the hook so that you are not disturbed during dinnertime.

31. WEDNESDAY. Variable. The morning is likely to be the busiest part of the day. Do not forget to write appointments on your calendar as soon as they are made in order to avoid the risk of double booking. Young children need more of your time and attention than usual. Their dependence is unlikely to be a cause for alarm; it is probably a passing phase of insecurity that all children go through. Later in the day is favorable for spending some time alone. If you have the option to work from home, this could be a good time for doing so. A small dinner party can be the perfect way to relax this evening with a friend or neighbor.

AUGUST

1. THURSDAY. Demanding. On this busy day there is a lot going on behind the scenes. At work you may be asked to keep certain information to yourself for the time being. Do not feel tempted to confide even in a colleague; such indiscretion is almost sure to be discovered. An increased workload is likely. This may be because you are covering for other staff members who are away on vacation or sick leave. A new business deal requires careful attention to detail. You need all the pertinent facts at your fingertips if you are going to prevent a plan from falling through. Exercise your right to ask for a second opinion regarding medical matters or other professional advice.

2. FRIDAY. Fair. Administrative duties can take up the major part of the morning. If you are working on a report, devote extra time to the layout and presentation of your material. Avoid leaving finished work lying around unprotected; a spilled cup of coffee could ruin it. The pressure is likely to be off this afternoon; you should be able to get away earlier than usual. This evening can be a good time for shopping for personal items, such as underwear. After dark also favors group activities, especially a reunion with a former colleague or old school friend. Someone with whom you were romantically involved could become a firm friend after passions have cooled down.

3. SATURDAY. Challenging. Aries who work on weekends can expect a busy morning. If you have worked a night shift you may find it difficult to get to sleep. If noise is the problem, you might have to ask other household members to be more considerate. A conflict of values with an older relative could be quickly resolved as long as you do not overreact. A get-together or formal party this afternoon can put your stamina to the test; being well organized is the key to success. Sports matches can be tougher than you expected. You might have to play into overtime or extra innings in order to get a final result. Win or lose, you will enjoy the competition.

4. SUNDAY. Unsettling. Aries people who had a late night may be feeling delicate this morning. Some fresh air could be just what you need to blow the cobwebs away. Friction within the family could cause some upset. Even if you are not directly involved, a brother or sister could turn to you for support. You may be asked to arbitrate a dispute or work out a pay-back agreement. If you are planning to go on an outing later in the day it would be a smart move to purchase tickets in advance. A concert can be disappointing. If you are eating out, keep a watch on your intake of sweets; too much can make you hyper and unable to fall asleep later on.

5. MONDAY. Cautious. This is not an easy start to the workweek. Just when you thought you had your finances under control another large bill can upset the applecart. If you cannot pay off the full amount, find out if you can spread the payments over the next couple of months. Do not ignore a household bill such as gas or electricity; there is a chance of it being disconnected. Guard against making too much work for yourself, especially at home. Some tasks may simply be unnecessary, not to mention boring. Refuse to spend any more of your time clearing up after older children who are more than capable of doing so for themselves. It is all too easy for family members to get used to you acting as their personal maid.

6. TUESDAY. Good. Aries who are looking for part-time work could be in the right place at the right time. A job can come your way if you keep your eyes and ears open. If you are unemployed or on a low income this is a favorable time for claiming government benefits. You may also be eligible for some help with other bills, such as tuition or school lunches. For Aries who work in sales, this should be a productive day. Your verbal skills and powers of persuasion are at their best. If you do not have time to work out at a gymnasium or health club, this is a good day for investing in weights or an exercise bicycle to use at home. Plan exercise as a routine part of your daily schedule.

7. WEDNESDAY. Tricky. Professional advice is a must if you are at the point of signing a binding contract. Someone may be trying to pull the wool over your eyes. Be patient enough to read the small print, several times if necessary. For Aries who are trying to sell property, this is a favorable time for switching to a better known real estate agent. You may have to consider dropping the price slightly if you are hoping for a quick sale. There is a greater risk of an accident at home. Make an extra effort to anticipate danger when handling sharp tools or carrying bulky items upstairs. Also be extra cautious on the road.

8. THURSDAY. Useful. If your child is experiencing problems with a friend, talk with the other parents involved. Together you should be able to come up with ways in which you can help. This is an excellent time for Aries business people to put together a new advertising campaign. Consider employing a professional agency for fresh ideas and a new look to your publicity. All personal artistic endeavors are favored. Creative writing can be fun as well as an emotional release. If you have an article or short story to sell, this is a good time for approaching an editor. Cancel evening plans in favor of staying home with your loved ones. A surprise visit or phone call will make being home worthwhile.

9. FRIDAY. Pleasant. If you are going shopping invite a neighbor to come along. This is a good day for buying new plants, especially of the flowering variety. An arrangement of dried blossoms can be an attractive addition to a room. If you are unemployed and able-bodied, consider volunteering your services for a local community project such as tidying up a park or coaching a junior sports team. This evening is good for a night out with friends. Aries who are unattached could be introduced to someone new. Take the initiative when it comes to exchanging telephone numbers. If you play hard to get you could miss an exciting opportunity.

10. SATURDAY. Mixed. Home may not be the most restful place this morning. Young children constantly bickering or people coming in and out can make you yearn for some peace and quiet. Jobs around the house which were started some time ago may still be unfinished; the mess and confusion could be getting on your nerves. It may be worth the expense of hiring some outside help in order to get the place back to normal. Try to keep active today; lazing around will probably only make you feel sluggish. Some mental activity can be just as therapeutic as physical exercise. This is a propitious time for typing up a job application along with your resume. Even if you are satisfied with your current work, it cannot hurt to check what else is available for a person with your skills.

11. SUNDAY. Deceptive. Aries people who live alone may experience a sense of isolation. This is probably self-imposed; make renewed efforts to keep in touch with your friends and family. However, guard against calling an old flame; doing so is almost sure to be against your better judgment and is apt to be regretted as soon as you make the connection. Your long-term prospects may be a source of anxiety. Aries are often unhappy without a clear sense of direction. But you might have to accept that there are no immediate answers just yet. Avoid overdoing stimulants such as alcohol or so-called energy pills and resist overindulging in fatty snack foods.

12. MONDAY. Enjoyable. This is one of those times when it is easy to go to work. There are several projects on today's agenda which you have been anticipating. If there are boring jobs to be done as well, make a point of looking for the fun element; this can have a uplifting effect not only on you but also on those around you. This is a good time for investigating school options for yourself or a child. Family members should enjoy the change in routine just as much as you. The beginnings of a new love affair for single Aries people can put a smile on your face and give you something to write home about.

13. TUESDAY. Calm. You may find that there is a lull in the demands of your work. This gives you the chance to assess your recent achievements and think creatively about plans for the future. This is a good day for entertaining new or valued clients. Providing hospitality at a sporting event, such as a ballgame or the races, should be ideal. Take the opportunity to get to know your contacts on a more personal level. In your social life try to concentrate on spending more time with those who have common interests. Stay away from negative thinkers. Your sense of self-worth can be boosted by the attentions. of a new admirer on the scene.

14. WEDNESDAY. Difficult.   The morning is the most productive part of the day. Break away from traditional lines of thought; original, even daring, ideas are almost sure to be the best. Events this afternoon can cast a cloud over what had started out as a promising day. Aries employees may find that a certain individual seems set on undermining your achievements. You could be getting caught up in a power struggle. Someone can twist your words to give them a meaning that you never intended. If you are returning unsatisfactory merchandise, make sure that you know your rights; do not be intimidated by an aggressive response, and do not take no for an answer.

15. THURSDAY. Starred.   Others seem content to leave you to your own devices. With difficult tasks, a little imagination can go a long way; you could hit on an easy solution to a problem. This is a lucky day for Aries who are interviewing. Do not be afraid to blow your own horn; others can be impressed by your confidence and knowledge of your own strong points. Make an appointment with your doctor if home remedies have not cleared up an ongoing health problem. If you want to obtain a second opinion, do not hesitate to pay for the very best. When it comes to your well-being, prevention is the best medicine.

16. FRIDAY. Variable.   If you are thinking of becoming self-employed, talk through your plans with someone who has done the same thing. You should be able to benefit from their experience. Plans for changes in your home or place of work could be in the final stage. Now is the time to speak up about details which you do not like. Remind yourself that it is better to change your mind beforehand rather than when the work is already under way. If you are entertaining at home this evening, guard against being too ambitious. Keep the number of guests manageable and the menu straightforward. You will most enjoy being able to maneuver in a casual atmosphere.

17. SATURDAY. Uncertain.   Married Aries need to devote time to loved ones today. A busy schedule during the working week means that you are in danger of losing touch with each other's everyday lives. Consider going out together this afternoon, perhaps to a museum or art gallery. Making plans for a second honeymoon can breathe fresh romance into your relationship. If you are recently separated or divorced, do not spend too much time alone this weekend. Remind yourself of the benefits of being single; friends can help you get back in the social whirl. A party or other get-together can be more fun than you had imagined once you get into the swing of things.

18. SUNDAY. Disquieting. The spotlight continues to be on your personal relationships. Someone may be in the mood for picking a fight over a relatively small issue. Do not fall into the trap of lashing back with equally petty criticisms. If you make an extra effort to laugh off thoughtless remarks you should be able to defuse the situation. Doubts about your compatibility with a new partner may come to a head; some differences are too important to overlook. If you often are out late at night, this is a good time to learn some basic self-defense techniques by taking a class in your local area. Avoid driving in high-crime parts of town.

19. MONDAY. Unsettling. This can be a difficult start to the working week. Someone in authority may try your patience to the hilt with their vague directions and lack of solid support. As impatient as you may feel, this is unlikely to be a good time for drastic moves. Guard against the Aries tendency to be hotheaded. If you walk out of your job without another offer to go to you are apt to regret your hastiness. Being in the company of children can be a highlight of the day. They can give freely of their affection just when you are feeling neglected by the adults around you. Social arrangements for this evening may be postponed due to a friend's illness.

20. TUESDAY. Lucky. Going into business or other joint venture with a partner can prove to be lucky. There could be an offer today of a loan or another form of financial backing. This may enable you to expand your plans or to launch them sooner than you expected. Shop around for the best price on insurance. A home policy may be cheaper than you had thought. For a small sum each month you can stop trusting to luck and instead feel secure. This is an excellent day for Aries who work in the music profession or with music as a backdrop to work. Live music this evening could make for a memorable night out.

21. WEDNESDAY. Mixed. This is a day when you need to deal in hard facts and not rely on your intuition, especially with regard to business concerns. Do not fall prey to someone's charm; there may be more to them than meets the eye. Seek professional advice before investing a large sum of money. It may be better not to put all your eggs in one basket. Avoid keeping a personal problem to yourself. The more you mull it over, the more confused you are likely to become. The objective opinion of an outsider can set you on the right path to a solution. Your partner may ask you to attend a business function with them this evening; be ready to change your own plans.

22. THURSDAY. Helpful.   If you are thinking of returning to school, this is a good day for obtaining the necessary information and forms. You may still be able to secure a last-minute place for this coming academic year. Career-oriented Aries may feel that progress up the professional ladder is too slow. You might have to commit to an evening class in order to secure the necessary qualifications for advancement. This is the perfect day for setting off on vacation. Travel plans should run to schedule. If you are traveling alone you are unlikely to be by yourself for long. Keep plans to a minimum so that you can enjoy whatever comes along.

23. FRIDAY. Demanding.   Someone close to you could receive disappointing news. The necessary changes in their long-term plans are likely to have an effect on you, especially if you have been providing financial support. This is a day when others are apt to seek you out for advice. However, do not let a certain individual drain your time and energy. They may be looking to you to provide the answers that they should really be working out for themselves. Legal matters can be time consuming. A setback in negotiations or a lawsuit may make you feel like giving up altogether. Do not rely on receiving a last-minute invitation to go out tonight. Call friends and organize an evening with them.

24. SATURDAY. Variable.   This is a good day for voluntary work in your local community. Consider helping out with transportation for elderly or disabled people. You may not be inclined to go along to an exhibition related to a family member's interests, but make an extra effort to show enthusiasm for their sake. Once you have stirred yourself into action you should enjoy yourself. Aries people usually have a positive outlook, but you may find yourself dispirited about your career prospects. Keep in mind that belief in yourself and your abilities can work wonders in dealing with other people. If you can make them believe in you, self-doubts should vanish.

25. SUNDAY. Misleading.   This is an important day for recognizing the importance of family unity. A child may welcome your efforts to reinforce a sense of security. A family outing or a sitdown dinner with all the family gathered at the same time can be enjoyable. Steer clear of touchy subjects. There is a greater risk that you could display some aggression just at the wrong moment. Someone close to you might not find it easy to forgive you if you lose your temper with them in public, no matter how justified you may feel about your outburst. There is a chance that you have the wrong facts about a new relationship. Listen to the other side of the story.

26. MONDAY. Fair. Business meetings are subject to upheaval this morning. Someone whose views are crucial may even fail to put in an appearance. A colleague can upset your usual routine by passing on unexpected work to you; try to be willing when it comes to helping them out. Being well organized is the key to getting through a mountain of tasks. If you are starting a new job you may find that you have inherited a mountain of paperwork. Make it your first priority to establish logical filing and replying procedures. This evening is the perfect time for a heart-to-heart talk with your partner about relocating at a distance.

27. TUESDAY. Quiet. A slower pace at work is likely. Superiors may be absent or simply too involved with their own concerns to have time to interfere with you. There is a chance to enjoy an extended lunch with your favorite colleagues. Aries who are interviewing may find it helpful to get right to the point. An informal chat could be more productive than any attempt to make an impression with graphs or other visual aids. Make a point of donating what you can afford if you are approached by a charity. No matter how large or small the amount, your contribution is sure to be appreciated. A get-together with close friends this evening can be a pleasant end to the day.

28. WEDNESDAY. Optimistic. Concerns about a health matter are likely to be unfounded. It is important to put your mind at rest; worrying in itself can lead to feeling unwell. Make an appointment to see your doctor for an expert opinion. The prognosis for a hospitalized friend or relative should be hopeful. If you are buying a pet, make sure to have a vet look it over. Bring vaccinations up to date. This can be an auspicious time for new business ventures, but it is best not to expect results too quickly. Patience and a sound strategy are the best approach to gaining recognition, especially when it comes to fending off your rivals and beating out competitors.

29. THURSDAY. Outstanding.   For Aries in the entertainment industry, this is a good day for auditions. An agent may be impressed by your talent even if they do not say so directly at the time. New business contacts could turn out to be invaluable in the future. File away business cards offered to you; you never know when they may come in handy. A recent tiff with your partner should have blown over without any real damage being done. It is up to you to forget your grievances; bearing a grudge can be counterproductive. This is a favorable evening for a cozy night at home with your mate or steady date.

30. FRIDAY. Variable.   One-to-one meetings could end up with you at loggerheads. A group situation is likely to be more helpful; an associate can support you and swing a decision in your favor. Other people's views may appear to be in direct conflict with your own, but make an extra effort to consider what they are saying. Do not hesitate to bow to someone else's better judgment; being able to admit an error is a strength, not a weakness. A formal occasion this evening is likely to be successful. Public speaking can be hard going at first, but if you inject some humor you can win over an audience and soon have them cheering you on.

31. SATURDAY. Deceptive.   Weekend guests can be hard work. Some may be inclined to treat your home as a hotel. Your best policy is not to suffer in silence. Remember that there are pleasant ways of asking for help with the usual chores, such as preparing food or doing the dishes. Aries singles need to guard against a tendency to idealize someone to whom you are attracted. Remind yourself that if you put someone on a pedestal they are bound to fall off eventually. Be realistic. Avoid a liaison with someone who is in the process of a separation but is still married. They may not be as available as they would have you believe.

SEPTEMBER

1. SUNDAY. Satisfactory. Be careful not to spend money that you do not really have. If you are going shopping, leave your credit cards at home; set a cash limit for yourself instead. If you are working around your home, avoid electrical work; there is a greater risk of a shock or of overloading the circuits. Call in an expert during the week ahead. Getting together with older members of your family could prove to be a lively occasion. Some heated debate over political or social issues may highlight the different viewpoints held by you and a relative. These are likely to be rooted in a generation gap, so try to make allowances while listening with an open mind.

2. MONDAY. Disconcerting. Money you were expecting to receive today may not be forthcoming. The reasons given might sound like flimsy excuses. If you want to be reimbursed quickly, you might have to take a tougher stand. Avoid laying out money for other people; someone may be slow to repay you or forget about it altogether. If you are at home you may suffer from feelings of restlessness or isolation. Get out for a walk or a round of golf; you are sure to feel better after some physical exercise. At work you may have a greater tendency to waste time through daydreaming. Come up with ways in which you can improve your concentration and focus your energies.

3. TUESDAY. Manageable. If you are sending mail or a package be sure that you have the correct postage. There is a greater risk of something going astray if it has to be returned for postage due. Mark your own address clearly both on the outside and inside. Aries employees need to be careful about making personal telephone calls from work, especially if they are long distance. There is a danger of being called to account by the boss and being presented with a large bill. A problem in a personal relationship may not be as serious as you imagine. There is little that cannot be ironed out with some honest talking. Do not hesitate to say exactly what you think or how you feel, but be polite.

4. WEDNESDAY. Strenuous. A backlog of paperwork makes for a demanding start to the day. You may not be able to progress with certain projects until this is properly dealt with. A variety of telephone inquiries could be time consuming, especially if you have to do some checking and then call back. It may be worth taking on some temporary staff at work for a few days to help you catch up. If you are learning a new skill you may have a crisis of confidence today. Resist the temptation to give up. It could be helpful to practice more in between your professional lessons; ask a friend to monitor your progress. Acquiring any new skill can be slow but worthwhile in the long run.

5. THURSDAY. Calm. This is a good day for some serious reading. Some books on the current best-seller list may be difficult to get at the library; consider purchasing a copy for yourself. A neighbor may need some company. Take a break from your chores for a couple of hours to enjoy catching up on local news or gossip with them. A brother or sister could prove to be a reliable confidante. A friend who is a single parent may ask you to babysit this evening. Make this an act of friendship and refuse payment. Do not put off writing a note of sympathy to an old family friend who has been kind and helpful in the past.

6. FRIDAY. Demanding. You may feel you are being pulled in several different directions. Expect some conflict of responsibility between home and work. It may be a question of trying to divide your time more equally. If you still have some vacation time owing to you, make sure that it does not slip by unused. Your mate or partner could be appeased by the prospect of getting away for a few days holiday together. Meetings of all kinds are likely to be tough going; you could find that you are simply talking in circles and getting nowhere fast. This is a day when perseverance may not be a virtue. Recognize when someone has outfoxed you. Beat a hasty retreat and prepare for the next round.

7. SATURDAY. Fair. The morning is the best part of the day for doing housework. You should be able to breeze through the usual tasks, especially if you get up early. If you have small children underfoot, consider asking your partner or a friend to take them out for a few hours. Aries may come up against bigotry or prejudice in a social setting. Your best policy is to treat it with the contempt it deserves. This evening is a favorable time for entertaining at home. An informal supper is likely to be enjoyed by all, including you. Board games or cards can be fun, but guard against being too competitive. Do not hesitate to play the role of matchmaker.

8. SUNDAY. Pleasant. This morning is a good time for tackling work in the garden, such as pruning and removing dead blossoms.

Add yard debris to a compost pile rather than disposing of it with your household trash. Later in the day can be a favorable time for sporting activities. Come up with some mild competition which you can do as a family, such as swimming or shooting basketballs. Team games can be more enjoyable if you play for fun rather than to win. For Aries who are unattached, a new romantic opportunity may crop up through an outside interest. It will soon be obvious that sharing the same hobby is not all that you have in common.

9. MONDAY. Good. Your ability to initiate and motivate places you in a position of leadership. Colleagues at work are likely to respond quickly to your ideas as your enthusiasm rubs off on them. This can be an auspicious day for any business deal which requires lengthy, careful negotiations. You should have little difficulty capturing the right person's attention. Information from an associate can be instrumental in closing a deal. In your personal relationships a little tact can go a long way. Remind yourself that it is not always what you say that is important, but how you say it. Showing true empathy can win the affection of someone special.

10. TUESDAY. Starred. Creative endeavors of all kinds are favored. An imaginative approach to your work can turn even a boring task into a challenge. You might discover talents you did not know you had. The office environment is a fun place to be today. A colleague with a lively sense of humor can help you put a problem in its true perspective. Amusing jokes or anecdotes can remind you that laughter is the best tonic. Aries parents should find time to help a child with homework. With patience you may be able to spark their interest in a subject which they worry about because it has been difficult for them in the past. Put an emphasis on reading at home.

11. WEDNESDAY. Helpful. If you are planning to travel abroad in the near future, this is a good day for checking that you are up to date with vaccinations. Do not overlook the importance of these; remind yourself that temporary discomfort is better than dealing with the real illness. A colleague who is constantly asking for your assistance can get on your nerves today. Your best policy is to devote more time to them rather than trying to ignore them. If you take the trouble to explain certain procedures in greater detail they should be able to manage alone. A trip to the theater or to a concert can make this an enjoyable evening with friends or co-workers.

12. THURSDAY. Promising. Both your physical and mental energy should be at a high level. Tackling long-standing projects with renewed vigor can be immensely productive. You may finally be able to bring certain matters to a satisfactory close. This can clear the way ahead for new interests. A fresh approach to a nagging health problem could pay off. Consider making an appointment with a new practitioner or trying an alternative remedy. If you have a spare room at home, this can be a lucky time for finding a lodger; a colleague may be able to recommend someone who is looking for a place to rent. This could prove to be an easy solution to balancing your personal budget.

13. FRIDAY. Sensitive. This morning favors interviews of all sorts. Temporary or part-time job opportunities could be easier to come across, but the competition may be tougher than you anticipate. Do not be afraid to sell yourself. Draw a potential employer's attention to your positive qualities and your past achievements. Aries in sales can expect a productive day on the whole, although you may need to call on extra reserves of patience with a customer who cannot make a decision. Your partner may be exhausted or irritable after a busy week at work. Make an extra effort to put their needs first this evening, even if this means canceling plans to go out.

14. SATURDAY. Quiet. This is a good day for devoting time to those who matter most to you. A new romantic relationship can flourish through just spending time together, doing ordinary things such as shopping for groceries and cooking a special meal this evening. Find out about each other's taste in music; listen to each other's favorites. If you are married, you and your spouse might consider opting out of social arrangements in favor of just doing your own thing. Aries people are usually known for single-mindedness. Now is the time to demonstrate just how willing you are to compromise. Hold back in stating your own views so that others can take the limelight.

15. SUNDAY. Deceptive. If you are unemployed at the moment the Sunday newspaper could be a gold mine of job advertisements. Be analytical about them. Something which sounds too good to be true is probably just that. Disturbing gossip may reach your ears. It is up to you not to take this for gospel truth. Find out the facts for yourself before you jump to any conclusions. There is a greater danger that certain facts are being deliberately misrepresented. If you have a joint bank account with your partner, this afternoon can be a good time for working out your financial position. One of you may have been over-spending while the other strives to save.

16. MONDAY. Disquieting. Concern about a child's health could cast a cloud over the morning. You may have no choice but to take off work or cancel other engagements in order to stay home with them. A visit to your doctor should set your mind at rest. Go over financial arrangements for your dependents. You might need to increase your budget allotment for clothing or recreation. Battles over alimony or child support can be stressful, but a good lawyer can help smooth out the worst areas of contention. This is also a good time for discussing life insurance needs with a professional adviser, preferably someone who comes recommended by a friend or colleague.

17. TUESDAY. Excellent. If you are expecting a large sum of money through an inheritance or an insurance payment, it could be in today's mail. A celebration could be in the cards. This can be a lucky time for new investments. Shares bought at this time are likely to yield a healthy profit in the future. For Aries employees, now can be a favorable time for approaching your boss about a pay raise; you could be in a stronger position than you realize. Money problems can be sorted out satisfactorily. Do not hesitate to call your bank manager; you may be surprised by the helpful, sympathetic answer you receive. Do not hesitate to apply for a loan if you know you can repay it soon.

18. WEDNESDAY. Fair. Long-distance traveling may take longer than you had bargained for. It may be wise to allow extra time for any journey. Aries who are traveling alone could strike up an interesting conversation with a fellow passenger. Legal matters may take a turn for the better just as you were on the point of giving up. Someone in a position of power may come up with helpful advice or practical support. This is a favorable day for Aries people who are preparing to take an examination. A good grade may well mark a turning point in your career. Choose a peaceful restaurant or other setting if you are going on a first date this evening.

19. THURSDAY. Variable. If you are looking for work, this is a time to be highly selective. Guard against taking the first position that you are offered; there could be something better in the pipeline. If you are applying for a position that was advertised, make sure that you ask for a full job description. There is a greater risk that a firm could be employing you only until someone returns. Teaching positions may be hard to get, but a friend in the same profession could come up with some inside information. Now is a good time to apply for a spot in a popular class to start this coming term. Fees may be harder to arrange, especially if you need scholarship aid.

20. FRIDAY. Disquieting. You would be well advised to ask for all verbal agreements to be confirmed in writing. Do not run the risk of getting in the position where it is your word against theirs. Double-check all travel and hotel reservations. It may be better to pick up tickets in person rather than trusting them to the postal service. Avoid buying tickets from a scalper; you could be ripped off. This afternoon could be a disappointing end to the workweek. A matter that you had hoped to complete could be subject to delays which are out of your control. Relax with friends this evening and try to put problems out of mind for a while.

21. SATURDAY. Good. This is likely to be a lucrative day for Aries people whose work involves serving the general public. You can expect to receive higher tips and other gratuities. Overtime could be well paid also. Information about a part-time job could come your way through word of mouth. This is a good time for paying attention to your health and general level of fitness. Consider becoming a member of a local health club or gymnasium; this could be an effective way of motivating yourself. You should also benefit from professional health and fitness advice. This evening is an excellent time for wining and dining to mark a special occasion.

22. SUNDAY. Fair. Devote this morning to household tasks. You are likely to enjoy yourself far more later in the day if you know that all your chores are up to date. This afternoon is a favorable time for inviting a group of friends for an informal lunch or dinner. If money is tight, ask everyone to bring their favorite dish; this way you do not have to break the bank in order to entertain. Conversation about political issues can be stimulating. You may find yourself revising certain views or feeling encouraged to join a different political party. This can also be a good time for lending your support to a campaign concerned with human rights violations and how to correct them.

23. MONDAY. Challenging. Business meetings can be hard going this morning. You may have to take a stand against considerable opposition, but do not allow yourself to be shouted down. Others will secretly respect you for sticking to your guns.

Support may come from an unexpected quarter. Aries parents may be struggling with discipline issues. Although you may be reluctant to impose your authority, this may be what is needed; firmness coupled with kindness can be the answer. Single Aries could be in competition for someone's attention. Your best policy is not to force your hand or be too available.

24. TUESDAY. Stressful. Aries people who work in a managerial capacity are in demand today. There is little point trying to work in privacy; expect a string of interruptions from staff needing your help. This is not a good time for keeping a secret from a loved one. The strain of what you believed to be a white lie is bound to show eventually; you might have to add more lies in order to support your original story. Make a clean breast of things and hope for a sympathetic response. An offer of a job transfer or early retirement should not be accepted in haste; think through the pros and cons before making a firm decision.

25. WEDNESDAY. Unsettling. Aries have a greater tendency to live in the past today. Although daydreaming can sometimes be therapeutic, guard against feeling too much regret or remorse. Remind yourself that what is done cannot be changed; make an extra effort to bring yourself back to the present. Try to banish painful memories so that you avoid sinking into depression. Listening to someone else's spiteful gossip can be uncomfortable; refuse to take any part in it. Putting in some overtime at work may mean having to reorganize your private life. Be prepared for some griping from your partner, who wants a prime role in your life.

26. THURSDAY. Unpredictable. The day starts on a pleasant enough note. A letter from someone who has been out of contact for a while can lift your spirits. But someone at work can soon put a damper on things. You will have to try hard not to let their pessimism rub off on you. Refuse to make a drama out of a crisis. Remind yourself that it is a sign of professionalism to keep your head when everyone else around you is panicking. A clear head can be your best asset. A difference of opinion with your partner may leave you feeling down. There is probably nothing to be gained from being passive; make your own feelings and needs known to those who care about you.

27. FRIDAY. Energetic. Working to a deadline today can actually be fun. A sense of urgency is the best motivator both for you and those working alongside you. Give yourself a big pat on the back when you deliver the goods on time. Later in the day favors shopping for clothes for yourself or for children. Some bargains could be found in out-of-season sportswear. This could be a lucky day for placing a bet at a racetrack; keep your stake moderate and you are likely to come out on top. A lottery ticket can also be lucky for you. A social gathering this evening is sure to be a lively affair and could easily continue on to the small hours.

28. SATURDAY. Tricky. You may not feel in the mood for doing much early in the day. This is probably a good morning for lolling in bed, especially if you know that you are short of sleep. Try not to let a work problem play on your mind. There is no point in spoiling your weekend over something which cannot be dealt with until next week anyway. Shopping with a friend this afternoon can be fun. However, guard against spending on the strength of next month's income. Do not buy secondhand electrical goods unless they come with a new guarantee. A friend going through a crisis may ask you to change your plans for this evening. Come to their aid as they have helped you in the past.

29. SUNDAY. Variable. Children can cause extra expense today. An outing may cost far more than you had planned; it is wise to have some spare cash in your wallet. Aries parents might be finding it difficult to keep up with the demands of children. This is a good time for increasing a teenager's allowance, but do this with the understanding that they learn to manage their own finances. It can do no harm to point out that you do not have a printing press to turn out money. Sports events can be fun. However, if you are competing yourself be careful not to take unnecessary risks; you could soon be out of the game. Try to take an argument with a loved one in stride, and resist personal jibes.

30. MONDAY. Changeable. If you are returning faulty merchandise make sure that you know your rights. A surly assistant can soon change their tune if you insist on seeing the manager. Finding daycare for a young child can be difficult. There is a chance that an older relative will offer to help out and so give you a wider choice. For Aries people who are unemployed, this is a good day for finding out about benefits you are entitled to. A welfare officer can be of help in cases of hardship. Different attitudes to money may be the root cause of an argument with your partner. Try to reach a mutually agreeable compromise.

OCTOBER

1. TUESDAY. Disconcerting. Be cautious when it comes to dealing with someone in authority, such as your employer. You stand a good chance of getting your own way if you can strike a balance between being respectful but forceful. Presentations to a gathering can have their sticky moments. A certain individual may just be testing you out, so try not to feel intimidated. This should be a favorable day for conducting business over the telephone. A mailing can be productive, but make sure that your mailing list is up to date. Married Aries may have to take sides in an argument between your parents and your partner.

2. WEDNESDAY. Disquieting. An argument with your mate or a neighbor could get the day off to a bad start. Guard against taking out your irritation on colleagues; they are less likely to be tolerant of any outbursts or sarcasm. Weigh your words carefully if you want someone to do something for you. You need to make sure that you are asking a favor and not giving a command. Mail which you were expecting might not show up. Certain items could be speeded up in reaching you if you make a few telephone calls. This is not a good day for investing in communications equipment of any kind, such as a computer program or a word processor. Wait until you are more certain about what you really need and will be able to use easily.

3. THURSDAY. Variable. If you are at home try not to spend too much time on housework or other chores. You will probably only end up feeling resentful, especially if most of the work has been made by someone else. Some small home decorating jobs can be fun to do as well as giving you a sense of achievement. Injecting variety into your usual working routine can make the day more enjoyable. A sense of urgency about certain tasks is likely to be uncalled for; try not to drive yourself harder than is strictly necessary. This evening favors inviting friends or work-mates to enjoy your home hospitality. Pick up a take-out meal if you do not feel like cooking for a crowd.

4. FRIDAY. Demanding. Aries who work at home may have to contend with numerous distractions. This could be outside noise or the loud comings and goings of other household members. Tasks which require total concentration might be better postponed to another time. An argument with a loved one could be weighing heavily on your conscience; you may be finding it difficult to admit that you were wrong. The best policy is to make a genuine apology. Further patience may be required if this is not accepted in the right spirit. If your partner is away, their absence may be hard to cope with. Try to keep yourself busy with personal projects.

5. SATURDAY. Mixed. House hunting can be a tedious business. It may come as a surprise that a real estate agent's descriptions are often quite different from the real thing. Try to cut through the jargon in order to get a more realistic picture of what is available in your price range. If you are moving, make sure that all your boxes are clearly labeled; this could save a lot of confusion when it comes to unpacking at the other end. Avoid keeping young children cooped up in the house this afternoon. Find a suitable way for them to expend some of their excess energy and make as much noise as they like, such as going to a local playground or amusement park.

6. SUNDAY. Quiet. This is one of those days best devoted to pure leisure. Remind yourself of the importance of having some time to do exactly what you want, when you want. Be as lazy or as active as you choose. For energetic Aries, this should be a good day for sports of the noncompetitive variety, such as swimming or riding. Children can be refreshingly good company; their straightforward outlook on life could be just the tonic you need. A new love affair should be blossoming. This could be an auspicious moment for single Aries parents to introduce a new partner to your children; they are likely to hit it off well.

7. MONDAY. Challenging. Nervous energy needs to be channeled into worthwhile pursuits. Make a conscious effort to prioritize the day's tasks. If you can harness your enthusiasm to a systematic approach, there is nothing that you cannot tackle successfully. Looking after children can drain your stamina. Just trying to keep up with them can be a job in itself. Use your creativity to come up with new games or activities; half the battle lies in capturing their imagination. If a romantic relationship is dominating your life and making you worried rather than content, question the wisdom of continuing along the path you have been treading.

8. TUESDAY. Unsettling. Make an extra effort to be flexible. The absence of a key family or staff member could mean that you have to handle extra work. Try to find the balance between covering for another person and not letting your own work suffer too much. A long-distance trip could be canceled at short notice; this is apt to upset your schedule for the rest of the week. Keep a weather eye on your health, especially your stress level. Now is a good time for a general checkup. If you are advised to find time to exercise, make sure that you do so; your health should always come first. You have the willpower now to begin a diet.

9. WEDNESDAY. Rewarding. Aries employers should find that this is a favorable day for putting together a team for a new project. There is a greater chance that you will find just the person you need. The best opportunities for job-seeking Aries are likely to come through current contacts. This could be a case of who you know rather than what you know. Do not hesitate to capitalize on such advantages. This is a good time for learning a second language with a view to improving your career prospects. Even if you are already employed you may be approached by a headhunter. Seek out the company of an intimate friend this evening for some relaxing conversation.

10. THURSDAY. Unpredictable. The day starts off at a relatively calm pace. Try to finish up the most important matters by lunchtime. This afternoon could bring all sorts of unforeseen issues to the surface. Meetings should go well overall, but there is a greater risk that they will run on much later than you anticipate. You may feel that there is too much talking and not enough action. In your personal relationships, make judgments based on what someone does rather than what they say. Promises are easy to make; keeping them is what really matters. Avoid overcommitting yourself to a community cause.

11. FRIDAY. Fair. Your partner's support should remind you to count your blessings. Although you may have had your differences recently, it is comforting to know that they are there for you when it really matters. Talking through a work problem with someone close to you can be helpful. Their objective viewpoint may yield possibilities which had not occurred to you. This could help you avoid a future confrontation. Try not to bring work home with you this weekend. A formal occasion this evening may be an obligation that you cannot avoid. Make a point of breaking the conversational ice with other guests rather than waiting for them to be formally introduced.

12. SATURDAY. Variable.   Try not to enter into arrangements with other people unless you are sure that you can honor them. Someone may be relying on you more than you realize. If being at a certain place at a certain time is doubtful, it is better to give fair warning ahead of time. Friction between you and a loved one is not as serious as they are making out. Your best policy is to take the line of least resistance in order to avoid a disagreement over nothing. This evening favors dressing up in your finest, whether you are going out for the night or entertaining guests in your own home. Go out of your way to make a newcomer feel part of your inner circle.

13. SUNDAY. Good.   Your powers of intuition are heightened today. Someone who has always been a puzzlement to you may now start to make sense. They may also have fresh insights into the way your mind works. Single Aries can afford to rely on instincts when it comes to meeting new people. If someone appears to be covering up their past, they probably are. But if you feel the person is merely nervous or shy, go out of your way to put them at ease; the rewards could be more than worthwhile. A new hobby can be absorbing. This afternoon is a good time for attending a workshop related to an outside interest.

14. MONDAY. Disquieting.   This may not be a promising start to the workweek. Someone close to you may not be working at their usual level. You may feel the need to offer your services to sort out necessary paperwork or handle other details for them. It is possible that they are facing difficult financial choices. Take this as a reminder to put your own affairs in order. This is a good time for overcoming superstition and drawing up a will. Lending emotional support to others could mean that your own needs are overlooked today. A child may be craving extra attention; make their care and welfare a priority.

15. TUESDAY. Mixed.   Your working life may be a grind at the moment. Efforts on your part to make things easier may not succeed as well as you had hoped. It is never easy to account for other people's reactions; all you can do is concentrate on doing what you think best at the time. A superior may be reluctant to admit an error of judgment. Try to resist the temptation to make an issue out of this; facts will speak for themselves given time. Stay out of arguments of all kinds. Fighting someone else's battle for them is likely to prove a thankless task. You have to go along to get along.

16. WEDNESDAY. Disconcerting. Work issues continue to dominate. A growing sense of dissatisfaction with your job can make you restless. However, this is not a day for impulsive decisions. Remind yourself that being employed at least means that you can pay your bills. At the same time there is no harm in making plans for the future. Having a light at the end of the tunnel could make all the difference in your outlook. Talk out a problem with a trusted friend or family member; remember that they are ready and willing to help and can be a source of inspiration. Look for solutions rather than dwelling on the problem.

17. THURSDAY. Cautious. This morning is the more enjoyable part of the day. A letter or call from someone you met earlier in the year could be a delightful surprise. Making plans to meet soon gives you something to look forward to. Later in the day can be a demanding time. You could suddenly be under added pressure when a deadline is moved forward. Someone in authority can be a thorn in your side. You may feel that they are taking you for granted in order to accommodate their own desires. Be strenuous in your objections if someone is delegating too much work to you or is not giving you the credit you deserve.

18. FRIDAY. Fair. The end of your working week has come none too soon. The pressures of work could keep your nose to the grindstone until the last possible minute. This is a good time for anticipating problems and talking them through. Point out to a superior that you are understaffed. This can be a favorable time for drumming up support for a community project. Obtaining financial sponsorship from a large company may be difficult, but they could be more than generous if you can give satisfactory answers to a barrage of questions. Make sure that verbal assurances related to money are confirmed in writing so that there are no future misunderstandings.

19. SATURDAY. Misleading. This morning is unlikely to be a good time to shop for costly items. A salesperson could talk you into buying something that is more expensive than your budget allows. Make sure that you have an option to return purchases for a full refund. An official document could be confusing. You may need an expert to decipher the small print of a contract. Later in the day can be a good time for social gatherings. An old schoolmate may put in a surprise appearance. If you are meeting a friend, it is sensible to recheck time and place; one of you could end up waiting in the wrong location. Keep money and friendship separate or you could lose both.

20. SUNDAY. Relaxing. Be content to let other people call the tune. Aries people are known for organizing skills, but go along with a friend's suggestions today and enjoy taking a backseat role. You often look after others; let someone look after you for a change. Sitting down to a dinner that you did not cook can be a real treat. A wish close to your heart may come true. Decisions affecting the whole household need to be made democratically. Give all family members the chance to have their say. Guard against making assumptions on behalf of someone who is absent while discussions are going on.

21. MONDAY. Changeable. For Aries people who are politically active, this is a good day to canvass for votes. Your ability to tactfully handle aggressive questions can stand you in good stead. Find the balance between giving orders and a friendly agreeable attitude. A troublemaker needs to put firmly in their place. Avoid participating in dangerous sports; there is a greater risk of an injury. At work, guard against making decisions without consultating a superior. You need to avoid taking sole responsibility if something does not go according to plan. Be sure to factor in a little extra when making budget plans.

22. TUESDAY. Helpful. Appointments are likely to run on time. Seeking a second opinion from a top consultant could be a wise move, either for yourself or a loved one. They may have alternative ideas which appeal to you. Consider some volunteer work. A charitable organization would probably leap at the offer of your time and skills. Heirlooms such as furniture or jewelry which have been in your family for several generations may need to be revalued for insurance purposes. A family treasure could be passed on to you through an inheritance. Research into your family roots can be rewarding as well as enjoyable.

23. WEDNESDAY. Variable. If you are at home, this is a good time to weed through accumulations in closets or the attic. There is a good chance of coming across belongings which you thought were lost. Reorganizing kitchen cupboards could create extra storage room. Space-saving ideas offered in a magazine could be useful. This is a favorable day for working closely with colleagues. Try not to let a superior impose their ideas when their knowledge of a particular project is clearly less than yours. Secrets concerning a friend's love life could be confided in you. Make sure that you do not repeat them or even hint about what you have been told in confidence.

24. THURSDAY. Stressful. Problems at work could come to a head. You may be tired of listing the same grievances over and over again to a boss who does nothing about them. If you want decisive action you may have to go out on a limb, such as threatening to resign if certain matters are not resolved. If attending a formal function, be sure to dress appropriately; guard against appearing flamboyant. Avoid making any drastic changes to your personal appearance, such as an unusual haircut; you may regret it as soon as it is done. It can be difficult to stick to a weight loss program. You might succeed better if you set a more achievable target to begin with rather than hoping for instant results.

25. FRIDAY. Rewarding. Hard work done earlier in the week is likely to produce rewards for you. Someone who thought you were on the wrong track regarding a business transaction may now have to eat humble pie. You can afford to follow your own judgment. Do not let an older person deter you from a chosen course of action. This evening is not good for being on your own. Going out can be fun and therapeutic. If you are single, call friends to see what is happening. You could find yourself included for a night on the town. A new romantic opportunity may make you glad that you put forth the effort. Love highlights the midnight hours.

26. SATURDAY. Challenging. For Aries who are struggling with ever-increasing debt, now is the time to take matters in hand. Interest payments could be crippling your attempts to get back to even. Talk the situation through with a professional adviser. If your family could help, swallow your pride and let them know that you need some assistance. Do not be tempted to cancel an insurance policy with the idea of saving money; this could prove to be a false economy. Conflict with a loved one needs to be sorted out. If you are stinging from a real or imagined hurt, have the confidence to bring it up and discuss it openly.

27. SUNDAY. Unsettling. Aries self-esteem may be at a low ebb. Consider whether you are giving a certain individual too much power. Try to attach less importance to what other people think. Have the confidence to stand up for your own beliefs even if someone scorns them. Realize that their attack may involve their insecurity, not yours. Listen with an open mind to a money-making proposition. Part of this may sound too farfetched to succeed, but there could be a sound idea at the heart of the scheme. Let yourself be treated to dinner tonight; you can always return the favor another time.

28. MONDAY. Mixed. If you are stocking up at the supermarket be prepared for a larger bill than usual. Make an extra effort to look for bargains, such as day-old goods or buying in bulk. Avoid high-price convenience foods. It is usually both cheaper and healthier to eat fresh produce which you prepare yourself. Later in the day is a good time for dealing with paperwork of all kinds. Do not put off writing a personal letter that you have been mentally composing. Someone may be feeling hurt that you have not been in touch. Studying can be more demanding than usual. Discussing work with a colleague can help you grasp the ins and outs of a difficult concept.

29. TUESDAY. Good. If a loved one is away, today's mail could bring a welcome letter. Certain business matters can be dealt with quickly on the telephone rather than waiting for a face-to-face appointment. Your personal popularity is soaring. Social invitations for the coming weekend may be pressed upon you. Aries who are unattached should not have to try particularly hard to attract someone you admire; the feelings are likely to be mutual. It may not be wise to risk spoiling an intimate friendship by letting it develop into romance. That special person in your life is ready and willing to spoil you this evening.

30. WEDNESDAY. Productive. Make an extra effort to arrive at work on time this morning or even slightly earlier than usual. You are under more pressure to produce. If you are at home, race through your chores in order to fit in a social arrangement. Avoid taking on too many new commitments. A certain individual may try to offload work onto you in the belief that you have spare time; it is up to you to put them straight. If you have a date this evening, allow plenty of time for getting ready; rushing can leave you flustered. You will probably feel more confident and relaxed if you are happy with the way you look. A new outfit can do wonders for your self-esteem.

31. THURSDAY. Successful. If you are in the process of buying or selling property, this can be an auspicious day for exchanging contracts. Securing a mortgage should be straightforward. Shop around to find a preferential interest rate. This is a favorable day for official ceremonies of all kinds. Booking the services of a local celebrity can add a touch of glamour to any occasion. Interviews related to promotion at work or a new position are likely to be successful. Do not hesitate to push for the pay raise you deserve. This evening is ideal for celebrating an anniversary or birthday in the family, even if it is just your pet's.

NOVEMBER

1. FRIDAY. Changeable. If you are considering becoming self-employed, look into certain financial details such as taxes and insurance coverage. Associates are apt to give conflicting advice, probably based on their own experience. Seek out the services of a professional accountant or other financial adviser. At work a superior may have a tendency to give vague instructions. You may have to supply the missing details by using your own intuition and common sense. You might find it difficult to settle down to any particular task. Your imagination is working overtime with regard to a scheme that you prefer to keep to yourself for now.

2. SATURDAY. Good. Sporting activities of all kinds are favored, whether you are actively participating or taking a spectator role. If you have young children now can be a good time to sign them up for swimming or dancing lessons; the younger they start, the better. Looking after a neighbor's children will probably cost you little effort, and they are sure to return the favor when you need some free time. A romantic relationship is becoming increasingly stable. This is a favorable time for talking together about your future plans. Today is also auspicious for an engagement announcement. Enjoy being the center of attention and savor the special moment.

3. SUNDAY. Tricky. If you have an important decision to make it is wiser to follow your own hunches rather than someone else's. You could strike it rich with a new scheme. Entertaining relatives or other guests at home can be hard work, both physically and mentally. Keep the conversation humming by introducing a controversial topic. Someone may take the hint to stop being polite and say what they really think. This is a favorable day for attending talks or workshops related to self-improvement. If a deep-seated issue is preying on your mind, consider working on this in more depth. If you cannot afford a therapist or other professionally trained counselor, try a self-help book.

4. MONDAY. Difficult. A full schedule means that you are inclined to overdo today. Make a point of stopping for a proper lunch break. Being able to switch off mentally for an hour can be just as important as physical sustenance. Check your calendar for nonwork appointments, such as a visit to the dentist. In the heat of the moment such things are likely to go out of your head. Some repair or cleaning jobs around the home may be too much for one person to tackle comfortably. Recognize your physical limitations; wait until there is someone else around to give you a helping hand. If you are doing more than your fair share of housework, speak up rather than being a martyr.

5. TUESDAY. Rewarding. This is a productive day on the job. A new contract can fall into your lap, probably by referral from a satisfied customer. This can make up for the times you have advertised with few or no results. Aries employees are apt to be in the boss's good books. Efforts which are beyond the call of duty are likely to be duly noticed, praised, and rewarded. If you are looking for a job, or are ready for a change, a career counselor can come up with original ideas for you to consider. Later in the day can be a good time for getting some physical exercise. Keeping fit can boost your energy level and put a new spring in your step.

6. WEDNESDAY. Easygoing. Today's tasks are unlikely to be complicated. You should be able to set your own pace. Much can be accomplished if you settle into a steady rhythm. This is an auspicious time to apply for a better job. You may not think you stand a chance, but this could be a case of nothing ventured, nothing gained. Now is a good time for going after what you really want. Auditions or interviews should go better than you had dared hope. This is a good day for having professional photographs taken of yourself and your family, especially if you want to mark a special occasion. Opt for a natural pose rather than a formal one.

7. THURSDAY. Fair. Someone in authority at work may not be giving you the opportunities that you need to get ahead. Your best policy is to prove that you are good at your job while also going all out to charm them. If you can win their friendship they will be more inclined to champion your cause. If you are planning a group vacation in the near future, trust a friend to make the arrangements. They may have contacts who could come up with a bargain price. Be willing to compromise with your partner this evening, especially when it comes to social arrangements. You could be accused of selfishness if you refuse to bend to their wishes or get together with their friends.

8. FRIDAY. Cautious. Be cautious about placing trust in a stranger. A certain individual is not beyond exploiting your good nature. You need to be more aggressive while avoiding underhanded tactics. Someone in authority might try to pull rank. Remind yourself that you are entitled to be treated as a person in your own right at all times. By refusing to be particularly impressed by titles or position you could soon knock the wind out of someone's sails. A romantic relationship is under some strain. Although you might find yourself hankering after your freedom, consider the companionship you would be giving up.

9. SATURDAY. Mixed. An argument with a friend can get the day off on the wrong foot. This may be caused by a misunderstanding. When you have time to reflect, you might want to set the record straight. There is no point in being at war with someone who matters to you. Try harder to take minor irritations in stride. Make a point of controlling your spending. The urge to splurge at a time when you cannot really afford it could push your budget into the red. If you share a bank account, ask your partner to show the same restraint. Avoid spending in an effort to make an impression.

10. SUNDAY. Promising. Think twice before turning down a social invitation for later in the day. You may not feel in the mood to go out, but once you do you could meet several people with whom you have many interests in common. A new relationship started today could prove to be a lasting one. Someone close to you can be a tower of strength. You may find yourself talking about issues which you have kept to yourself for a long time. By sharing your worries with them you can get important new insights. If you have an important day at work tomorrow or an interview pending, detailed preparation is vital this evening. Pick out your clothes for tomorrow before going to bed tonight.

11. MONDAY. Starred. This is likely to be a busy morning. Exercise extra caution if you have to authorize company expenditure; do not overlook necessary paperwork. This is a good day for reorganizing your filing system. Being able to put your hands on important documents at a moment's notice should improve your overall efficiency. This is a favorable time for installing new communication equipment, such as a fax machine. Talking through a problem with a friend can yield results if you are willing to listen with an open mind. But do not expect them to say just what you want to hear; be prepared for the blunt truth.

12. TUESDAY. Difficult. This is likely to be a demanding day. It may seem impossible to make real headway with a project due soon. It may be better to put it aside for a couple of hours while you clear your head. Long-distance traveling can be time-consuming. Expect delays or cancellations; make sure that you have work or a good book with you to help pass the time. You may have to give up discussing a certain subject with a loved one because it is increasingly apparent that you are never going to see eye-to-eye on this matter. This is a time when you just have to agree to disagree. Give a child the extra attention they crave.

13. WEDNESDAY. Disquieting.   Aries could be in for a rough ride today. If you are attending an important meeting, be sure that you have all the necessary paperwork on hand. Someone is looking for the chance to catch you off guard and unprepared. If you have an interview of any kind, allow extra time for getting to it. Arriving late can start the whole process off on the wrong foot. This is unlikely to be a good day for taking a stand regarding work issues. Just concentrate on getting on with the job and doing it well. A formal occasion this evening can be boring. An attempt to break the ice may fall flat because you do not know the politics of those with whom you are talking.

14. THURSDAY. Productive.   This is a better day when it comes to career concerns. If you make your dissatisfactions known, the boss may go to extraordinary lengths to improve matters. Even if you are not indispensable, it is in their best interests to keep you happy. If you are applying for a new job or a transfer you should be able to secure an excellent reference from your current superior. A community project could succeed beyond your expectations; recognition for your efforts makes your hard work seem especially worthwhile. Advertising for a forthcoming event may produce an overwhelming response; plan on a larger crowd than anticipated.

15. FRIDAY. Fair.   The inefficiency of other people can cause holdups or mistakes at work. Make an extra effort to be tolerant of their shortcomings. You can then expect the same latitude on an occasion when you are at fault. Someone's work may be affected by the stress of a personal problem. Try to take the pressure off them for the time being. This is a favorable day for Aries people who work behind the scenes. Your efforts are apt to be publicly acknowledged and may even result in a bonus. A night out with friends starts the weekend off with a bang. Sports are under favorable influences, and so is a wager on a game.

16. SATURDAY. Sensitive.   Lend support to a charitable project even if a friend who had shown the same interest opts out of helping. Their commitment to social issues may not be as strong as yours. Try not to be judgmental even if you feel let down. Your religious or political beliefs could come under attack. Someone's flippant attitude toward a subject they clearly know nothing about can try your patience. Remind yourself that you do not have to defend your views to anyone; on this occasion it is probably not worth wasting your breath. Do not sit around waiting for a call from someone who is away. It is important to show that you have a life of your own.

17. SUNDAY. Magical.   If you have recently ended a relationship do not be surprised if you receive a telephone call today. This person may not be prepared to go down without a fight. You might consider giving the romance a second chance. Patching up your differences may not be as difficult as you had thought. This can be a favorable day for giving full rein to the romantic side of your nature. A small gift or a bunch of flowers can make your partner feel like a star. If you are celebrating an anniversary or birthday, do not cut corners. Splurge on some champagne or vintage wine to make the occasion extra special.

18. MONDAY. Stressful.   Guard against criticizing someone who is not present to put up a defense. A momentary lapse of discretion is almost sure to get back to them, maybe with added embellishments. If you have a bone to pick with someone, your best policy is to do it face to face and in private. You may sense that there is a lot going on behind the scenes. There is probably no point in probing for information just yet. Trust that what concerns you directly will eventually be brought to your attention. Focus on what you have been assigned to do. Drop on argument with a loved one if you do not want to be accused of nagging.

19. TUESDAY. Routine.   Even if you have not prepared thoroughly for a meeting, decisions are likely to go in your favor. This is a time when can easily think on your feet. Valuable facts can come to mind just when you need them. Single Aries may become aware of an admirer. Someone may have you up on a pedestal without your even realizing it. Married Aries might need to resist the temptation to stray; remind yourself of what you have to lose. If you have mislaid something valuable do not write it off. Contact the police or lost property office; an honest person could have found it and handed it in.

20. WEDNESDAY. Fair. Extra responsibility is probably unavoidable. Self-discipline is a must if you are going to complete the day's agenda. A colleague may come to the rescue with an offer of help. If you are chairing a meeting, guard against holding center stage for too long. One person talking on and on can be boring for others. Make a point of posing questions and gathering in the responses. Try not to belabor a minor point with someone close to you; doing so will probably only make them more stubborn. If someone asks you for advice, give an opinion but not a sermon. There is more than one way to achieve a desired result.

21. THURSDAY. Misleading.   Aim for moderation in all things. Being overly enthusiastic, especially at work, can be mistaken for bossiness. Aries people are usually bold in all that you do, but remind yourself that someone of a quieter disposition could find you intimidating when you are being your most forceful. Bite back impatience and give others a chance to have their say. You have a greater tendency today to indulge in food or drink, but if you are normally careful about your diet an isolated binge will probably do little harm. Be generous with your time; a friend needs some moral support and encouragement from you.

22. FRIDAY. Disquieting.   This morning is unlikely to get off to a tranquil start. You could argue with a family member over matters which are essentially trivial. An apology later in the day may be called for and should deflect a bad atmosphere setting in for the weekend. Apologize even if you were only partly to blame. If you are single, be careful about setting your cap for someone who is on the rebound. You might find yourself playing second fiddle to an ex-partner who is still very much on the scene. Avoid lending money; you may never get it back. This evening is a good time for a trip with friends to visit someone confined to bed after an accident or illness.

23. SATURDAY. Exciting.   Capitalize on the chance to earn some extra cash. One job could lead to other offers. A friend may suggest the idea of a vacation, perhaps over the holiday period. If you have no other plans, this could be an attractive proposition. Even if you have already used up most of your annual leave, you could find that your employer is willing to give you some extra time off, although it will be unpaid. You may feel the urge to do something different this evening because you are tired of your usual haunts. This could be a good time for seeking out some live music or comedy performed by amateurs hoping to break into the entertainment industry.

24. SUNDAY. Challenging.   This morning is a good time for reviewing your financial affairs. Calculate exactly what your bank

balance is at the moment; it could be healthier than you ha
thought. Unexpected money from a relative is a possibility. A
brother or sister may appreciate a gift certificate so that they can
buy exactly what they want. Aries students may have to devote
part of the day to some intensive work, especially if you are up
against a final deadline. Set a time limit so that you can be free
for a social event later in the day. Let someone else do the driving tonight, but still urge caution and safety on the road.

25. MONDAY. Frustrating.   Dealing with a backlog of paperwork can be tedious. If your work involves a lot of administration
you might need to improve your system. This is not the time to
be technology shy. If you have yet to learn to use a computer or
word processor, now is the time. Ask your boss if the company
would send you to a training course. Once you point out the
advantages of upgrading your skills they are unlikely to refuse.
Stress can show in your overall health. Avoid taking too many
pills if you have a tension headache; finding ways in which you
can relax should be more beneficial and healthful in the long run.

26. TUESDAY. Routine.   Aries business men and women can
be most productive staying in the office. Certain projects need
your undivided attention. A staff member may be waiting for
some of your uninterrupted time; be prepared to work through
their problems in depth. If you are planning an office Christmas
party, now is not too early for making a restaurant reservation.
Getting in early means that you should be able to book the place
you want. If you work in sales, this is a good time for chasing
down leads before they go cold. Set this evening aside for relaxing at home. A good book can be your best choice of company.

27. WEDNESDAY. Pleasant.   This promises to be a productive
day. The efficiency of those working with and for you means that
you will complete tasks earlier than anticipated. This is a starred
day for buying an object of beauty for your home, such as a picture or a new lamp. You may find some bargains in furnishings.
Working from home can be enjoyable. If you are part of a large
household, related or not, this evening favors a sitdown meal with
everyone gathered at the table. A sense of unity can count for a
lot. If you are living alone, invite a friend or colleague to share
dinner with you. A late phone call will give you a reason to dream.

28. THURSDAY. Variable.   Today's plans on this Thanksgiving
holiday present some challenges. You may have to increase your
usual tempo. There may not be enough hours in the day to give

as much attention to preparations as you would wish. Working against the clock can create tension. There is no need to take family members' sharp words personally. Hold on to your sense of humor. Some physical exercise can alleviate the strains and stresses of the day. A relative may join you for a long walk or a ride in the country. Travel can be slower than usual. If using public transportation, allow extra time to make connections. Driving demands full attention to the road.

29. FRIDAY. Mixed. Looking after children can be easier if you keep them occupied with individual tasks. Joint activities are likely to end up with bickering or tears. You may have to work harder at not losing your temper. A new hobby may be falling by the wayside as a result of other pressures. Make an extra effort to find time to do the things you enjoy. If you reserve a definite time slot in your weekly calendar you are more likely to succeed. A new romance may be faltering because you are not spending enough quality time together. Consider planning a weekend away so that you can relax together far from the usual pressures and interruptions.

30. SATURDAY. Stressful. Everyone may seem to be getting on your nerves. You need to spend some time alone so that you can please yourself without having to worry about other people's feelings. Staying in someone else's home can be difficult. You might realize that this is a worn-out friendship and that you no longer really have anything in common. All you can do is make an extra effort to be pleasant while you are there. Avoid staying in a romantic relationship for the wrong reasons. Making a break can be hard, but remind yourself that it is better to be single than to be with someone who does not make you happy or bring out the best in you.

DECEMBER

1. SUNDAY. Good. This can be a good day for a family outing. A zoo or amusement arcade can be just as much fun for the adults as the children. If the weather is bad try organizing games at home that everyone can participate in. A child's innocent remark can give you a fresh angle on a personal issue. Sporting activities are likely to be high on the agenda this afternoon. If you are playing a competitive match you have a good chance of being on the winning side. This is an auspicious time for announcing an engagement, pregnancy, or adoption. The news should meet with approval and delight all around. News from someone at a distance can be cause for celebration and gift buying.

2. MONDAY. Disquieting. It may be more difficult than usual to get out of bed on time this morning. Resist the temptation to roll over and go back to sleep, this will almost certainly put you behind schedule for the rest of the day. If you are suffering from low energy, take a look at your diet. Consider extra vitamin supplements during the winter months. Try to cut down on the things which you know are bad for you. Conducting a long-distance business or personal relationship can be difficult. You might want to schedule a visit soon for a face-to-face meeting. Overtime at work could put a social arrangement later in the day on hold or force you to cancel it.

3. TUESDAY. Variable. Guard against using aggressive tactics in your business dealings. You may get what you want this time, but there is a greater risk of damaging your prospects for the future. Do not win the battle at the expense of losing the war. Be cautious about accepting extravagant hospitality from a mere acquaintance; there could be strings attached. If you work with machinery, be sure to follow safety procedures to the letter. Personal injury can be avoided with proper care and caution. Do not leave potentially dangerous objects lying around at home. Put them away as soon as you have finished the job. Be sure that all medicine is out of the reach of youngsters.

4. WEDNESDAY. Demanding. You may feel that you cannot put a foot right this morning. A certain individual seems determined to find fault with you. Your best policy is not to rise to their bait; a shouting match is unlikely to benefit anyone. If someone is on the warpath, stay out of their way as much as possible. Aries in new relationships need to tread gently. There is no point pushing someone into making a commitment to you. They may genuinely not be in a position to give you what you want right now. Be patient and try not to think too much about the future. Remind yourself that what really matters is making the most of the here and now.

5. THURSDAY. Starred. This can be a lucky day if you get out and about. Someone in an influential position may take an instant liking to you on first meeting. This can do much to boost your confidence and reputation. An offer to work in a different location should not be dismissed out of hand; it could be a golden opportunity. Talk through the proposition with family members. They may be more willing to embrace change than you had realized. This can be an excellent time for committing yourself to obtaining further education or taking an on-the-job training course related to your career. Discussing your goals and aspirations with a loved one could make you aware of your true vocation.

6. FRIDAY. Deceptive. All that glitters is not gold. If someone you hardly know starts turning on the charm, it is wise to hold back; their motives could be unclear. Nurture a healthy skepticism and do not fall prey to flattery. This is unlikely to be a good day for entering into a new partnership. Do not ignore suspicions or doubts flashing warning signals at the back of your mind; they should be heeded. Delay signing any binding contract until the beginning of next week. Refuse to be rushed into making decisions of any kind today. Certain information could soon come to light which can put a whole new perspective on matters. Making a loan to a friend could cost you not only money but the friendship as well.

7. SATURDAY. Productive. If you have not started your holiday shopping, this is a good day for doing so. Get to the stores early to avoid the worst of the crowds. If you are unsure of what to buy for certain relatives, simply ask them what they want. This could save you from making expensive mistakes. If you have a partner, make sure that you do not double up on gifts for each other's family. For Aries who are unemployed at the moment, this can be a good day for finding seasonal work, which may be more lucrative than you realized. This evening favors an intimate candlelight dinner with that special someone in your life. Let go of inhibitions so that love can grow.

8. SUNDAY. Stimulating. A person with mystical beliefs can capture your imagination. Even if you have no strong religious convictions, a lot of what they say could sound like common sense. If you have had psychic flashes yourself, now is a good time to work at developing them. Aries tend to be creative; making something for your home can bring a great deal of satisfaction. Odd repair jobs around the house which were started some time ago should be tackled today. It will be a relief to get them out of the way. In your personal relationships this is not a time for playing mind games. Be honest about your feelings if you want someone to take you seriously and open up to you.

9. MONDAY. Fortunate. This is an excellent start to the work-week. Some fast thinking could save you from losing a valued customer or losing the edge to a competitor. A deal which you believed was lost may now be resurrected. This can be a favorable time for business mergers; pooling resources can open up new opportunities. If you work as part of a team, pass out praise to the other team members for recent achievements. A certain individual needs this boost to their confidence. Refigure expenses for Christmas. Some careful planning now could help you stick to a budget. Gifts that you make rather than buy are sure to be appreciated.

10. TUESDAY. Stressful. Aries business people may have to fit in a long-distance trip before the holiday season begins. Make arrangements now so that you can be sure of securing appointments with the people you need to see. Business plans for the coming year should be discussed fully with other staff members or associates. Do not let someone feel they have been passed over or ignored. Full-time Aries students may be racing against the clock to finish written work before the holiday break. Legal matters may slow to a crawl. Someone may be dragging their feet in the hope of delaying a final decision for as long as possible. Heed advice from a lawyer or other professional.

11. WEDNESDAY. Mixed. If you are looking for a new job it may be difficult to schedule interviews before the holiday. If unemployed now, your best policy is to look for seasonal work as a stopgap. Pressure in the office is likely to be higher than usual. You may have to forgo a lunch break or put in some extra time this evening in order to meet a deadline. Meetings could run on and on; someone may challenge you over every point you make. Family obligations can play havoc with social arrangements for later in the day. It might not be possible to keep everyone happy, but do not allow someone close to you to exert emotional blackmail in an effort to get their way.

12. THURSDAY. Good. This is an excellent day for entertaining business clients at lunch. Going out together shows your valued customers how much you appreciate the work they have steered your way this year. This should be a favorable time for helping out with a charitable project in the community. Be generous if asked to make a donation to a good cause. Aries retailers who are now approaching the busiest time of year might consider a final advertising push. The extra revenue that you attract should more than cover costs. This evening is favorable for an office party. Take the chance to get to know someone on a more personal level.

13. FRIDAY. Sensitive. A friend's turbulent love life can be a cause for concern. They may need both moral support and some frank advice. Although it would probably be unwise to make decisions for them, you may yet be able to get them to think twice about a rash course of action. This is a busy end to the working week. Make an extra effort to be well organized or you could feel as if you are going around in circles. Last-minute bookings for a Christmas vacation can be hard to come by; you might have to spend more than you had budgeted. Tickets for the theater or a children's performance should be reserved now. Keep a promise to a friend no matter what other offers come along.

14. SATURDAY. Rewarding. Make a point of doing the bulk of your holiday shopping today. Get an early start if you can. A good friend can come up with some invaluable suggestions when it comes to deciding on gifts for those close to you. Keep on the lookout for excellent bargains in books. A subscription to a favorite publication could make the perfect gift. This is a good time for mailing off greeting cards or gift parcels; they may not arrive on time if you wait any longer. You are apt to have a choice of social events for this evening. A party which you know will be well attended by good friends is likely to be the best option. If you cannot relax and be yourself you will not have much fun.

15. SUNDAY. Cautious. This is a favorable day for relaxing in the comfort of your home. Your energy level may be flagging, especially if you have been burning the candle at both ends. Plans for some of the holiday period may have to be altered. If you have been planning a long-distance trip, a traveling companion may pull out altogether. Find out about refunds on train or air tickets before you make any final decisions. Single Aries may still be undecided about where to spend the vacation. You are unlikely to be short of offers. Consider breaking with tradition, even though a relative may find this hard to understand or accept. A need to assert your independence may be motivating you.

16. MONDAY. Useful. Today's mail could bring a card from someone you had lost touch with. A note from an old flame could rekindle romantic feelings. This is a good day for tying up loose ends at work. Administrative tasks can be brought up to date if you lock your office door for a few hours and turn on the telephone answering machine. You can always return calls later in the day. If you have not already sent out all your Christmas greetings, make sure that the rest go out today. Find a safe hiding place for gifts for your partner or children. An invitation to an exclusive party could be a pleasant surprise. If unsure what to wear, it is better to overdress than to be too casual.

17. TUESDAY. Fair. If you are at home today try to get all of your chores done in the morning. This way you will be free to accept a social invitation from a friend, maybe to meet for lunch. Matinee tickets for a theatrical performance can be good value. At work the pressure is likely to ease off as the day goes on, but be prepared for a frantically busy morning. If you need to make an official complaint, do not be stalled by someone who is clearly not in a position to make decisions; demand to see the person at the top. This evening favors an impromptu get-together. Invite friends both from work and your own social circle to drop by for dessert. A new cycle beginning today favors harmonious social relations.

18. WEDNESDAY. Promising. Be completely honest in all of your business dealings today. There is no point in promising to meet a deadline if you know that you are cutting it fine. Assurances from a superior at work may be sincere at the time, but they could be quickly forgotten. It is up to you to remind them of verbal promises or to put requests in writing. If you are planning to leave on vacation during the next couple of days, now is the time to finalize paperwork such as picking up tickets and writing instructions for the person who will be caring for your pet. Deliver a gift in person if possible. If a friend has forgotten to repay a loan, call with a kindly reminder.

19. THURSDAY. Deceptive. The details of business functions need to be double-checked. A change of time or location may not have been passed on to you. A speech can be boring or just too long; you may find it difficult to concentrate on what is being said. Guard against drinking any alcohol at a business lunch, especially if you have to return to the office. You need all your wits this afternoon in order to deal with an unexpected problem. If you go shopping later, keep a close watch on your personal belongings. Pickpockets can be a bigger risk than usual at this time of year. Do not contribute money to a charity you have never heard of.

20. FRIDAY. Calm. This is a leisurely end to the working week. The festive mood is in full swing by now; an office party can be fun. Someone may use this as an excuse to flirt with you, but do not take their attentions too seriously. For Aries who are paid today there could be a welcome Christmas bonus. For those who work on commission, this should be an especially lucrative day. If you are expecting guests at home over the holiday period, do not put off planning menus. Make sure that you do not forget to make provisions for someone who is vegetarian or allergic to certain food. Bring along a small gift for your host or hostess if you are going to a party tonight.

21. SATURDAY. Good. If you work on the weekends serving the general public, this can be a lucrative day. People are more inclined to leave generous tips. If you have put off your Christmas shopping until the last minute there is no need to worry too much. Today you should be able to find just what you are looking for without too much effort. Someone in the family may know exactly what certain relatives are hoping to receive. This evening is an excellent time for entertaining at home. Make it a grand occasion; use your best linen, silverware, and china. Candles and mistletoe can create a romantic atmosphere for you as well as your guests.

22. SUNDAY. Disconcerting. If you were expecting someone home for the holidays, there may be news of a change in plans. They might have to postpone their trip until the new year or cancel altogether. Try not to let this disappointment spoil the festivities for you. If you are traveling a long distance be prepared for delays. Allow extra time for getting to your destination; local traffic is likely to be much heavier than usual. If your car has been acting up, ask a mechanic at your local garage to have a look at it before they close for the holidays. A party this evening can be fun, but do not risk drinking and driving. An early gift could be the best of all.

23. MONDAY. Quiet. The business world is likely to be in a state of limbo, with many of your associates already on vacation. Aries employees who have to be in the office will probably have very little to do. To avoid boredom, concentrate on administrative jobs which get pushed aside when you are busy. You may want to reorganize your filing system or bring your address lists up to date. Make a call to someone who was inadvertently left off your Christmas card list. Shops may be open late this evening; you might be able to pick up last-minute presents or extra wrapping paper at a bargain price. If you are perplexed about a gift, money is always appreciated.

24. TUESDAY. Unsettling. If you are going away for the holiday period give extra thought to your home security. Do not make it easy for a burglar to break in. Double locks and timed light switches can be helpful. Do not forget to cancel home deliveries, such as mail or newspapers. If you are staying home for the holidays, you are likely to be busy with last-minute tasks. Being with members of your family whom you have not seen for a while may be hard going at first; someone may not be in a particularly festive mood. But the atmosphere should lighten up as the day goes on. Burying the hatchet over a past argument can be a relief not only for those involved but for all family members.

25. WEDNESDAY. MERRY CHRISTMAS! If you are celebrating the day at home you could be in for an early start, especially if you have young children. Urging them to go back to bed for a while is unlikely to have any effect; you might as well enter into the spirit of things straight away. Opening presents can be a boisterous affair and could take up most of the morning. Plan on having your main meal slightly later than usual. A good movie on television can be relaxing later in the day. This evening is favorable for more active pursuits, such as board games or putting together a new toy. Talking late into the night with a loved one can be revealing.

26. THURSDAY. Mixed. This morning is a good time for getting some fresh air, especially if you overdid the food and drink yesterday. A walk in the park or more strenuous exercise could be just what you need to feel more lively. For Aries who have to work today, the morning can be demanding. It may be difficult to switch into a work mode, but there is a good chance that you can get away earlier than you had expected. If you have young children plan on taking them out this afternoon. For Aries who are unattached, a party invitation for this evening is something to look forward to; you may come face to face with a fascinating character who soon will become your love interest.

27. FRIDAY. Happy. If you are at home make a point of devoting the day to pure leisure. Having time to indulge a creative hobby to its full extent can be a special joy. Young children can be a pleasure to have around; their enthusiasm and sense of fun will surely rub off on you. This afternoon favors taking part in some sport. Exercise that is fun can help take off the few extra pounds that you may have put on over the past few days. If you are away for the holiday period, this can be an excellent day for sightseeing or learning more about local culture. An evening spent only with your love partner is likely to be a time of great contentment.

28. SATURDAY. Relaxing. Young children may be restless now that the excitement of the festivities is wearing off. They can be easily entertained if you are prepared to play games with them or go out to the park. This is a good day for spending money which you received as a Christmas gift. Browse through stores that have already started their sales. Make a point of buying something which you would normally regard as a luxury item, such as brand-name colognes or toiletries. Consider adding to your music collection or getting special supplies for a hobby. If you have been apart from your loved one, a reunion this evening can be a very special occasion.

29. SUNDAY. Disquieting. Long-distance traveling today can be tiring. A flight may be rescheduled. If you are returning from another country, the time change could be just what your body does not need. It may be best to stay awake and go to bed at the usual time tonight; this should make the adjustment easier. Aries students may have to fit in some studying today. Try not to expect too much of yourself; start with something which is relatively easy to tackle. A guest may be overstaying their welcome. You may not be able to say anything directly, but do not let them stop you from keeping your usual social commitments and chatting with friends.

30. MONDAY. Variable. Aries employees who are back at work may find it difficult to get going this morning. However, the day should become easier than you had expected. Exchanging news with your colleagues can be entertaining. If you are out of work at the moment, this is a favorable time for planning a strategy for the new year. If you sign up now with some employment agencies they may be able to line up interviews for you at the beginning of January. A minor health ailment may be on your mind. A friend or colleague can recommend a book to read that gives you insight into the problem and possible cures. Make an appointment with your doctor or dentist to put your mind at ease.

31. TUESDAY. Fair. Work commitments or domestic chores can take up most of the morning, but you should be able to race through these more quickly than usual. This is not a good day for relying on others to do things on your behalf. You should get on much faster if you just do them yourself in your own way. Although someone else's slowness can be irritating, make an effort to stifle the criticisms that spring to mind. Even if you do not normally make much of New Year's Eve, this is one which you should not miss. Welcome 1997 with a loved one at your side. If you are throwing your own party, it is almost sure to be a roaring success extending into the wee hours. Happy New Year!

November–December 1995
NOVEMBER

1. WEDNESDAY. Mixed. Do nothing that will arouse the jealousy or resentment of trusted acquaintances. Do not take their friendship for granted, and avoid asking financial favors of them. Business profits can be diminished through unforeseen overhead, bank charges, or taxes. In humanitarian and altruistic ventures, make sure that personality factors and conflicts are firmly excluded; power struggles must be prevented for success to result. Influential people tend to be most helpful if you catch them at their most informal. Individuals who operate behind the scenes are also cooperative. Do not expect too much of people who are ill.

2. THURSDAY. Unsettling. By the end of today you may feel you have become a pawn of fate. There is a greater risk of personal wishes being thwarted and frustrated. With all the best intentions in the world, it can still seem that people are only too ready to misunderstand you. Do not overestimate your ability to change situations or people's attitudes. Where financial affairs are concerned, individuals who appear to be granting you a favor are probably doing the opposite. In business and career activities there is a greater risk of lengthy negotiations proving useless.

3. FRIDAY. Positive. You can do more than you may have realized to appease a bad conscience and be free once and for all from regrets that have been nagging at you for some time. Make a commitment to yourself to break negative habits; you will find it surprisingly easy to keep. Consider new approaches to old problems in business and career affairs. Time-saving technology may prove invaluable and perfectly suited to your personal needs. Put away any extra savings or income into long-term investments. Aries intuition is probably worth following and investigating. Do some digging and delving behind the scenes.

4. SATURDAY. Good. Press ahead with personal plans and schemes. Use that Aries dynamism and willpower to get yourself where you want to go. Let the sky be the limit; be prepared to realize what other people only dream of achieving. A positive attitude is all important. Tell yourself that you will succeed and find greater fulfillment in your life, and that is precisely what will happen. Conditions are good for making an unscheduled journey, possibly somewhere at a distance. Take the bull by the horns when dealing with people you hardly know; they will respect your honesty and forthrightness. Sign up to take a self-improvement course.

5. SUNDAY. Deceptive. You may not be at the peak of your form today and should not pretend otherwise. If tired or under the weather, there is a greater risk of making mistakes or errors of judgment. Avoid making commitments and then shirking or avoiding them. Face up to aspects of yourself that you would like to change. Overindulgence must be tackled if you are to become the person you really want to be. Do not use unhealthy habits as a way of forgetting yourself and your problems. Be careful on slippery surfaces or high places; there is a greater risk of minor accidents. Guard against shady or underhanded dealings even if you consider your motivations aboveboard and honorable.

6. MONDAY. Disquieting. Use plain good common Aries sense where finances are concerned. Do not waste time and energy asking people questions to which you already know the answer. Individuals who try to make financial decisions for you are hardly likely to be acting in your own best interests. Keep your wallet in a safe place and well guarded. There is a greater risk of pickpockets or simply of mislaying valuable items through carelessness. Plastic money undoubtedly has its advantages, but it may also involve you in hidden expenses. When making purchases be sure to obtain and keep receipts. As soon as possible, check everything you buy for possible manufacturing defects or missing parts.

7. TUESDAY. Variable. People on whom you depend can be slow off the mark, especially where financial affairs are concerned. Applications for a pay raise are less likely to be accepted. Litigation proceedings are best postponed if possible; judges or lawyers may fail to give your side of the story a proper hearing. The day favors attempts at achieving results by more devious or roundabout routes. Avoid publicity. Business and career interests can be furthered by keeping important new projects under wraps and keeping discussions behind closed doors. Influential people tend to be more concerned about maintaining their own positions and can be unwilling to support anything that might compromise them.

8. WEDNESDAY. Frustrating. Avoid making mountains out of molehills where money matters are concerned. Do not let financial differences between you and your loved ones degenerate into power struggles or arguments over who has the last word. Information that is vital to your business or professional activities can cost more than you had expected. In research projects or investigations, do not lose sight of the forest for all the trees. Keep a sense of perspective, and above all do not ignore data just because it does not fit in with your preconceived ideas. Your romantic partner may need to travel to distant places, resulting in a temporary separation. Absence will make the heart grow fonder.

9. THURSDAY. Difficult. This has not tended to be the smoothest or easiest of weeks, but it is important that you not let impatience and frustration get the better of you. Stick to doing one thing at a time. Avoid attempting to cram too much into a single journey. Schedules are likely to be tight, and you will probably have less time to spare than you had anticipated. When traveling leave enough time to make connections. Otherwise you will arrive at your destination tense and tired. If driving, guard against speeding. Inconsiderate neighbors may cause some minor problems. The best course is to let them know they are annoying you.

10. FRIDAY. Mixed. You are likely to reap the rewards for actions performed in the past. On the other hand, there is also a greater risk of past actions catching up with you and enforcing some limitations on your plans for the future. Keep detailed records of important conversations and transactions; you will need to refer back to them at some later date. Bankers tend to be more helpful. If trying to win a contract with a large company or corporation, you can be very lucky if you manage to get through to the person at the top. The fact that someone is ill and needs looking after may require you to make significant modifications.

11. SATURDAY. Good. Pay full attention to that project that has been simmering on the back burner for quite a while. At the very least, getting it finished will mean that you have less on your mind. And more positively, you may find that you have a very lucrative scheme on your hands and could wonder why you did not act on it much sooner. Conditions are favorable for visiting members of the family, or inviting them to your place for the weekend. This is a good day for home entertaining, and especially for renewing the acquaintance of people you have drifted away from over the past few months. Shop for something special to brighten your home surroundings. Self-improvement endeavors are starred.

12. SUNDAY. Variable. This is another favorable day for all matters relating to the home. Do whatever you can to make it an even more peaceful place, so that it can become a welcome shelter from the pressures and demands of living. Finish off that do-it-yourself job which you keep postponing. You will be surprised at how easy it is to do some practical and basic jobs. Double-check all work that involves plumbing and water systems; any leaks that you unwittingly cause could mean considerable inconvenience. The health of a member of the family or household is likely to improve, perhaps considerably. Evening is good for entertaining.

13. MONDAY. Disquieting. Creativity and freedom of expression may become major issues today. Do what you can to introduce that special personal touch into all of your tasks and chores. Aries men and women are likely to get ahead much better in jobs where your artistic side is not only tolerated but encouraged. However, there is a greater risk of conflicts with co-workers. Resentments can flare up over nothing. Language problems may create a serious misunderstanding. Even cultural differences can create complications if you assume that people from distant places will perceive things the same way as you. A potential conflict with older relatives may flare up and come to a head.

14. TUESDAY. Fair. The morning can produce missed opportunity, especially if you spend too much time on the telephone. Youngsters are unlikely to heed your words, and they are apt to forget to pass on a message. In artistic projects and endeavors, be more spontaneous; think with your heart, not your head. Check that financial information is accurate before dealing in stocks and bonds. This is a favorable day for romance. Take the opportunity now before it is too late to get to know someone from a distance to whom you are especially attracted. Actions speak louder than words. Discussions of a philosophical or religious nature can be particularly stimulating.

15. WEDNESDAY. Happy. You may at last receive confirmation of certain arrangements and can put your mind at rest. Information received from people who operate behind the scenes can prove especially useful, particularly where investment and other financial affairs are concerned. There is a greater risk of children landing in trouble with teachers or the authorities. But do not be too harsh on them, as the situation is probably not as black and white as it might seem. Guard against creating problems at work where no problem need exist. Feelings of inferiority about your supposed lack of qualifications are quite unnecessary. Lack of formal training is not the impediment you imagine.

16. THURSDAY. Good. Outwardly this should be a fairly relaxed day. You can produce good results at work with a minimum of effort. Pay more attention to your health. Spend some time in a health store to see what is new in the way of vitamin and mineral products. There may be something ideal for your needs and your situation. Influential people can be crafty and pull off a special feat on your behalf. Honor their wishes if they ask that you keep the matter strictly confidential. A strong sense of impatience and dissatisfaction with the direction that your life is taking may come to the surface. Seriously consider making that journey.

17. FRIDAY. Stressful. Deep inside yourself you know that everything is for the best. However, this may not make it altogether easy to be philosophical where certain aspects of your life are concerned. Your romantic partners can succeed in pressing all your emotional buttons and even making you feel rather guilty. But do not give in to these pressures. Stand strong against what might be a subtle form of emotional blackmail. If working to help the poor or underprivileged, expect little or no thanks for your efforts, especially from the very people you are trying to help. Health needs protecting. You deserve some peace and rest.

18. SATURDAY. Useful. Stick firmly to your goals and your ideas. They can make all the difference, transforming what would otherwise be petty and pointless difficulties into interesting trials and tests of your character. Look for ways to develop your intellectual and spiritual interests, possibly through reading accompanied by serious discussions with friends. This can be a favorable day for attending spiritual gatherings or going to visit a healer or medium. It does not mean that you have to accept everything you are told; what is important is to broaden your own vision and raise your vibrations. A confidential discussion can be beneficial to your long-term career prospects.

19. SUNDAY. Fair. This is a particularly auspicious day for love and romance. A new romantic beginning made now may mark a turning point in your life. If you and your partner share the same thirst for self-improvement and spiritual values, there is no limit to what you can achieve together. Romance can be a perfectly valid reason for moving your home base and going to live elsewhere, possibly at a distance. Marriage is especially favored and, surprisingly to some, is likely to lead to greater freedom for both of you. With the right attitude and aspirations, whatever you do today will tend to work out satisfactorily. Pay no attention to idle gossip and certainly do not repeat it.

20. MONDAY. Profitable. Changes in your personal life are likely to be reflected in your professional and business affairs.

Influential people can spot the fact that you are no longer the same person, and this may lead to forming an entirely different relationship with them. There is less need either to compromise or to conform. People are probably looking to you to set the pace and initiate new trends. Sound financial proposals can win major backing for large organizations or corporations. Similarly, daring ideas may receive substantial backing from the most unusual sources, possibly in the form of a grant. Aries involved in research work can come up with spectacular results.

21. TUESDAY. Good. The best results today are achieved through modesty and self-effacement. If you try being more open to new ideas, people will tend to respect you more, waste your time less, and be more explicit about how much you mean to them. There is no need to push ahead with your business and career affairs. You have already set the wheels in motion; all you need to do now is watch how matters proceed and interfere as little as possible. There is a greater chance of benefiting from legacies or inheritances. Try different tactics in advertising or in ways of attracting public attention. Newspaper coverage can boost your prestige and reputation in the most positive ways.

22. WEDNESDAY. Successful. This is a favorable day for making new starts, especially in partnership and cooperative ventures. Focus on the financial side of such activities. Sound handling of money matters is a must, and the key to success. Conditions are good for initiating new business deals with conglomerates and large corporations. Investigative or detective work can uncover important facts and information. New ideas of yours may be a breakthrough. If they relate to design or industry, do not delay in applying for a patent. Love and romance can leave you breathless.

23. THURSDAY. Unsettling. Do not fly up to cloud nine just because of a trivial piece of good news. Overconfidence or too much optimism can make you careless. Breakthroughs and achievements, however great or small, need to be consolidated before you can afford to celebrate. People at or from a distance tend to be more helpful. However, foreign officials are likely to prove bureaucratic and may seem almost to enjoy creating unnecessary problems. Having to care for or take responsibility for someone may mean that your hands are tied and that you are unable to take full advantage of an attractive new opportunity. Avoid engaging in power struggles, especially outside your own territory. Relax and give thanks on this holiday.

24. FRIDAY. Quiet. You can afford to take things easier and relax more. But this is not to say that you should forget your higher aims and ambitions. Use any tranquil moments for reviewing your progress over the past few months. Plot how far you have come along the route to the fulfillment you not only crave but also deserve. Qualifications, or the lack of them, may prove more crucial to your success than you realize or are willing to admit. Now is not too late to enroll in special training or correspondence courses. Ivory tower types can offer some expert advice. Participating in organized sport should be a way of letting off steam.

25. SATURDAY. Variable. Something you have mislaid or forgotten can disorient you and make you lose your bearings. Make sure that you have access to a spare set of keys, especially to your home or car. People tend to be more unreliable, particularly if you are hoping to get some extra work or business done over the weekend. Try to be more self-dependent. If someone is gossiping behind your back, confront them about the matter directly and leave no possible room for further doubt in their mind. Time spent alone later in the afternoon or evening can be profitable and is also likely to give you a greater sense of self-awareness and purpose.

26. SUNDAY. Fair. Household arrangements can easily degenerate into confusion and chaos. With family members wishing to shift responsibilities to other people, it may well be you who are left holding the bag. Try to be more understanding if loved ones feel a sudden need to visit or even stay for a while with their folks. Something unexpected can happen which is likely to produce a distinct shift in your life values, ambitions, and wishes for achievement. This can be disconcerting, but in the long run it will open up more possibilities for genuine fulfillment. Social events can be a good context for meeting or getting to know influential people. Consider making a special journey tomorrow.

27. MONDAY. Good. This is an auspicious day for all kinds and modes of travel. In particular, a journey to distant places can pave the way for the fulfillment of your most secret hopes and dreams. Grab at any opportunity which will enable you to broaden your horizons. Offers of work received from abroad are well worth following up. You can excel in all aspects of the importing or exporting business, as well as in teaming up with foreign experts or university people. Special study courses may provide the skills that will give a truly international dimension to your work or career. Close friends of yours can be lucky today, and their luck may well rub off on you.

28. TUESDAY. Manageable. The morning is favorable for pushing ahead with plans you started to put into action yesterday. Friends or acquaintances continue to be a source of good luck, inspiration, and energetic support for your own personal plans and schemes. Do not take no for an answer, especially in dealings with people at or from a distance. Call in a knowledgeable friend to help you with a language difficulty. Review thoroughly for an examination and you are likely to shoot to the top of the class. But later in the day calls for more modesty and self-restraint. A particular strategy that has worked well for you once or twice may no longer prove so successful. Romance is sure to be happy.

29. WEDNESDAY. Disquieting. This day can bring occasional small disappointments. But look on the bright side. There will also be plenty of opportunities for learning from your mistakes and understanding where you have tended to go wrong in the past. Do not engage in activities that go against the grain, make you uneasy, or jar against your inner sense of right and wrong. You may have good reasons for wanting to smother the voice of your conscience. However, in the long run it is best that you listen to it now before it is too late, even if doing so means having to turn down an attractive opportunity. Keep your plans simple.

30. THURSDAY. Mixed. A sense of wonder at the sheer mystery of life can spur you on to investigate areas you would otherwise have left alone. Remember that there is much more to living than what can be understood rationally. Work at developing and nurturing your intuition; it can stand you in good stead not only in your personal affairs but also in your career or profession. There is nothing immoral in taking advantage of other people's confusion or dishonesty, provided it does not hurt anyone who is innocent. Avoid trying to overcome obstacles through naked force.

DECEMBER

1. FRIDAY. Good. Employers, superiors, and government officials tend to be on your side. Even if you are strictly an amateur in your field of interest, professional or academic people can give you formal backing and confirm the correctness of your ideas. Conditions are favorable for all college and university work. Aries teachers and students are likely to find their work becoming more and more fulfilling from the personal point of view. Those of you who lack typing or writing skills should consider enrolling in a course that will provide you with them. Being able to get your views across to a wide audience is imperative.

2. SATURDAY. Deceptive. The day is likely to start on an optimistic note. But as always with Aries people, there is a danger of overestimating the extent to which others may be willing to go along with your more daring or enterprising schemes. Travel is favorable, but something you leave behind at home or at work may make the journey less than totally successful. In dealings with people you know only casually or not at all, give them the benefit of the doubt up to a certain point. However, if you place too much trust in them there is a very real danger of deception. Do not expect routine business matters to look after themselves.

3. SUNDAY. Positive. This is a favorable day for putting in some overtime at work if you have the desire and if the opportunity presents itself. You can make particularly rapid progress with your tasks and chores, and enjoy them at the same time. For Aries professional people able to determine your own schedules, it is possible that working the occasional weekend and taking a midweek break will have definite pluses and allow you to get the necessary advantage over your competitors. Tackle that financial matter you have been putting off and keep avoiding. The task itself is much less distasteful than you had imagined, and through it there may be ways of adding substantially to your income.

4. MONDAY. Disquieting. This is another favorable day for routine financial affairs. Sheer hard work and perseverance can lead to bonuses and other monetary perks. Someone may repay you a sum of money which you had lent them a while ago and never expected to see returned. Give a little something additional to charity. Take extra care to record all your financial transactions. Failure to do so in the past may now be causing some complications, or possibly may mean that you are unable to claim certain expenses to which you are entitled. Contacts with people at a distance can be burdened with misunderstandings. Someone may still be holding a grudge against you from long ago.

5. TUESDAY. Variable. You may be able to pick up a real bargain in computerware or other modern technology. Time-saving devices, whether for work or home, can be a genuine investment. Extra offers of income from an unexpected source are well worth looking into; there may be opportunities for earning big money. It is a good day for holiday shopping; opt for something unusual and your present is sure to be a success. Keep your plans flexible today and also for the rest of the month. Learn to adapt more to other people's wishes and to changing circumstances. Avoid becoming obsessive about one particular idea.

6. WEDNESDAY. Stressful. You may feel you are coming under crossfire, especially in matters relating to career or business planning. There are a lot of factors to juggle when drawing up plans and schedules for the coming few weeks and months. Your favored project could meet with opposition from influential people. But do not become discouraged. Today emotions and tempers can flare up out of all proportion to the actual issues involved. People may try to raise matters of so-called principle as a cloak for furthering their own ambitions. Persist with your own plans, but discreetly. Avoid challenging authority, and keep a low profile.

7. THURSDAY. Difficult. Again your personal plans and interests can come under attack. But at least today it will be easier to see people's true motives and motivations. Lengthy discussion and negotiations tend to be unproductive. Those with whom you are dealing will simply start to shift the goalposts when they see that their own interests are threatened. When trying to ensure that justice is done, correspondence is likely to be ineffective. Personal meetings will be more successful, but trying to arrange such an interview today can prove quite impossible. Plans for travel can go haywire. A missed connection may mean having to stay overnight in less than ideal accommodations.

8. FRIDAY. Fair. You cannot necessarily blame family or household members for becoming angry; you are not altogether as innocent as you might imagine. Be more careful with delicate objects around the home, especially if they are valuable; there is a greater risk of breakage. Meeting deadlines may prove more difficult than anticipated. Do your best, but do not worry if you cannot achieve the impossible. This is an altogether more auspicious day for travel, provided that you leave your domestic affairs in good order. Conditions are also favorable for negotiations with people at or from a distance. These could have an energizing effect on your life over the next few months or even years.

9. SATURDAY. Mixed. Your plans for a perfect weekend may not work out quite as anticipated. It is possible that you will end up spending more time alone. However you may pretend to dislike solitary activity, it can prove a blessing in disguise. A minor disagreement with loved ones should cause you no concern. Your romantic partner is almost bound to come around to your way of thinking by the start of next week. A more introspective attitude is especially valuable. The still small voice inside you can amaze you with its wisdom and experience. Consider spending more time in natural surroundings.

10. SUNDAY. Disquieting. Trying to break old habits can prove more of a wrench than you had anticipated. The departure of a family or household member to live elsewhere may leave you feeling rather unsettled and lonely. But there are plenty of opportunities for finding greater fulfillment through your own interests and activities rather than trying to live through other people. All creative and artistic endeavors are favored. Take up a new hobby, especially one that will help you broaden your horizons. Stick well within the limits of the law, especially if traveling in a foreign country. Do not let the pain of past disappointment stand between you and the future.

11. MONDAY. Good. This can be an altogether reassuring and positive start to the workweek. Employers or superiors can be particularly cooperative. They may allow you more opportunities for combining work and pleasure. Those of you who are self-employed or considering taking up self-employment can find that you are eligible for special grants or government assistance. Theater projects may win substantial backing. This can be a memorable day for romance. An old flame may reappear out of your past; if you are single, this can mean that your days of loneliness are at an end. Those of you who are married or in a serious relationship are likely to achieve deeper intimacy with your loved one.

12. TUESDAY. Quiet. Pressures of routine work tend to be diminished today. Do not work at top speed if there is no real need to do so. In creative endeavors, the key to success lies in doing what you most enjoy. Aries employees may find that a change in management policy gives you more opportunity to do jobs in the way that you prefer. A day off from work can be a good idea if you are able to afford it. Spend more time with children; catch up on their news, their interests, and share their growing-up problems with them. Also, learn to relate to the child in yourself. Being too worldly-wise can limit you and make you forget about the simple marvels of life, nature, and the universe around us.

13. WEDNESDAY. Fair. Worries about your health are probably exaggerated. If in doubt, make an appointment to see a specialist. Similarly, it is possible that you are blowing your fears about a certain task or job out of all proportion. If you have been entrusted with a particular responsibility that you feel may be beyond your powers to carry through, do a trial run. Break the task down into its component parts and see precisely where, if anywhere, the real difficulty lies. You can do more than you realize, but you need to do them in the right order. Learn to walk before you try to run. A brilliant piece of work that you hand in today can pave the way for a promotion.

14. THURSDAY. Variable. Do not force yourself to keep going if you feel tired and run-down. The holiday period is always hectic, and this year is certainly no exception. Keep warm, especially in old buildings. Try to avoid the company of people who have infections that are obviously contagious. Charm can work wonders in your place of work. A flirtation with a co-worker may point the way to something more serious, but do not rush matters. You should have no trouble at all in winning the heart of the public. Influential people can be less cooperative and may even feel threatened by your success. Employers are likely to remain tight-lipped about their plans for the future.

15. FRIDAY. Misleading. You still have the tendency to overreach in routine work affairs. The best policy is to take things one step at a time. Do not be too ambitious, and do not expect others to make long-term commitments just for your sake. Avoid overindulgence in food or drink; there will be plenty of opportunity for that later in the month. A change of routine or environment can produce a marked improvement in your health and general sense of well-being. The afternoon and evening are favorable for partnership ventures, especially those aimed at expanding existing business through diversification. Later, have a profound, heart-to-heart talk with your loved one or spouse.

16. SATURDAY. Deceptive. Be more patient with loved ones and partners, even if they seem determined to do whatever they can to provoke you. If they are under particular pressure, try to help by sharing their burdens. This is sensitive day for all career and professional affairs. Do not try underhanded tactics to obtain the results you want, even if you consider your actions morally justified. Charm is likely to get you nowhere. There is a greater risk of Aries being discriminated against, but you do not have enough solid evidence to be able to prove this is the case. Do not expect romantic partners to stand by you in your most ambitious aims. On your own you can reach new heights.

17. SUNDAY. Variable. This is another sensitive day for partnership affairs. There is a greater danger of misunderstanding arising through not making your intentions perfectly clear. With loved ones feeling more insecure than usual, it is important to do and say nothing that will make them feel uneasy. Similarly, avoid jumping to conclusions on the basis of throwaway statements made by loved ones. They may simply be wanting to test your love and sincerity. Later in the day is likely to bring a fresh breeze of cheerfulness and optimism to lighten up your mood. Draw up career plans for implementation during the coming few weeks. Look on the bright side, and be daring in your schemes.

18. MONDAY. Good. This day can be particularly auspicious for projects and affairs relating to places at a distance. Faraway travel is more likely to be successful and rewarding. Influential people, including government and other officials, tend to be especially cooperative. If considering setting up a base of operations for business overseas, start now to put your plans into action. Conditions are favorable for all publishing and printing ventures. Work of yours that comes into print today stands a good chance of winning public acclaim. All research and investigative projects are under auspicious aspects. Examinations can be passed with flying colors. Academics may be extremely helpful and informative.

19. TUESDAY. Fair. With the Christmas vacation coming up, you tend to have less time on your hands for the activities that matter to you the most. However, you will be pleased to notice that problems tend to solve themselves, and that the most important concerns in your life actually require less of your time and energy. In business and career affairs, it is quality that counts, not quantity. Do your research thoroughly and you can achieve targets you previously thought were impossible to attain. Later in the day, a conflict between work and family may lead to a strained situation. Do not demand too much of yourself or of others, and do not be too much of a perfectionist. Recognize your own limitations.

20. WEDNESDAY. Mixed. Finish up any last-minute holiday shopping. Books, especially on nonfiction subjects, can be hits as Christmas gifts. So can objects made in foreign parts of the world. This is also a good day for stocking up on basic food and other supplies for end-of-year partying. Do nothing to ruffle the feathers of your romantic partner or loved ones. They tend to be more moody and jumpy than usual, and a word out of place can cause them to overreact. Reaching an agreement with them regarding career interests can be difficult, especially if you are both professional people. This may even prove the rock on which short-term romantic attraction goes aground.

21. THURSDAY. Buoyant. The future is likely to look rosier than ever. There is even a danger of Aries being unwilling to believe your fortune and good luck where a new situation or opportunity is concerned. With the support you are likely to obtain from influential people, major new moves in your life can mean a turning point after which there is no turning back. Continue with academic or self-improvement endeavors in which you are already engaged. Enrolling in new university or college courses starting after the holiday break, or in the fall of 1996, can be an excellent idea. This is also an auspicious day to apply for a job that will take you overseas.

22. FRIDAY. Tricky. Test out the ground where new business possibilities are concerned, but do not commit yourself definitely as yet. With impulsive Aries people there is always a danger of rushing prematurely into new ventures and losing the natural advantage that comes from appearing more cool and noncommittal. Give people time to bargain with you; if necessary, play hard to get. Advertising can be helpful in promoting particular business products or attracting applications for job openings. This is an auspicious day for romance. An existing friendship can blossom into love, providing the firm foundation for a mutual relationship based on true compatibility.

23. SATURDAY. Deceptive. There is no use pleading ignorance in career and professional affairs. Own up to mistakes, even if you are only partially to blame. If nothing else, this will at least be a reminder of what not to do in the future. This is not a day for locking away skeletons in closets or trying to brush problems under the rug. The inevitable panic and confusion preceding the vacation period tends to make it unwise to commit yourself to any definite business moves. If someone tries to pressure you into making a snap decision, be firm and tell them they must wait. Evening favors attending a special social occasion or party. Steer the conversation away from business and work.

24. SUNDAY. Good. A chat with someone you have not spoken to for a long time can be especially revealing. Be prepared to learn from the greater experience of older people. Do not let any gems of wisdom that come your way today pass unheeded. If you have a spare moment on your hands, look back over your notes and records for the last year. Your successes will be encouraging and your temporary failures will provide good food for thought. Visit someone who is going to have to spend the vacation where they would rather not be. If nobody you know is in this situation, make a trip to a hospital, nursing home, or homeless shelter to see if you can help in any way.

25. MONDAY. MERRY CHRISTMAS! Sometimes this holiday is little more than a rush and a big chore, especially if you have children. But this year should be an exception. A marvelous time can be had by all, yourself included! Do not worry if your social calendar for the day becomes fully booked. One party can merge into another, small festivities into larger ones. Social gatherings can be ideal opportunities not only for reunions with old acquaintances but also for making new and lasting friendships. Travel can be fun and a welcome change. Devoted business people may make major breakthroughs if you keep at work today. Stick to your guns and do not give up on what you feel is right.

26. TUESDAY. Quiet. With most of the main festivities over, you can afford to relax a little. Try to spend more time by yourself. Moments of solitude will give you an opportunity to unwind. They are also sure to provide the chance for introspection and some important insights into yourself and what makes you tick. Do not worry over areas of indecision in your life; problems will tend to resolve themselves in their own good time. Be more sympathetic to other people, especially those afflicted by ill health or poverty. But remember that their problems are ultimately theirs, not yours. Learn not to identify too closely with the predicament of others.

27. WEDNESDAY. Variable. For a headache or hangover first thing in the morning you only have yourself to blame. Dress in layers if the weather is cool or damp; there is a greater risk of catching a cold. Do not hang on to any little resentment. The person you are angry with probably does not even know he or she has done anything to offend you. This is a good day for catching up with work and career activities, possibly from your own home. You will tend to get the most done and produce the best results if you can work alone without external distractions. Later in the day may bring some disappointing news from people or places at a distance. Do not rely on in-laws to keep their word.

28. THURSDAY. Deceptive. Be more careful what you do, even at the most basic level. There is greater risk of ending up on the wrong side of the law. Putting up with the personal eccentricities of people occupying positions of influence and power may prove difficult, not to mention distasteful. But some degree of compromise is the best course. Keep a clear sense of purpose and boundary in business and professional activities. There is a greater risk of being diverted by irrelevancies, or letting your concentration drift away from your original plans. Conditions are auspicious for romance. Go to a party or social gathering together and you are sure to have a great time. The day is favorable for all humanitarian endeavors.

29. FRIDAY. Stressful. It is essential that you get your priorities right. Your better nature can easily lead you astray. Learn the art of discrimination. You cannot help everyone in the world, and sometimes it is only through helping yourself that you are to serve others. A sense of edginess and insecurity can make you more impatient than usual. Measure your words; people will not understand if you get angry with them for no apparent reason. Avoid the tendency to overdramatize. Take extra care when behind the wheel. On no account should you mix drinking and driving. Also be prepared outdoors; the weather can change unexpectedly.

30. SATURDAY. Mixed. Today you may get clear indications of what to do and what not to do in the year to come. An attitude of optimism and cheerfulness tends to spread easily to others. This is especially important if you are involved professionally in the art of communication, teaching, or supervising others. True success begins not outside yourself, in external circumstances, but with the right attitude within. Plan for the future. Follow your vision of how the future should be, and do not change course simply out of expediency or opportunism. Conditions are favorable for travel, but the change of environment can prove more tiring than you had anticipated. If flying, allow for jet lag.

31. SUNDAY. Disquieting. This last day of the year strikes a cautionary note, especially where money or romance is concerned. Overspending by loved ones can create a financial burden which you should try to avoid. Socializing may prove more expensive than you had expected, especially if it involves providing food or drink for others. Your humanitarian impulses can be misunderstood and, if wrongly directed, they may even cause harm rather than good. A certain degree of nervousness about your career is understandable. But pay no heed to conflicting advice you receive from various sources, however well intentioned. Take in stride last-minute changes for New Year's Eve. Welcome 1996 with optimism and hope.

Your Own Personal
PSYCHIC
Our Truly Gifted Psychics are ready to talk LIVE about, Love, Money, Success, Health and Happiness.
Available 24 Hours
One-on-One • Totally Confidential
1-900-773-2737
$2.99 per minute • 18 years or older
For entertainment purposes only • Vision Quest Media • Deerfield Bch. FL

STRAIGHT TALK
That's What You Get When You
Call La Toya Jackson's Psychic Network.
La Toya's Psychics Tell It Like It Is...
Just Like She Does!
LA TOYA JACKSON'S PSYCHIC NETWORK
1-900-420-8998 ★ $3.99 per min
Use Your Credit Card And SAVE $1.00 Per Min.
1-800-994-1800 ★ $2.99 per min
Must Be 18 or Older to Call • For Entertainment Only
The Zodiac Group, Inc. • Boca Raton, FL

The Witches of Salem Network
★ If You Like Talking To Psychics...
You'll Love Talking To Witches...
Witches Are The World's Oldest And
Most Accurate Psychics!
1-900-820-9889 ★ $3.99 per min
Use Your Credit Card And SAVE $1.00 Per Min
1-800-799-5959 ★ $2.99 per min
Salem Connection, Inc. Salem, MA • Must Be 18 Years Or Older To Call • For Entertainment Only
Brigitte Neilsen

SUCCESS
ROMANCE
MONEY
LOVE
DESIRES
SUCCESS
ROMANCE
MONEY
LOVE
DESIRES
SUCCESS
ROMANCE
MONEY
Isabel "WEEZY" Sanford Star Of
"The Jeffersons"
Knows what her futures holds...
WHY???
Because She Calls...
The National Psychic Association
1-900-451-3604 ★ $3.99 per min
Use Your Credit Card And SAVE $1.00 Per min.
1-800-452-4334 ★ $2.99 per min
We Are Here To Help You 24 Hours A Day!
Galaxy Communications Corp., Boca Raton, FL • Must Be 18 Years Or Older To Call • For Entertainment Only

ANDREIKA

© 1984 California Astrology Assoc.

I WILL CAST A SPELL FOR YOU!

I can cast a spell to make one love another, or cause a person to change his mind about a relationship, or bring two people together.

My magical powers are beyond your imagination. I can cast a spell in your behalf regarding a relationship, your financial situation, future events, or whatever is important to you. I have the power and I use the power.

I am Andreika, and I can change the course of destiny. Pay me and I shall cast a spell for you. Tell me what it is you want and I shall go about my work. Is it someone or something you desire to have? Do you want wealth, or happiness, or a mate?

I will cast only one spell at a time. Do not ask for more. My energies must be massed toward one specific target; otherwise, my powers are lessened. Send me your most important desire and I shall work my powers in your favor.

Tell Andreika what you want! Send your request to "Andreika" c/o California Astrology Association, Dept. KH-1, P.O. Box 8005, Canoga Park, CA 91309. Include $15.50 plus $1.00 shipping.

UNCONDITIONAL GUARANTEE

If for any reason you are not completely satisfied, we will be happy to return your money in full at any time.

All letters to Andreika are confidential! The following letters have been printed with the permission of the writer.

Dear Andreika:

In December you cast a spell for me per my request for money. Just 10 days later I hit the lottery for $2600! It has really relieved the pressure of pressing bills, and I thank you from the bottom of my heart!

D.G.
Temple Hills, MD

Dear Andreika:

I knew you were for real! I believe in you! You made my wish come true. My husband is back home with me, and I am so happy and so thankful to you. You are the only one that has truly helped me. Thank you!

J.M. Smith
Ft. Pierce, FL

Dear Andreika,

Three months ago my husband walked out and left me with two children and an unpaid mortgage. I was unemployed at the time and my savings were diminishing fast. I wrote you my letter and asked you to help me financially. Within weeks I had won a local raffle with winnings totalling over $7,000. Two days later I was hired for a manager's job. Needless to say, my life has changed 100 per cent, and I owe it all to you.

D.K.
Ossining, NY

AMAZING PSYCHIC PREDICTIONS
Now you too can experience the Astonishing Accuracy of the world's most gifted psychics!
Discover YOUR Destiny! Ask About
LOVE • SUCCESS • MONEY
Live Answers to All Your Questions!
CALL NOW!
1-900-993-4315
Open 24 hours! Only $3.99 per minute. Must be 18+.
© 1991 Phone Vision, Inc. P.O. Box 194, Mill Valley, CA 94942